ALL THAT GLITTERS
IS NOT GOLD

The Olympic Game

WILLIAM O. JOHNSON, Jr.

Also by William O. Johnson, Jr.

SUPER SPECTATOR AND THE ELECTRIC LILLIPUTIANS

All That Glitters Is Not Gold

THE OLYMPIC GAME

G. P. Putnam's Sons, New York

Copyright © 1972 by William O. Johnson, Jr.

SBN: 399–11008–9
Library of Congress Catalog Card Number: 72–76741

PRINTED IN THE UNITED STATES OF AMERICA

ACKNOWLEDGMENTS

MUCH of the material in this book is to appear in *Sports Illustrated* magazine in the summer of 1972. I am grateful to Managing Editor Andre Laguerre, for allowing me to do the series and to Assistant Managing Editor Ray Cave for his good guidance and to Senior Editor Gilbert Rogin for his patience and aplomb and for his fine editing and advice. I must thank my wife, Ruth, for her patience, aplomb and advice also and for her excellent typing technique. Most of all, I must thank Nancy Pierce Williamson, the splendid *Sports Illustrated* writer-reporter who worked with me for nearly a year doing the interviews and library research necessary. Her work was, as usual, invaluable; the book could not have been done without her. Nor could it have been done without the magnificent material contributed by the correspondents and stringers of the Time-Life News Service and the correspondents of *Sports Illustrated*. They filed tens of thousands of words about Olympians from all over the world; their insights, descriptions and interviews form the foundation for the book.

Germantown, N.Y.   W. O. J., Jr.
January 20, 1972

CONTENTS

CONTENTS

A PROLOGUE:
The Ancient Games

NOTHING like the Olympic Games was seen on the planet for the first 500,000,000 years or so. Oh, perhaps the physical skills and agile cunning of primitive man were a kind of harbinger. No decathlon champions were crowned then, but the feats of the Neanderthal were similar—stone throwing, spear flinging, fierce and desperate footraces fraught with jumps both high and long in pursuit of (or headlong flight from) various beasts of the day.

There is no point in belaboring the metamorphosis that brought us over hundreds of centuries to our present state of affairs. Gradually the actions required for sheer survival gave way to less desperate acts we call sport—archery 20,000 years ago, polo in Tibet, fisticuffs in Egypt, wrestling in Mesopotamia about 3000 B.C. Men moved into the Neolithic Age and polished their stone tools. Then came the Bronze Age. Men began to concoct religions, some kind of definition, however dim, to explain away their terror of lightning and maniac thunderclaps, as well as their wonderment over the regular reappearance of fresh foliage, wild flowers and new fruit. After religion came the rituals to express it. And there entered the earliest festivals of sport.

Men worshiped the dead then. They believed that blood sacrifices could enhance the fertility of the world. They believed that the dead could utilize the desperately spent energies of the athletes, as they used the freshly spilled blood of sacrifices, to make the earth bloom.

The earliest Olympic Games in Greece—around 1370 B.C.— seem to have risen from such primitive and occult observances. Records are dim and all but nonexistent from that Neolithic Age, but most scholars believe that those first Games were performed before a cult of the dead, perhaps even relying on gifts of human blood.

It is agreed that the year 776 B.C. marked the recorded "modern" beginning of the Olympics in Greece. That was the year from which the Greeks dated their calendar. The Olympic Games were held on the rock-encircled grassy plain of Olympia, where there was a temple of Zeus, and they were at first only a provincial event on the order of a county fair. There were other such Games around the country—at Delphi, Corinth and Nemea, all quasireligious carnivals often held in conjunction with funerals. Sports and death walked hand in hand for several centuries.

Eventually, all Greece wound up having its quadrennial festival at Olympia, and The Olympic Games lasted for 1,168 years, a very long time for a mere festival. They were finally eradicated by the Roman Emperor Theodosius the Great, A.D. 393. He ordered all of Greece's religious landmarks to be destroyed and its pagan ceremonies outlawed, the better that his chosen religion, Christianity, could prosper. By then Rome had occupied Greece for three centuries, and by then the Olympic Games had deteriorated into a tawdry, though still very large, spectacle.

The historical horror story most often told of the shabby latter days of the ancient Olympic Games occurred in A.D. 66, when the demented Emperor Nero brought along 5,000 bodyguards from Rome and entered himself as a contestant in many events. He won them all easily, being judged the best singer, the best musician, the best herald and the best chariot driver. He won a chariot race despite the fact that he fell out of his chariot in mid-race and narrowly escaped being mashed beneath the wheels. Seeing Nero alive after the accident all the other charioteers in the race politely and prudently reined in their horses and waited until the emperor had regained his chariot and whipped his horses back into action and on to victory. Such was the charisma of a man with 5,000 bodyguards.

Nero notwithstanding, few institutions in history have been so thoroughly mythologized and devulgarized as those ancient Olympic Games have been in the last few decades. It is widely believed now that men competed strenuously for the mere honor of wearing a chaplet of laurel or wreaths made from wild celery or pine twigs or olive leaves. It is widely believed that pure idealism reigned.

The truth is the athletes of ancient Greece were a pampered class, a corps of swaggering narcissists who did little but build their bodies and massage their egos from one year to the next. No man could compete, of course, unless he could prove he was a freeborn and full-blooded son of Greece. Thus no slaves were allowed. It helped a lot to be very, very wealthy: No man entered the Olympic Games unless he had spent the previous eleven months exclusively in training. Many of the athletes were immortalized in marble sculpture, praised in the odes of Pindar, even quite openly worshiped at altars built when they died.

11

Nothing counted but victory. When Diagoras did win an Olympic championship, a friend said, "Die, Diagoras, for thou has nothing short of divinity to desire!" Losers were lepers. Pindar wrote: "They slink away, sore smitten by misfortune, nor does any sweet smile grace their return."

Soon enough, this sort of grotesque idolatry of athletes became offensive to intelligent men. As early as the sixth century B.C., while the Olympics were considered in their Golden Age the philosopher Xenophanes complained that the culture of Greece had actually reached a point where people praised a wrestler's strength over a philosopher's wisdom. Euripedes scorned the elitism and body adoration rampant among the athletes.

Aristotle more gently criticized the life of athletic specialization when he wrote, "The best habit is that which comes midway between the athletic and the valetudinarian—the exertion must not be violent or specialized, as is the case with the athlete; it should rather be a general exertion directed to all activities of a free man."

Long before the Romans occupied Greece, the Olympics had begun to deteriorate into overt professionalism. Many athletes were paid outright by their hometowns. Others became full-time pot hunters, picking up prizes of oxen and drachmas and other rewards at various games throughout Greece. The famed Theagenes won more than 1,400 prizes in boxing, running and the pancration. This pancration was a singularly brutal sport in which no holds and no blows were barred and the contest continued until one man raised his hand from the ground to signal his defeat. Indeed, the savagery of the pancration is completely out of keeping with our modern myths celebrating the gentlemanly sportsmanship and civilized manners which supposedly ennobled the ancient Games. In one pancration battle, perhaps

12

only a legend, a boxer named Arrachion was wrestling with an opponent on the ground and he held the other man's foot in an agonizing grip. As Arrachion twisted viciously, his rival desperately locked Arrachion's neck in a stranglehold, and they lay in those throes for a short time. Then Arrachion died. But as he died, he gave one last violent twist to his opponent's ankle, the man raised his hand in defeat, and Arrachion, now stone dead on the ground, was declared the victor.

A few years after the ancient Olympics were declared dead by Theodosius, a band of Goths pillaged Olympia and burned the Temple of Zeus. For fifteen centuries the world celebrated no more carnivals of sports in the grand style of the Olympic Games.

In fact, until our own Olympics, only the ancient Romans matched the Greeks for overall magnitude and spectacle in sports. The Circus Maximus held 350,000 people. This is more spectators than witnessed any single public event in the history of the world until our own gargantuan twentieth-century baby —television—was born.

The Roman viewer actually enjoyed more violence in the Circus Maximus, the Colosseum and other public arenas than we are offered on television today. The Romans were delighted by lions, tigers, elephants, giraffes and crocodiles either devouring each other or doing the same to hapless criminals, prisoners of war or Christians. At the gala show which marked the opening of the Colosseum 5,000 wild animals and 4,000 tame ones were butchered. Once, to commemorate a great military victory, 11,000 animals were killed while thousands cheered in the stands.

It was in that bloody arena that Julius Caesar invented the bullfight. Another favorite of the thirsty crowd in the Colosseum was the naumachia, a sea battle fought to the death before

13

their eyes. The arena was flooded for the occasion by a network of sluices. Opposing fleets were manned by prisoners of war or criminals. The game was simply to keep fighting until one side was exterminated. In one such fight, this one arranged on Lake Fucinus by the Emperor Claudius, 100 ships and 19,000 men were involved, and the water turned pink before the spectacle was over.

After those Roman debacles, the world seemed sated with sporting extravaganzas. Throughout the Dark Ages, people did most of their spectating at church or at gloomy little doings like witch burnings and public hangings. Some 30,000 turned out to see Marie Antoinette lose her head to the guillotine. There were county fairs and jousting tournaments, to be sure, but lavish carnivals for spectators did not really surface again until a French aristocrat named Baron Pierre de Fredi de Coubertin launched his new Games in Athens in 1896.

By then the Industrial Revolution had cut its swath through the lives of men, and a certain amount of leisure time was beginning to accumulate for all but the most deprived of workers. At first, these leisure hours were spent in personal participation in games. But soon this palled for many millions, and rather than play games themselves, they chose to sit down and watch others who excelled. Thus, the age of the spectator dawned at just about the same time the modern Olympic Games were born.

ALL THAT GLITTERS
IS NOT GOLD

The Olympic Game

Part I
The Olympic Games

I. Humbug and Hypocrisy

TO write properly about the Olympic Games of the twentieth century is to write about almost everything in the twentieth century. About plastics and politics and racism and the demise of rigid Biblical morality and the rise of situation ethics. About avarice and airplanes and vitamin pills and chauvinism and free love and selling refrigerators on television and urban renewal and electricity. . . .

The Olympic Games are a unique and most peculiar phenomenon. Never in the history of the world has there been a regularly scheduled, floating public spectacular that is so enormous, so expensive and that so thoroughly enfolds the peoples of the planet. Yet, despite the breadth of their acceptance and the depth of their impact, the modern Olympic Games have come to be defined almost entirely within the terms of their own stilted mythology. People see the Olympics as a mystical and antiseptic festival of sports that features huge portions of international brotherhood and enlightened friendship, panoramic sights and unforgettable feats of sporting skill. It seems to be a celestial event that bobs like an emperor's zeppelin above reality. It seems untouched by social troubles. It seems unstained by man's proclivity for sin and folly. Mainly it seems very *serious.* Even sacred.

The spiritual essence of the Olympics is said to be rooted for all time in the soil of Greek antiquity. The operating ideals of the Games are said to be forever anchored in a century-old code written by gentlemen amateurs who are now long dead and buried—"It is not the winning, but the taking part, not the conquering, but the playing fair. . . ."

This all has come to be humbug in this era of commercialism and opportunism.

Of course, the mass of men never come closer to an Olympics than to look at it through the flickering dark glass of television. There the myths are embroidered and the heroes enlarged —and the truth of it is blurred even more than would ordinarily be the case. Television specializes in simplicity, and what appears on the tube is too fleeting, too anxiously compressed to do more than hint at the realities behind—or beyond—the moment of competition.

So let us proceed with this treatise on the modern Olympic Games and how they have changed in themselves and (far more fascinating) how they have changed those who have participated in them. We will ignore the Winter Games because they involve a relatively small section of the world and because they are relatively new (born in 1924) and because they lately have been performed under such a heavy shadow of alleged corruption and dark doubt concerning the eligibility of the world's best skiers that it is almost impossible to maintain a clear perspective on them.

The bulk of this chronicle will be built with a multitude of scattered and separate anecdotes and quotations and thumbnail

20

profiles and life stories. This will be a rather antic presentation, episodic, skeptical, fraught with the absurdities and ironies and foibles which are never recorded in official Olympic mythology. When it is finished, perhaps there will be an answer to a pertinent question about the Olympic Games of the twentieth century: *What the hell have we wrought?*

The phenomenon of the modern Games is only seventy-six years old, and the statistics of sheer growth are impressive. Whereas only 285 athletes appeared at the I Olympiad in Athens in 1896, there would be upwards of 7,000 at the XX Olympiad in Munich in 1972. That number of contestants does not make the Olympic Games the largest athletic event in the world. No. Two bigger are the Vasaloppet cross-country ski race in Sweden, which has attracted as many as 9,000 contestants for the annual stampede across the snow, and the annual swim across the Sea of Galilee in Israel, which draws more than 10,000 water chestnuts who churn elbow to elbow across 2.4 miles of those historic waters. Neither the Vasaloppet nor the Sea of Galilee Swim can touch a candle to the Olympics when it comes to prestige.

As for growing Olympic costs, the Games of '96 cost the Greeks 3,740,000 drachmas. If we apply that currency to Munich '72, the latest Games will cost over 6 billion drachmas. To make the currency exchange clear, let us recall that in ancient Greece 5 drachmas were worth one ox. In the economy of late-nineteenth-century Greece, 5 drachmas were worth 60 cents. Thus, those first modern Games cost 748,000 ancient oxen, or $448,800. Using the same currencies, the XX Olympiad in Munich will cost a total of 1.2 billion ancient oxen, or $720,000,000.

Beyond the numbers of it all, it is impressive to realize just how pervasive the Olympics is on the planet. No other institu-

21

tion or religion or political ideology or cultural form can match the universality of the Olympic Games now. They have captured the imaginations of all disparate manner of human beings —of brown equatorial natives and Japanese cavalrymen and East European socialists with steel teeth and Latin American dictators and French movie stars and Pakistani camel drivers and barbers in Iowa as well as the apostles of Jomo Kenyatta and Billy Graham and Buddha and Che Guevara and Golda Meir and Ronald Reagan.

A Turkish wrestler named Mustafa Dagistanli, a mighty man who was undefeated in hundreds of matches over many years and won gold medals in the Olympics of 1956 and 1960, spoke recently in wonder about the grand reach of the Games. "It is amazing. Participants of countries still at the door of the Stone Age come to the Olympic Games in these modern days," said Dagistanli. "They compete, they win, they are beaten perhaps, but always they are praised and applauded by other Olympic contestants. Then they return to their homes in the Stone Age. The Olympics is so beautiful, so bighearted, so open to everything on the earth."

Well, there is indeed beauty, and even a big heart perhaps, to be found in today's sprawling, expensive, hyperglamorous Olympic Games. No institution so thoroughly ribboned in the trappings of ceremony—a really thrilling ceremony which owes its origins to an incomparable amalgam of the snappiest military parade and the solemnest religious pomp—can exist entirely without an impressive esthetic dimension. And no institution so steeped in the ritual and vocabulary of "brotherhood" can exist without at least a modicum of real affection for fellowmen. But over the years there have been some remarkably overblown declarations made in definition—and perhaps defense—of the purpose of the Olympic Games.

Baron Pierre de Coubertin, the determined little French aristocrat who was responsible for the revival of the Games, ascribed grandiose potential to his brainchild: "The Olympic movement," said the baron, "tends to bring together in a radiant union all the qualities which guide mankind to perfection."

But even the good baron's transcendant expectations were outdone by Count Henri de Baillet-Latour, a Belgian, who in 1924 became Coubertin's successor as president of the International Olympic Committee. (The IOC is a blue-ribbon board of blue bloods—millionaires and aristocrats—which has controlled the destinies of the Olympic Games over the past seventy-six years.) Count de Baillet-Latour faced a sticky situation in 1936, the year the Olympics were to be held in Berlin under the auspices of Adolf Hitler's Nazi government. The count was concerned that the Führer would make an overt attempt to take over the Games as a Nazi publicity vehicle—through his own dazzling rhetoric or public decor or with throngs of Nazi manpower. Baillet-Latour had to think of something to say that would keep Hitler's hands off. With lofty superiority, the Belgian aristocrat drew himself up and informed the Führer: "The Olympic Games are not held in Berlin, in Los Angeles or in Amsterdam. When the five-circled Olympic flag is raised over a stadium, it becomes sacred Olympic territory and theoretically and for all practical purposes, the Games are held in ancient Olympia. There I am the master."

The reply of the Chancellor of the Third Reich to the Master of Ancient Olympia was not recorded, but he did not meddle personally in the Games at all that year.

Over the past two decades, the world's most outspoken Olympic oracle has been IOC President Avery Brundage, an octogenarian construction millionaire from Chicago. On occasion, Mr. Brundage has surpassed even Baron de Coubertin and

Count Baillet-Latour in granting the Olympic Games quasi-divine influence and superhuman power to cure any number of ailments which have plagued humanity since Eden. In speeches over the years, Avery Brundage has said the following:

> The Olympic Movement is a Twentieth Century religion. Here there is no injustice of caste, of race, of family, of wealth. . . .
> The Olympic Movement appears as a ray of sunshine through clouds of racial animosity, religious bigotry and political chicanery. . . .
> The Olympic Movement is perhaps the greatest social force in the world. It is a revolt against Twentieth Century materialism, it is a devotion to the cause and not to the reward. . . .

Mr. Brundage is a brass-bound old soul, a man of stern and immovable principle, and he devoutly believes what he says about his Olympic religion. So did Baillet-Latour and Coubertin. So do a lot of other people in the world today—perhaps millions of them.

However, such a blind faith in the Olympics as a force which can turn stadiums and running tracks and jumping pits and swimming pools into "sacred territory" probably does not serve the Games as well as a less starry-eyed, less sanctimonious approach might. In fact, the Games are a profoundly human institution, and there is charm, beauty and truth to be found in the realities which remain after the pomp and ceremony are done, after the rhetoric of the Olympic popes has dissipated and after the public heroics of Olympian competitors have been duly applauded and registered in the record books. The Olympics has always had more to offer the world than mere gold medals and impossible dreams.

The construction of Olympic facilities was responsible for

vast and badly needed urban renewal and housing projects in Rome and Tokyo and Mexico City. Indeed, for the Japanese, the Olympics of 1964 served as a gleaming vehicle to launch enterprises far more ambitious than games. The government of Japan earmarked nearly $3 billion for the Tokyo Olympics; restructuring of Tokyo was part of the Olympic mission, but there were even bigger fish than that to fry. Dr. Ryotaro Azuma, then mayor of Tokyo and chairman of the Japanese Olympic Committee, said in 1971: "Without the Olympics, Japan probably would not have risen to its high position in world trade so rapidly. Our national prestige depended on the Tokyo Games being a success and I doubt that we would be what we are today if they had failed."

For Mexico, the 1968 Olympics meant an almost total transformation of the nation's image in the eyes of the world. Officials there firmly believe that because word of their efficient Olympic efforts was transmitted around the world through television, their reputation had changed from that of a backward, *mañana* republic into that of a brisk, ambitious nation ready to take its rightful place in the twentieth century.

Ah, and beyond that, the Olympics of Mexico City produced one of the most admirable reversals of public policy in decades. Mexicans still talk about the 1968 unveiling of their lovely naked Diana as one of the greatest events since Mexican independence. Diana is, in this case, a statue—a magnificent zoftic nude which was erected at the entrance of Mexico City's Chapultepec Park more than twenty-five years ago. Unfortunately, when Diana was first revealed in her altogether, the shocked outcry was deafening. Cowed city authorities quickly surrendered to the legions of prudes and declared that Diana could not stand without clothing.

A small iron dress, a kind of steel Aztec miniskirt, was

designed and wrapped about her flanks, and thus she stood until 1967. Then it suddenly occurred to a few people that since Mexico was going to be the focus of millions of eyes during telecasts of the Olympic Games, the country just might become a global laughingstock because while the rest of the world frolicked in sexual revolution, Mexico persisted in hiding the naked charms of a statue. Thus, in the interests of presenting a more liberated Olympic image, the authorities rescinded the decree outlawing Diana undressed. The iron miniskirt was removed and Diana's beautiful derriere was revealed. The night she was first fully uncovered, it is said, there was dancing in the park because everyone who turned out for that historic event could plainly see that everything was up to date in Mexico City.

Olympic mythology does not tout that incident, though it should. Nor does it dwell proudly on the fact that the Olympic Games inspired Irving Berlin to write both the lyrics and the melody to a song for the first time in his career. It happened in 1909, and the title of the piece was "Dorando." The song originated with a bizarre and wonderful thing that happened at the 1908 Olympics in London. The hero was Dorando Pietri, a poor, courageous little Italian marathon runner who had wobbled into Wembley Stadium ahead of the pack, exhausted and stumbling like a broken toy. The stadium was filled with British spectators who suddenly became exuberant at the sight of Dorando. They were exuberant because this was an Olympics already scarred with recriminations between Americans and Englishmen and the British crowds wanted *anyone* to win but an American. Ah, but their roar for Dorando soon turned to anxious silence, for just behind the staggering Italian came an American, Johnny Hayes. He was moving sluggishly but steadily. Panicked that the Yankee might overtake the Italian, English officials at the finish line leaped onto the track and bodily car-

26

ried the nearly comatose Dorando Pietri to victory ahead of Johnny Hayes. The crowd bellowed its pleasure.

Poor Dorando was disqualified. But his brave struggle in London and later races as a professional in the United States appealed to the young songwriter Irving Berlin. He first wrote the lyrics of "Dorando" for a vaudeville comic who wanted something topical in his act. Berlin's effort was ultimately rejected by the vaudevillian. He tried selling the lyrics to the Seminary Music Company. The firm was not wildly enthusiastic, but it did agree to buy it for $25 if Berlin threw some music into the deal. He did, but it still was no bargain even at $25. Here is a sampling of "Dorando" by Irving Berlin:

> Dorando! Dorando! He run-a, run-a, run-a, run
> like anything.
> One-a, two-a hundred times around da ring.
> I cry, "Please a nun ga stop!"
> Just then, Dorando he's a drop!*

If the Olympic Games helped further the career of Irving Berlin and improve the trade of Japan, they must also be credited with contributing to the world at least three Hollywood Tarzans (Johnny Weissmuller, Glenn Morris, Buster Crabbe), one Flash Gordon (Crabbe), one Jungle Jim (Weissmuller) and one Sonja Henie, the richest athlete ever to perform. *The Guinness Book of World Records* (the Bible of trivia lovers) reports: "The greatest fortune amassed by an individual in sport is an estimated $47,500,000 by Sonja Henie of Norway, the triple Olympic ice skating champion." Miss Henie, the dimpled doll from Oslo, starred in many movies and owned her own ice show. Her first Olympic competition occurred in 1924, when she was eleven years old, and she won gold medals in the Games of 1928, 1932 and 1936.

The real Olympic Games—as opposed to the mythical—have been the vehicle for satisfying all manner of profit motives, personal ambitions and governmental policies. Yet of all the wayward and sensational things which have come to pass in the name of the Games, none was so bizarre as the Love Garden which was located in the woods near the Olympic Village the Nazis built for the 1936 Games in Berlin.

An athlete who participated in those Olympics and was particularly revered at the time was Dr. Paul Martin, now seventy years old, an osteopathic surgeon who has always lived in Lausanne, Switzerland. He had enjoyed the friendship of Baron de Coubertin, and he was a most determined competitor. Although the only Olympic medal Dr. Martin actually won was a silver for second place in the 800-meter run in Antwerp in 1920, he is still famed among Olympians because he competed as a runner for the Swiss in five consecutive Games. The last was in Berlin where he was individually honored and awarded a

Diplome de Mérite from the International Olympic Committee as the only track competitor ever to enter five straight Olympics.

Dr. Martin recently recalled the strange and sexy facts of the Germans' Olympic Love Garden: "The Olympic athlete in Berlin was elevated to a godlike creature. We were gods of the stadium. The Germans had even reserved a sort of heavenly forest near the Olympic Village for those gods. And there the prettiest handpicked maidens would offer themselves to the athletes—especially to the good Aryan types. Olympic babies born out of such encounters were cared for by the state. There was every indication that this Woods of Love was a matter of state policy by the Nazis.

"The maidens were usually sports teachers or members of Hitler's *Bund deutscher Mädchen* [German Girls' League] and they had special passes to enter the Village woods and mingle with the athletes. It was a lovely beech forest which had a pretty little lake, and the place was tightly ringed by *Schupos* [Berlin city police] so no one would disturb the sportive couples.

"It was interesting that before submitting to the Olympic god of her choice, the girl would request her partner's Olympic badge. In case of pregnancy, the girl would give this information to state or Red Cross maternities to prove the Olympic origin of her baby. Then the state would pay for the whole works."

Dr. Martin said that since Aryan racial improvement was apparently the object of the young ladies' affection, they avoided blacks and seemed to favor Americans, Scandinavians, Finns, Dutchmen and, of course, Germans.

Dr. Martin had also been in Los Angeles for the '32 Games, and he recalled, "Very pretty girls with big automobiles would turn up at the Olympic Village to try and meet the athlete of their choice. But there, of course, race improvement was decidedly not the prime incentive."

The Olympics has come to mean many things to many men and women, and to reduce its definitions to mere grandiose and idealistic generalization is neither fair nor accurate. It is a kind of fountain of youth, an athletic Shangri-La where no one grows old. Bill Toomey won the decathlon at the 1968 Olympics in Mexico at the fairly ripe age of thirty-one, and Toomey said not long ago, "It's like being Peter Pan. You feel as if you'll always stay young if you compete. The Olympics is one man doing it against one man. It's like a window on your soul and you don't feel you will ever die."

The Olympics is an endangered species, perhaps on the brink of extinction. Henry Wittenberg, forty-five, a professor of physical education at City College of New York who was coach of the 1968 U.S. wrestling team and a medal-winning wrestler at the Olympics of 1948 and 1952, spoke quite sternly about the present state of the Games: "The Olympics is like the SST or the dinosaur. It will keep getting bigger and bigger until it dies. We often confuse growth with quality, and now we have to reassess our standards and deflate the Olympics down to reality—and practicality. Right now, the Games are so big that they won't be able to survive their own environment. They're also too damn *serious*. God, in Mexico City the Olympic Village was like a big, frantic factory—chug, chug, chugging all the time. We used to have *fun* at sports. Nowadays we even emphasize the hostility between nations so we can hone the competitive edge of an Olympic athlete. We *trick* the kids into performing like champions."

The Games are an extension of man's worst proclivities toward hypocrisy and self-delusion. Harry Edwards, twenty-eight, is an associate professor of sociology at the University of California at Berkeley, and in 1967 he was the inspiration for a movement among black athletes to boycott the Olympic Games in Mexico City. Ultimately, the rebellion faltered, but Harry Edwards goes on, an outspoken, articulate, iconoclastic critic of the Olympic Games. He said, "Sports and war are born from man's same needs. The same training, the same drives work for both. The same rituals prevail—anthems, martial music, prayers for victory, medals for heroes. The same organized structures that support war support the Olympic Games. Nationalists and politicians, hymn singers, American Legion Neanderthals. The Olympic Games as an ideal of brotherhood and world community is passé. The Olympics is so obviously hypocritical that even the Neanderthals watching TV know what they're seeing can't be true. With access to total information—*instantly*—like TV gives us, even Neanderthals know that the Russians stomped the Czechs and that the Jews despise the Arabs and that racists rule the U.S. So, all of a sudden, the Olympics comes on TV—all this smiling and handshaking, and even the Neanderthal has to sit up and say, 'Hey, what the hell? How can that be? All year I watch nothin' but hate on TV; now they come on with the love! It's gotta be phony. The Olympics gotta be a put-on, man.' "

The Olympics is strictly a matter of profit and loss, a game played in red or black ink on a balance sheet. Zack Farmer, a grizzled ex-cowboy who got rich in California during the twenties, was chairman of the 1932 Olympic committee which produced the Games in Los Angeles. Zack Farmer saw it all as a matter of cash flow: "The '32 Games were the first ones that ever paid off—all the others came in at a loss. And, don't forget, 1932 was the rock bottom of the Depression. We showed a profit of one million three hundred thousand dollars after every-

31

thing. Yeah, after four years of hard work gettin' ready for it, we gave them a wonderful Olympics and a profit to boot. Hell, it's all just a business proposition."

Possibly. In television, the Olympic Games are valued highly, for they are known as a "wholesome sales vehicle." In this case "wholesome" simply means that it is safe for an advertiser to be associated with the Olympics on television because viewers do not consider it controversial or troublesome.

The networks are perfectly aware of all this, of course, and they do not hesitate to invest heavily in the Olympics. In fact, TV's largess has done much to transform the modern Games into the massive multimillion-dollar athletic Disneylands which they have become. In 1968, the American Broadcasting Company won the American rights to televise the Games from Mexico City. The final figures were arrived at through secret bids, and ABC offered $4,500,000, which was a rather expensive overbid of $2,300,000 more than the National Broadcasting Company offered. Later Roone Arledge, the president of ABC Sports, was asked if he regretted the fact that he had bid so much more than NBC, and the jaunty Mr. Arledge replied, "I'd a hell of a lot rather blow a couple of million bucks on the Olympic Games than on the Bluebonnet Bowl."

Perhaps that was not quite as high praise as the gods of Olympia might have felt their Games deserved, but it was heartfelt. In reality, of course, Mr. Arledge did not in any way feel that he had "blown" his money on the 1968 Olympics. He and ABC came back four years later, fighting for rights to the 1972 Games in Munich. The price this time was $13,500,000. ABC's motives were in no way based on the Olympics as a socioreligious movement. As Roone Arledge made clear, it was a matter of profit and the network's public image: "The Olympics is the biggest sports event on earth and it is worth every penny—

every single million bucks—you have to spend to get it. Because then your network is 'The Olympic Network' and people see your image as something special. And nothing carries prestige like the Olympic Games among viewers—and advertisers, of course."

The idea of peddling their goods and services on "The Olympic Network" appealed to quite a number of advertisers in 1968. They paid up to $60,000 a minute to mount their products upon the wheels of ABC's "wholesale sales vehicle." The XIX Olympiad did its part in selling many things—soda from Coca-Cola, cars from the Ford Motor Company, tires from Goodyear, plane travel from Pan American, metal from Reynolds Aluminum, beer from the Jos. Schlitz Brewing Company, gasoline from Texaco and politics from the Nixon-Agnew Campaign Committee.

So. We have defined the Olympics variously as a fountain of youth and a fountain of hypocrisy, as a black-ink business proposition and a pure-white sales vehicle, as the strong right arm of a nation's world trade policy, as a dinosaur and as an entertainment property worth more money than the Bluebonnet Bowl. Let us briefly view the Olympics as a political arena.

This is heresy, of course. It has long been an untouchable tenet of the Olympic creed that Sports and Politics Shall Not Mix. For years, Olympic leaders have tried vainly to halt the practice of journalists who insist on compiling box scores showing which nation won the most medals and thus "won" the Olympic Games. In 1952 at his inaugural speech as president of the IOC, Avery Brundage waggled a thick finger and said, "We must keep a happy balance between justifiable national pride and the use of sport for national aggrandizement. If the Games become contests between the hired gladiators of various nations with the idea of building national prestige or proving that one

33

system of government is better than another, they will lose all purpose."

The theory is inspired, but in practice it does not prevail. The forces of patriotism—and its uglier brother, chauvinism—have descended upon the Olympics with a vengeance. It is rare that the victory of an individual does not somehow become translated into a victory for some far larger entity than one man alone. When the great Finnish distance runners—Kolehomainer, Nurmi, Ritola—first appeared to sweep the Olympiads in the second and third decades of this century, their triumphs were said to herald the arrival of icy, isolated Finland as a full-fledged member of the twentieth-century world. When American blacks, led by the incomparable Jesse Owens, won medal after medal in the Berlin Olympics of 1936, their inspiring individual efforts were lumped together and labeled a sort of black cultural triumph over Hitler's racist philosophies. When U.S. athletes gathered many more medals than the Russians during the 1952 Olympics in Helsinki, it was judged an overwhelming cold war coup—proving, of course, that capitalism was a far better system for all mankind than Communism. In the 1960 Games in Rome, when the Russians were easy winners over the Americans, the pendulum swung back, and the rating of opposing political systems had to be reversed.

Well, it is folly—obviously—to let a mere athletic festival stand as proof of a way of life. And yet even thinking men in the Olympic movement tend to speak in terms of *national* achievement rather than individual success when they discuss Olympic results.

Arthur Lentz, for example, is a candid, clear-thinking fellow who has been executive director of the U.S. Olympic Committee for eight years. Recently, Lentz discussed the $10,000,000 which had to be raised to field an American Olympic team.

Art Lentz explained that such a great amount was needed for one major reason: "When the U.S. enters anything, it has to be reasonably sure the team will do well. Otherwise we downgrade our American image. People look to us big nations for the top talent. When you do poorly, it looks as if you are weak. India and Pakistan think of the U.S. as a lower-class nation. They always beat us in field hockey—*ergo*, they think they are stronger than we are."

(*Ergo*, one might well pray for the day when Olympic field hockey champions really *are* judged the strongest nations on earth—thus doing away with nuclear arsenals, jet fighter planes, armies and all that nonsense.)

Perhaps Art Lentz should be forgiven the taint of chauvinism in his statement, for there is a theory that since the world has come to possess the means for its own extermination—the Bomb—the Olympic Games actually are a more viable influence on world politics and power balances than ever before. C. P. McIntosh, a British author who wrote a book in 1962 called *Sport in Society*, advanced the idea this way:

> There are few governments in the world which do not now accept the political importance of success in international sport. In 1962 both global and local wars are likely to be suicidal ways of influencing people and winning support, and sport as a means of influence has assumed correspondingly greater political importance. What could then happen is that the Olympic Games would be no more than a testing ground for two great political units [the United States and USSR]. There would be no difficulty in training elite teams of participants whose efficiency and skill would be superb, but who would cease to be sportsmen. The competitions would be keenly contested but as predominantly political occasions they would cease to share with humbler events that playful unreality which is essential to sport.

There are those who feel that long ago the world reached the point where "playful unreality" was in no way an element of the Olympic Games. Richard Mandell, in his book *The Nazi Olympics*, wrote: "A trend that was strengthened by the results of the 1936 Olympics was to view athletes increasingly as national assets, procurable like fighter planes, submarines or synthetic rubber factories. After 1936 a stable of athletes became necessary for a national standing."

The question of equating Olympic athletes with submarines or synthetic rubber factories is not so controversial or so surprising as one might imagine. Recognition of the phenomenon is widespread and reaches across a wide spectrum of philosophies and life-styles.

Mrs. Elizabeth Robinson Schwartz, sixty, was the first American woman ever to win a gold medal in Olympic track; she did it in 1928 when she was sixteen, winning the 100-meter dash in Amsterdam. In 1939, she married Richard Schwartz, the wealthy owner of an upholstery fabrics firm, and they live in a fine brick house in Glencoe, Illinois, an expensive suburb of Chicago. The affluent Mrs. Schwartz said, "Often I still weep when I remember how it felt to win that day. Looking back, I don't think there's any doubt about the fact that it's really for your country. These days I don't think it's fair that we insist our athletes be amateurs—if a competitor has to take time off to represent his country, he should be reimbursed. He's representing his country as a soldier or a sailor is. That doesn't make him a professional; it makes him a patriot. I don't care if it's political or not, the athletes are the most important, and they should be taken care of so they don't lose anything in representing their nation."

John Carlos, twenty-seven, is the angry black sprinter who (with sprinter Tommie Smith) shocked the world during the

1968 Olympics by bowing his head on the victory stand and raising a black-gloved fist during the playing of "The Star-Spangled Banner." John Carlos, too, feels that his performance as an Olympic competitor was used to enhance American prestige. He hated it. "The Olympics is nothing but a full political scene—everything in world athletics is," said John Carlos. "You tell a kid the Olympic Games is the highest form of athletics. That it's man against man, soul against soul. But when you get to the Games it's all different from what you've been told all your life. It's country against country, ideology against ideology. The people you run for—the officials—overshadow you with their political ambitions, with the *face* they want *you* to put on your country. The Olympics could be beautiful if they just let the athletes get together and run it together, instead of having us all stand up on some podium so the world can count how many medals each country won."

The demand for wringing some national advantage from Olympic athletics has caused enormous investments of manpower and money over the years. In the early thirties, Hitler launched an exhaustive and expensive talent hunt throughout Germany for potential Olympians who would bring honor to the Third Reich in the Berlin Games. In the late forties, Russia spent millions on full-time training facilities so that its athletes would rank with the best in the world when they were at last unveiled —for the first time since 1908—at Helsinki in 1952. It is common practice in Africa and Europe to give Olympic-caliber athletes salaried jobs as nonworking customs officials, firemen or military functionaries. In East Germany, which has been working full time for years to produce a powerful Olympic team for the Munich Games, the environment is like a Brave New World breeding factory. Marc Hodler, a member of the IOC and president of the Fédération Internationale de Ski, is a resident of

37

Switzerland and has had occasion to analyze the East German Olympic-athlete assembly line. He said, "They are finding their Olympians while they are still in their cradles, and they are taking them into full-time camps and training them as if they were thoroughbred horses or racing dogs. They are not humans. One feels they are counted in the gross national product as if they were so many pounds of butter—in the national arsenal as if they were so many guns."

So just what *is* Olympic amateurism? Ah, that is a complex and troublesome subject which will be discussed at further length in a later chapter. For now, let us simply state the fact that hypocrisy has come to be the lifeblood of the Olympic movement because of the issue of amateurism.

It is true. Each athlete who participates in the Olympic Games must sign an oath swearing that he has obeyed the letter of the law—that he has, in no way, been paid or supported or benefited materially because of his athletic prowess.

To swear to this simply calls for a blatant, unadulterated lie for the great majority of Olympic athletes. Be they subsidized by the government in Russia, paid for not working as a customs agent in France, awarded an army position in Finland which allows full days for training or given a college scholarship in the United States for being a gifted athlete, they cannot meet the qualifications of Olympic amateurism.

Jack Kelly, president of the Amateur Athletic Union, said recently: "Most of us are aware that as many as two-thirds of the athletes signing the Olympic oath are committing perjury. What should concern us is the extent to which we damage the character of a young competitor by a code which has lost its relevancy. Instead of teaching the great lessons of our sport—honesty, integrity and fair play—our code sanctions the worst."

The insistence on pure amateurism as an absolute Olympic

virtue possibly produces more dishonesty among Olympians than among any other category of mortals alive on earth today.

But everything in the Olympics is not sliced from the pudding of pomp and cooked in the juice of hypocrisy. The Olympics is not *only* a matter of profit motives and movie careers and beer commercials and box scores kept by nationalists. The Olympic Games are also the stuff from which dreams are made; they are capable of creating that rarest of twentieth-century commodities—heroism. The feats of Olympians can cast a spell for decades. They bring reveries to little boys lying abed in the twilight of summer evenings, and they offer a precious chance for open admiration and genuine wonder among grown men.

Certainly, the heroism generated by a mere sporting event is a feeble and insignificant brand of the commodity when compared to brave acts of life-saving or to the sacrifices of men who will their own destruction in defense of principle. Yet in some cases, an Olympic performance is so compelling, so unforgettable that even the heroics of an athlete can make him seem immortal in his own lifetime. If that happens, he is rarely able to lead his life without its being somehow molded and controlled more by that famous, fleeting triumph than by his own will.

No man symbolizes better the heights of deathless Olympic heroism—as well as the formidable aftereffects that scaling such a peak can have—than James Cleveland "Jesse" Owens, a man recognized all over the world as the Greatest Olympian of Them All.

2. A Professional Good Example

THE morning in the summer of 1971 was warm and sunny in Binghamton, New York. On the infield and everywhere on the track runners were busy at warm-ups, the distance men floating with a long gliding gait, the sprinters chopping furiously through starts on the grass. Jesse Owens came down the stadium steps and walked onto the green infield with the short, bouncy, confident stride that appeared so often in the newsreels and the movies from Berlin in 1936. He was erect, square-shouldered, and all the fluid power that used to explode in his sprints still seemed available if he just decided to call for it. But certainly not. Jesse Owens was fifty-eight years old now, pouched around the eyes and a full twenty-five pounds heavier than in 1936. Even without the pencil-line mustache and the receded hairline, the features of the older man scarcely resembled those of the younger.

In Berlin, there were the calm bright eyes, the serene face, the brown silken skin and the magnificently supple physique which seemed to be able to do any superhuman feat asked of it.

40

The body was a combination of grace and strength so over-whelming that Leni Riefenstahl, Hitler's own official cinematographer for those Olympics, all but deified the young Jesse Owens with her cameras in making him a major focus—a kind of living Olympic icon—in her film of the Berlin Games, *Olympia*, which is simply one of the most beautiful documentaries ever made. In these Olympics, Owens competed in twelve events, including preliminary heats; he set or equaled Olympic records nine times. He won the 100-meter dash, the 200-meter dash, the broad jump, and was on the winning 400-meter relay team. Four gold medals, and there were parades and audiences with kings and prime ministers. No track athlete ever lived who was like Jesse Owens, and in 1950 he was voted by sportswriters to be the best of the first fifty years of the twentieth century, polling twice as many votes as Jim Thorpe and Paavo Nurmi combined. That was all because of the young man Jesse Owens had been in Berlin.

This event in Binghamton, New York, was a track meet for teen-agers sponsored by the Junior Chamber of Commerce, and along with the churning legs of competitors, the infield was alive with the grins of go-get-'em junior executives and the smiles of rising young salesmen. Jaycees moved in from all sides to shake hands and welcome "Mr. Owens, sir, to our Sports Spectacular." Jesse Owens was enormously friendly, untiringly enthusiastic, not unlike a Jaycee himself. Jesse Owens signed autographs, always relaxed, always loose, always chatting. "Your name's Darlene? Harya, Darlene, ol' buddy. Mike? Harya, Mike, ol' buddy, you gonna be a runner?"

Then the kids stopped running, and the Jaycees stood quietly, and so did the 100 or so people scattered like blown leaves here and there in the grandstand, and so did Jesse Owens. "The Star-Spangled Banner" played through a PA speaker from a tiny cassette tape recorder. Then a young Jaycee rather tremulously introduced Jesse Owens—"I give you America's greatest Olympic hero!"

Loose and casual, Jesse Owens spoke into the microphone, in a deep and impressive voice, his words well enunciated. Jesse Owens was at work, of course. He said, "On behalf of the Ford Motor Company and the Lincoln-Mercury Division of Ford, we're glad to be a part of this fine Sports Spectacular here with the Junior Chamber of Commerce in Binghamton, New York. . . . A lot of good luck to all of you, and God bless."

Jesse Owens began to walk from the field when a Jaycee said, "Wait, Mr. Owens, we've got the Olympic torch ceremony to go." A runner appeared at one end of the track carrying a funnel-shaped object, which turned out to be the torch—unlighted. "Dammit, the fire's out," muttered a Jaycee. The runner loped a couple of hundred yards along the track to a large dish-shaped receptacle which was to hold the "Olympic flame" during the day's meet. The Jaycee stationed there looked rather dazedly at the unlighted torch, fumbled through his pockets for matches, then shrugged and held out empty hands. Another Jaycee jogged over with a cigarette lighter, and after a few minutes' struggle he too turned and looked inquiringly at other Jaycees. One shouted, "Put some more fluid on!" A can of charcoal lighter appeared, was squirted into the receptacle, and soon the Olympic flame in Binghamton, New York, was blazing merrily.

Jesse Owens left the field then, grinning, waving, signing every autograph requested. He climbed into the back seat of a gleaming gray 1971 Lincoln, furnished by the local Lincoln-Mercury dealer. The president of the Binghamton Jaycees was at the wheel, and he drove to the Schrafft's Motor Inn in downtown Binghamton. Outside was a white plastic sign with movable red plastic letters. On one side of the sign the letters were arranged to spell DINNER SPECIAL SEAFOOD PLATTER; on the other side they said WELCOME JESSE OWENS.

It was time, said Jesse Owens, for lunch, a fried egg and ham sandwich and a cold bottle of beer.

When Jesse Owens speaks, even with a bite of fried egg and ham sandwich in his mouth, grand oratorical echoes roll through every dithyrambic phrase. If you ask him, for example, how he liked the Games in Mexico City, Jesse Owens is apt to say, "I saw ten thousand people competing there, and it was the aim of every girl and every boy to be victorious. Yet there they were— eating together, singing together, dancing together, *rapping* together, and I thought, 'If this does not bring the nations of the world together, whatever will?' . . ." Or if you ask what advantage Olympic medals may be to the futures of the athletes, Jesse Owens might say, "The Olympic movement is functioning in a highly economic world, and if a boy takes advantage of his medals to enhance his chances as he enters the greatest of all competitions in life—to seek prosperity and to make a living— then I ask, why not? Why should he not have further reward for being an extraordinary individual who has covered himself with extra glory?" Or if you ask how much money a gold medal is worth, he may reply, "Material reward is not all there is, sir. No. How many meals can a man eat? How many cars can he drive? In how many beds can he sleep? All of life's wonders are not reflected in material wealth. . . ."

And so on and so forth. This is a natural way of talking for Jesse Owens unless he is very relaxed. He is a kind of all-around super-combination of nineteenth-century spellbinder and twentieth-century plastic PR man, a full-time banquet guest, eternal

43

glad-hander and evangelistic small-talker. Muted, tasteful, inspirational bombast is his stock-in-trade.

Jesse Owens is what you might call a professional good example.

For this he is paid around $75,000 a year. Some of the income comes from the eighty or ninety speeches he makes at $750 or so per speech, some from the corporate clients he "represents"—meaning, in essence, that he sells them his celebrity and his personality and his reputation for use at public events where his clients wish to display their "Jesse Owens Image" (as one advertising executive called it). Among the clients of the Jesse Owens Image are the Atlantic-Richfield Oil Company, Sears, Roebuck, the American League, United Fruit, U.S. Rubber and, of course, the Ford Motor Company, where he serves on a "sports panel" with such as Al Kaline, Bart Starr and Dave DeBusschere. Jesse Owens offers other endorsements, too. He appeared for Schlitz Beer in its TV commercials during the 1968 Olympics, and not long ago he was in magazine advertisements with Rafer Johnson boosting Jim Beam whiskey.

In pursuit of his career, Jesse Owens says he travels 200,000 miles a year. On the average he spends four days of every seven sleeping in some hotel and eating his meals with Jaycees, salesmen and other strangers.

A dispatch sent by International News Service under Jesse Owens' byline and datelined London, August 17, 1936, (one day after the Berlin Olympics ended) said: "I am turning professional because, first of all I'm busted and know the difficulties encountered by any member of my race in getting financial security. Secondly, because if I have money, I can help my race and perhaps become like Booker T. Washington."

Jesse Owens had many offers of big money after the Olympics—a Harlem club said he could earn $10,000 in a single night, and Eddie Cantor wired him in London to "hold tight" because there was $50,000 to be made on a personal tour. Some of these offers fell through. Nevertheless, people were startled in the autumn of 1936 when Jesse Owens announced his choice for his first big-paying job. It bore no resemblance to the career of Booker T. Washington. He was going to campaign for the Republican Presidential candidate, Governor Alf Landon of Kansas, the Sunflower State.

Looking back now from Binghamton, New York, Jesse said with a smile, "Poorest race I ever ran. But they paid me a *lot*. No, I won't say how much—but a *lot*! Joe Pew of Sun Oil Company got me to do it. I was the guy who was the beginning of the celebrity stable in political campaigns, I guess."

Alf Landon won just two states, the lonely eight electoral votes of Vermont and Maine. Only Booker T. Washington might have done worse. The use of champion athletes as political assets was plainly in its pioneering stages. Here, for example, is part of a speech Jesse read before an adoring crowd of 9,000 Republicans on October 13, 1936, in Baltimore: "There are people here old enough to be my daddy and mother, and I am not old enough to tell you how to vote. . . . I am not knocking the President [FDR]. Remember, I am not a politician, but remember that the President did not send me a message of congratulations because, people said, he was too busy. Governor Alfred M. Landon did send me a message, and he was very nice to me. I had the opportunity to talk about a half hour with Alf M. Landon. We did not talk about politics, but talked about horseback riding. I do not care much for horseback riding because of the effects, but I told him that when he is President then I will come and go horseback riding with him. . . ."

And so on and so forth.

In Binghamton Jesse Owens spoke of his growth as a public orator. "I was once a stutterer, and when I was at Ohio State I took a course in phonetics, from a master teacher. I cured my ailment, and now I have probably spent more hours public speaking than I have sleeping. Ever since I was a college student, I've admired the great orators of my day, even more than the great athletes. . . . Roscoe Conklin Simmons and Perry W. Howard and, of course, Martin Luther King and Adam Clayton Powell. When I was young, I used to go to banquets just to watch the mannerisms and the style of public speakers."

Jesse Owens' own style of oratory is grandiose and soaring, perhaps more notable for its transcendental delivery than its scholarly thought. "Mostly, I'd say the substance is sheerly inspirational," said Jesse Owens. "I work for my payday like anyone else, and things fall into routine. I have a speech on motivation and values, one on religion, one on patriotism. Some parts are interchangeable, but I'm talking to kids most of the time. I tell them things like this. . . ." His voice made a slight adjustment, and suddenly it was deeper, and it became a kind of dignified holler that bounded about the restaurant of Schrafft's Motor Inn.

"Awards become tarnished and diplomas fade," said Jesse Owens in full cry. "Gold turns green, and ink turns gray and you cannot *read* what is upon that diploma or upon that badge. Championships are mythical things. They have no permanence. What is a gold medal? It is but a trinket, a bauble. What counts, my friends, are the *realities* of life: the fact of competition and, yes, the great and good *friends* you make. . . ."

His voice readjusted some to show he was no longer orating. But an intrinsic consciousness of the sound of his voice remained. "Grown men," he said softly, "stop me on the street now and say, 'Mr. Owens, I heard you talk fifteen years ago in Minneapolis. I'll never forget that speech.' And I think to myself, that man probably has children of his own now. And maybe, *maybe* he remembers a specific point I made, or perhaps two points I made. And maybe he is passing those points on to his own son just as I said them. And then I think"—Jesse's voice drops close to a whisper—"then I think, that's immortality. You are immortal if your ideas are being passed on from a father to a son and to his son and on and on. . . ."

"People said it was degrading for an Olympic champion to run against a horse," said Jesse Owens, "but what was I supposed to do? I had four gold medals, but you can't eat four gold medals. There was no television, no big advertising, no endorsements then. Not for a black man, anyway. Things were different then. You know, I didn't even get the Sullivan Award. Never. In 1935, the year I broke three world records and tied one in one day, it went to some golfer named Lawson Little. And in 1936 the AAU gave it to Glenn Morris, who won the decathlon in Berlin. A lot of people don't realize what blacks had to do then to get money—we had to resort to personal promotions and use our resources to scrape up what there was around."

Eddie Cantor had welched on his offer, and Alf Landon proved to be terribly temporary, so Jesse Owens turned to a series of offbeat ways of making a living. He traveled for a time with a circus-basketball team called the Indianapolis Clowns. "We'd get into these little towns and tell 'em to get out the fastest guy in town and Jesse Owens'd spot him ten yards and beat him." He had his own basketball team, the Jesse Owens Olympians, which traveled with the Harlem Globetrotters for a time. He fronted for a dance band for a year or so. "Well, I couldn't play any instrument. I'd just stand up front and announce the numbers," he said. "They had me sing a little, but that was a horrible mistake. I can't carry a tune in a bucket. We played black theaters and nightclubs all over hell. One-nighters. Apollo Theater in Harlem and the Earle Theater in Philly—that was big time for blacks. We went to garden spots like Monroe, Louisiana. Sometimes I'd slip in a running exhibition at a ball game. It was rough going; there'd be knife fights right on the dance floor some nights. Promoters'd run off with all the dough after a dance. Whoooo-ee. It was a long way from the Olympic ideal. I wound up with a strep throat in Richmond, Virginia, and I very nearly died."

His first big exhibition race against a horse was in Havana in December, 1936. Jesse Owens was to receive $2,000 for the race. "Batista was the kingpin down there then. I was scared to death because they had a huge crowd. But it all came off all right—I won. Of course, there's no way that a man can *really* beat a horse, even over a hundred yards. The secret is—first, get a thoroughbred horse because they are the most nervous animals on earth. Then get the biggest gun you can and make sure the starter fires that big gun right by that nervous thoroughbred's ear. By the time the jockey gets the horse settled down, I could cover about fifty yards. Once that horse started galloping with twenty-, twenty-two-foot strides, man I'd have to go like *hell* to win in a hundred yards. And we also found out that you should never, never race a quarterhorse, because the gun doesn't bother him at all, and you don't have a chance."

The day Jesse Owens returned from Europe in 1936, there was a wild and exuberant parade through Harlem. He and his wife, Ruth, perched on the back of a convertible, and they were pelted with papers and balloons and all sorts of things thrown by throngs along the curb. After the parade they went to the apartment of the dancer Bill "Bojangles" Robinson, who had befriended the Owenses long before the Olympics. "We had a great little party at Bill's house, and I was so thankful for his taking care of Ruth while I was gone that I gave him one of my gold medals that day," recalled Jesse Owens. "He kept it all his life, I know that. Then I remember it was time to get to the station to catch the train back to Cleveland. And we just picked up all the stuff from the convertible and from Bill's house and piled it on the train. As we were pulling out, we started to sort through what we had, and there was this little brown package, like a sandwich. It had rubber bands around it. It had been thrown into the convertible and landed on the floor. So I opened it up, figuring maybe it was someone's lunch or something and—I couldn't believe it—I'd never seen so much money in my life. There were twenties and tens and hundred-dollar bills. Ruth and I counted it. There was ten thousand dollars! We couldn't believe we were right. Larry Snyder, my college coach, counted it too—ten thousand dollars in a brown paper sack! To this day I have no idea at all who gave us that money. No one has ever stepped forward."

Jesse Owens shook his head. "But I'll tell you, I never spent any money in my life better than I spent that ten thousand dollars cash. People had been so beautiful to me that I just started spending on them. Ruth and I spent it on my mother and father and on Charlie Riley, my old high school coach, and on Jack Clowser, a great newspaperman at the Cleveland Press, who had helped me write some speeches. We bought Riley a brand-new car—it only cost eight hundred dollars then—and gave it to him with a big red ribbon around it. We bought bikes and watches for the Clowser kids, and we bought my mother a house with all the furniture. . . ."

Jesse Owens now has a summer home in Michigan and a

spacious new house in Scottsdale, Arizona, with the great brown hump of Camelback Mountain within his view. His prosperity seems assured, but no man with Jesse Owens' background ever takes wealth for granted. "My parents were not literate people —how could a sharecropper in Alabama in the first twenty years of this century get to be literate? The only thing we had was a belief in God, and we lived according to the Bible. We picked cotton all day long. When I was seven, I was picking one hundred pounds a day. In the morning I'd wait in the wagon until the dew dried off. The cotton stalks were taller than me, and I'd practically drown until the sun was high and the dew dried some. But it was hard, and we'd sell the crops after the season, after working like demons for the summer, and then there still wasn't enough money to last the winter.

"My father decided to try it in the north, and he went up to Cleveland. He was there a year ahead of us. Then he said come on up. It was a horn of plenty there, we thought. We had a house.

"My dad had a defective left eye. One day he stepped into the street and didn't see a taxi coming, and he broke his leg. It never healed right, and they wouldn't let him work. I pumped gas and delivered groceries for twenty cents an hour. . . ."

Jesse Owens paused, then said, "Hell, I can't forget my upbringing. I started at the bottom—and look at me now. I've got two homes, and I'm free to travel, and I know where my next meals are coming from.

"It's the Establishment that gave that to me. I tell the kids I talk to that the Establishment has been too good to me to knock it. I tell them that if they damn the system, *condemn* the system, then they have to have some ideas to *improve* the system. . . ."

Whether Jesse Owens is being himself or the "Jesse Owens Image," he is a man of candor. He has been called an Uncle Tom for his views on American racial problems, and he has been called an opportunist for using his Olympic status to advance his career—indeed, to *create* his career. Yet he does not equivocate in what he says. Here are a few samplings of quotes from Jesse Owens which help greatly to define him and his times:

• Jesse Owens was found guilty and fined $3,000 in 1966 for failure to pay $68,166 in federal taxes. "At the time," he said, "I was tied up in a lot of business deals—in trucking and insurance and radio and public appearances. There was a lot of money, and I let someone else take care of the records. It was my fault. I was a poor captain of my team, and I won't holler wolf. You find out who your friends are, though. People could've dropped me cold, but they stuck by. Listen, I like America for things like that. There's nowhere else in the world where when a guy is down, someone'll come and pick him up." The fine was considered fairly light, and Judge Joseph Sam Perry, who could have sent Owens to jail for four years and fined him $40,000, said, "I've taken into consideration the fact that it is well known that you have suffered more than others."

• On the hustings for Alf Landon in Kansas City in 1936: "Hitler didn't snub me—it was our President who snubbed me. The President didn't even send me a telegram."

• At the Schrafft's Motor Inn in Binghamton, 1971: "Hell, today every marble champion gets to the White House, but none of us heard a word from Roosevelt. We figured we'd really done something, too."

• "Until the thirties, the Negro had no image to point to. Then there were two—Joe Louis and myself. We were riding the wave of newfound pride that the Negro had then. And I hope we've never let them down."

• "When I was at Ohio State on trips with the track team, I stayed across the tracks on the black side of town. In Columbus, either I ate on campus or I couldn't eat anywhere *near*

51

campus. In 1961 my daughter was elected Homecoming Queen at Ohio State. There's some kind of progress there. . . ."

• "The black fist is a meaningless symbol. When you open it, you have nothing but fingers—weak empty fingers. The only time the black fist has significance is when there's money inside. There's where the power lies."

The banquet following the Jaycees' Sport Spectacular in Binghamton, New York, was held in a large, brightly lighted meeting room at the Harpur College union building. Jesse Owens was dressed in a fine beige suit of modified Edwardian cut, a muted green shirt and a wide, loud tie. Jesse Owens was ushered into the banquet room by himself, while a few hundred banquet guests waited in the lobby. He stood for a moment at the head table and stared out at the neatly set dinner tables that covered the otherwise empty room. "God, I *always* have these damn butterflies before I talk," he said. "Wouldn't you think I'd get over it?" Soon the crowd came in to eat, and Jesse sat at the head table, a Jaycee on one side, an administrator from Harpur College on the other. The usual babble and clatter of a banquet being consumed (an oddly soporific sound) rose over the room. Jesse bent occasionally back and forth between his companions, speaking small-talk. A shy child was prodded by her father to ask Jesse for his autograph, and he put on a pair of large horn-rimmed glasses in order to see where he signed. Then the master of ceremonies introduced Jesse Owens—"I give you the greatest Olympian of them all, *Jesse Owens!*"—and Jesse stood easily at the podium while a robust ovation burst over the room for more than a minute. Everyone settled down then, and Jesse Owens began to speak his evangelism: ". . . there'll be winners and losers . . . friendships born on the field of strife are the real gold of competition . . . awards become corroded, but friends gather no dust . . . youth is the greatest commodity this nation has . . . honor thyself and honor thy God. . . ."

Jesse Owens had eaten yet another meal among strangers, and now the greatest Olympian of them all and the image of the greatest Olympian of them all were working nicely in tandem again.

Part II
The Olympic Establishment

3. "I Hereby Assert My Claims for Being the Sole Author of the Whole Project"

IN his waning years he was often seen by citizens of Lausanne rowing alone on Lake Geneva, a small and melancholy silhouette bending and pulling, bending and pulling to propel himself in slow circles upon the glassy water. The time was the 1930's, and he was quite poor now, his ancient family fortune spent and little more money to be expected despite his fame as founder of the Olympic Games and his title. Baron Pierre de Coubertin and his wife, Marie, and his only daughter, Renée, were living in a hotel suite given to them by the municipality of Lausanne.

His wife, barbed and shrewish in her old age, refused even to grant him a few sous for pocket money. His daughter, once a sunny gentle child gifted as both a watercolorist and a poet, had come to be what close relatives cautiously called "funny"—"She was not mad," said a cousin, "just something a little funny." Since late childhood, Renée had been forced by her mother to wear masculine clothing and forbidden any use of ribbons or lace, powder or rouge. This, relatives agreed, was caused by the

57

dark and towering Victorian guilt Baroness de Coubertin had created in herself over the bizarre tragedy that had befallen a baby son many years before. The boy had been two years old when his mother left him exposed for several hours beneath a fierce summer sun. When he was found, the baby had suffered a stroke, and though he lived for several years, he never again showed the faintest sign of human intelligence. The Baron and Baroness de Coubertin had no other children.

As if the strife and shadow that crowded into their little hotel suite were not enough, the baron was also desperately disappointed when he failed to win the Nobel Peace Prize in 1936. His name had been submitted to the jury in Oslo by some of the most celebrated names in Europe's fading bouquet of aristocrats and frock-coat politicians. The baron had assumed that with their support, his resurrection of the Olympic Games would win him election as the peace laureate of 1936. Instead, the jury chose the first Latin American ever to be honored, Carlos Saavedra Lamas, an Argentinian lawyer, professor and diplomat.

Baron de Coubertin was heartbroken. He had wanted the Nobel Prize as a kind of legacy which would somehow validate his dream of the Olympic Games as a source of true peace on earth. The baron really had believed that the Games *could* eradicate war even while war machines were clanking just beyond every horizon.

"He was very disillusioned, very sad, at the end of his life," the baron's nephew, Geoffrey de Navacelle, recalled many years later. "Remember, in 1914 the Olympics were in their infancy. No one really believed they could stop war then. But in 1936 I'm afraid my uncle was forced to realize that even a full-grown Olympics had never been the means, perhaps, that he had been searching for. He was quite distraught. Things had not gone as he intended."

Baron de Coubertin died "of a stroke of apoplexy," it was reported by the Associated Press, while he was strolling in a public garden of Geneva on September 2, 1937. He was seventy-four. In his will the baron declared that his body was to be buried in Lausanne where the headquarters of the International Olympic Committee stood. But first, his heart was to be removed from his breast, encased in a marble column and buried separately at Olympia in Greece.

This request caused some raised eyebrows among the baron's aristocratic friends, but of course, it was done. His wife lived long years after her husband. She did not die until she was a hundred and one years old. She maintained an active interest in the Olympics until her death.

The life of a child of the aristocracy in nineteenth-century France was both stifling and elegant. Pierre de Coubertin grew up in a castle at St.-Rémy-lès-Chevreuse, a town house at 20 Rue Oudinot in Paris and a seaside chateau near Le Havre in Normandy. His was a naïve and gracious existence—at times quaintly anachronistic even for those days. The family title dated back to the reign of Louis XI in the fifteenth century and the Coubertins had never come to accept the tides of republican government in France after the Revolution. To them, Napoleonic democracy was simply a passing ripple, a bubble to be burst soon enough by God's own finger. The only government man could properly expect to enjoy was the divine right of a king. The Coubertins were still stubbornly royalist when France had been a republic for nearly three-quarters of a century. When Pierre de Coubertin was sixteen, his family made a pilgrimage across Europe to Vienna; there they paid clandestine homage to the pretender to the French throne, the man whom they believed to be "King Henri V." The family knelt before him and kissed his sword. Young Pierre was appalled at what he saw, a shattered and rheumy-eyed bit of human wreckage, a sad and lonely old crock.

The folly of waiting, of praying for this poor old man to dash into Paris and seize France for the royalists was all too clear to the boy. He dropped any pretense of allegiance to a French kingdom-come and even began to shock the blooded patricians who visited his parents' homes by declaring that *all* republicans were not *all* wrong. Eventually the baron would refer to himself as a "revolutionist," and ultimately he spoke in favor of workers' colleges in France. He was genuinely shocked over the segregated plight of American blacks when he visited the United States in the late 1880's.

In time, the baron was accused of being a socialist. Of course, he was not. For all his life the baron's warmest, most influential friends in Olympic as well as personal matters were to be counts and marquis and archdukes and princes and kings and extremely rich men from a few limited walks of life.

The baron was quite tiny, barely five feet three inches tall. Early in life he cultivated a fine sweeping cowcatcher of a mustache beneath his generous aristocratic nose (it was the nose of a much taller aristocrat). He wore the mustache all his life, and it turned snow white when he grew old in Lausanne. The gentle baron did not indulge greatly in competitive sport himself. Mostly he rowed or rode. He adored flowers and loved music; he enjoyed all manner of drawing-room chatter and particularly reveled in private concerts put on for him by his niece, a harpist. Beethoven's Symphony Number Seven was his favorite, and more than once it was included in Olympic ceremonies to please him.

Writing was the baron's favorite pastime, and he produced words in prolific bulk, hundreds of pounds of papers and pamphlets and letters and books over the years. It was mostly pedantic, dusty, unpoetic stuff which dealt with weighty themes and obscure patterns in education, politics or history. He argued that the study of history was actually a handmaiden to war rather than to peace, for it taught Germans to hate French and French to hate Germans. Also, he could not see why the "facts" of Waterloo should be taught differently in England from in France, and he suggested a "universal" international history. In 1898 the baron argued in a tract that students of France must be given more voice in the way their schools were run. This same argument was heard again seventy years later, when rioting French students took to the barricades to demand more freedom within the same antiquated educational system that Coubertin had opposed.

Despite a high voice, the baron cut a dandy figure at the speaker's rostrum, and he did a great deal of lecturing and public speaking during his life. Indeed, at one point he actually endowed a chair in public speaking at the University of California at Berkeley.

For all the words he wrote and spoke, it is ironic that two of the more famous quotations attributed to the baron were not really his own creations. Perhaps the most-repeated inspirational bromide said to be his is this: "The most important thing in the Olympic Games is not to win but to take part, just as the most important thing in life is not the triumph but the struggle." It is true that the baron said it many, many times, but he seized upon it only after he had heard the Bishop of Pennsylvania say it first in 1908.

The Olympic motto—*Citius, Altius, Fortius* (Swifter, Higher, Stronger)—sprang not from Coubertin's forehead either, but from a chunk of chiseled stone over the entrance to a progressive parochical school run by a celebrated Dominican gadfly-priest, Henri Martin Didon. Père Didon was a fiery orator, a razor-tongued left-wing assailant of the Roman Catholic Church, who flailed away at standardized church views of divorce and the Trinity. Père Didon was also an aggressive crusader against the ongoing decadence of France, and he adopted many of Baron de Coubertin's then-radical educational ideas for injecting physical competition into his curriculum.

France in the latter half of the nineteenth century was still deafened and baffled by the ringing defeat suffered in the six weeks' war of 1870 at the hands of the hated Germans. There were a few critics who shouted that French ways were too effete and too cerebral. There were some who said that no nation built on a foundation of musty salons and nourished on a pale diet of circular intellectual discussion could long endure in the robust knockabout world to come. Some said that, but not many.

Inertia was considered essential to develop great thought. Sport was gauche and rarely discussed by anyone who considered himself either stylish or sensible. No one minded that a leading newspaper once carefully explained to its readers that soccer was a game played with rackets and small, hard balls. People minded even less, perhaps, when another newspaper struck back to correct that error by declaring that soccer was in fact properly played only with long, flat mallets. Intelligent Frenchmen all knew soccer to be a game of cracked brains and unseemly bloodshed in public places—a game to be abhorred, however it was played.

Into this marshmallow swamp waded the brave Baron de Coubertin, braying pro-athletic bon mots through his nose and tossing around blizzards of pedantic papers which proclaimed sport to be the potential savior of the French spirit, if not of the world itself. He preached about "physical degeneracy" in his nation, and he cried out that he wanted to *rebronzer* French youth. He praised the comparatively robust British educational system: "It is the application according to modern requirements of the most characteristic principles of Grecian civilization: To make the muscles be chief factor in the work of moral education." He lauded fresh air and sweat and vast green playing fields within French cities and footraces for scholars and calisthenics for librarians.

Of course, he was denounced as a vulgarian.

The baron was not a vulgarian; he was an astute politician and ultimately a convincing advocate of his ideas. In only a couple of years he had enlisted in his crusade to bring sports into French schools the philosopher Jules Simon, Georges de Saint-Clair (who in 1887 organized the world's first international track meet), the director of l'École Monge (who reduced class hours to allow students to play)—plus two Presidents of the French Republic, Sadi Carnot and Armand Fallières. The baron also traveled to England, where he discussed his schemes with former Prime Minister William Gladstone, and to the United States where he found a sympathetic and influential audience in Professor William Sloane of Princeton. This is not to mention the legions of assorted noblemen and aristocrats to whom the baron could turn in time of need. His were not the common connections of a vulgarian, not at all.

Perhaps no one will ever know precisely why the baron became so enmeshed in the controversial matter of physical fitness in a country which so cherished its inertia. Some say it was merely the *noblesse oblige* of a nicely reared aristocrat asserting itself. Others insist the baron was a raging, secret superpatriot, a man so obsessed by the military humiliation of France in 1870 that he envisioned his plan to *rebronzer* the young as a paramilitary policy that would make France husky and mean and warlike—equal to Germany or Great Britain. Others maintain he was simply reacting to the creeping suffocation of life among nineteenth-century bluebloods, that he could as well have spent his rebellious energies promoting horseless carriages or birth control devices as in reinventing the Olympic Games. But we shall never really know.

It is not known, either, precisely why the baron hit upon the Olympic Games as a vehicle for promoting sports and peace. He was not reputed to have any overweaning interest in antique Greece. Perhaps it came about in 1890 during a visit to England and to a strange little festival held in the rocky green countryside of Shropshire near the border of Wales. This event, too, was called an "Olympic Games." It was sponsored by an eighty-two-year-old Englishman, a Dr. W. P. Brookes, who had named his estate the Olympian Fields and had founded a group called the Olympian Society of Much Wenlock. (Much Wenlock was the village nearest the doctor's home.) The festival included footraces and horse races, tennis and cricket matches, soccer and spirited mock battles between amused farmers and villagers dressed as medieval jousters. There was a lot of foofaraw and pageantry—sipping at silver champagne bowls and kneeling before fair ladies and wafting showers of flower petals about the landscape. Old Dr. Brookes also hung banners in the trees with ancient Greek mottoes emblazoned upon them.

The baron was very impressed. He later made the ancient

Dr. Brookes an honorary member of the group that would ultimately be the world's first International Olympic Committee. But no one can be quite sure why Baron de Coubertin chose the Olympic Games to put life in his vision of physical education as the redemption of mankind.

November 25, 1892, was the night the baron chose to make the first public announcement of his scheme to improve the world through producing a new Olympic Games. The audience was supposedly friendly and warm and thoroughly in favor of both sports as a way of life and the baron as its prophet. The occasion he selected was the fifth anniversary of the Union des Sociétés Françaises de Sports Athlétiques, an organization of which the baron was president. The place was the Sorbonne, and later the baron wrote: "It seemed to me that under the venerable roof of the Sorbonne the words 'Olympic Games' would resound more impressively and more persuasively on the audience."

The essence of the baron's speech dealt with the value of internationalism in sports. He spoke with fervor: "There are those whom you would call Utopians since they speak of the disappearance of war, but there are others who believe in the diminution of the chances of war, and I don't see that as Utopian." He cried out that the "cause of peace would receive a new and forceful boost" if nations competed in athletics rather than arms. Then he unleashed the historic notion: "We must join to found a base conforming to the conditions of modern life, this grandiose and beneficent work: *the re-establishment of the Olympic Games!*"

The baron paused and glared significantly at the gathering. The gathering looked back blankly and did nothing at first. Then people became restless.

They had no idea what the baron was talking about. At last men began scrambling to their feet to ask questions:

"Do you mean a theatrical reproduction with fake athletes?"

"Oh, *non*," said the baron, "the real thing. . . ."

"Then will the athletes be nude?" The audience was laughing. "Will it be forbidden for women to watch? Who will participate? Only the French? It used to be only the Greeks. . . ."

"I foresee the Games on a world scale," said the baron, but the audience scarcely cared what he said, for now he was only a poor butterfly pinned at the podium for their amusement.

"Oh, then we'll have Negroes and Chinese and—and—redskins!" shouted one man, and the halls of the Sorbonne rocked and shivered with laughter.

Next, there occurs a scene in which Hollywood could cast only Jimmy Stewart as Baron de Coubertin. No one else will do. He is walking alone out of the Sorbonne after the speech, his shoulders are stooped, and his face is very sad. As he pauses, gazing at the streetlights of Paris, a young girl steps to his side and places her small hand upon his arm. She is played by June Allyson. No one else will do. June Allyson is playing the part of Marie Rothan, the petite daughter of a wealthy but untitled Alsatian Protestant. She speaks this line to the baron (as reported in a biography of Coubertin by Marie Thérèse Eiquen): "Your idea was too much for them. It will be necessary to give it to them little by little. This time, their reaction is not important."

The baron looks down at her. His Jimmy Stewart eyes seem to grow warm. His mustache moves a little to indicate that he is smiling now despite the fiasco that has occurred inside.

They leave the Sorbonne arm in arm, and the romance blossoms. However, there are thorns in the blossoms, for Pierre-Jimmy's parents do not approve of his Marie-June on four counts: (1) She is a commoner; (2) she is a Protestant; (3) she is an Alsatian, and their province had changed hands so often over the centuries that they are not considered to be true blooded Frenchmen; and (4) she is two years older than he is.

Baron de Coubertin-Stewart faces his family down, of course, with a wonderful warm speech that wins hearts in the balconies of all the Bijous and Roxys in every land: "Our match is perfect. Alsace is a lost province and one must love it more than the others. I am Christian, as are the Protestants. There was a time, certainly, when our family was common. And we both are old enough to know what we're doing."

They were married on March 12, 1895. Ahead lay the Olympic Games and, alas, Lausanne.

There was entertainment and convention fun the likes of which no Shriners ever knew in Paris during June, 1894. Baron de Coubertin had convened from around the world physical educationists and sporting dignitaries of many ilks, ostensibly to discuss such problems as the bane of professionalism in sport and the hope for more international competition. Of course, his chief object was to sell the Olympic Games. For eight days the delegates were wined and dined and soireed. After one massed banquet, the lawn of the Croix Catalan was framed by a thousand blazing torches while the baron's dazzled delegates watched horse races, mock skirmishes between armored men on horseback and waterfalls of fireworks in the sky. The ancient "Hymn to Apollo" had been unearthed recently by German archaeologists at Delphi, and this was performed to music composed by Gabriel Faure.

Besides these nocturnal diversions, the baron kept the delegates occupied during the day with a wretchedly complicated agenda that included eight lengthy items. Seven of the items consumed the arduous, droning sessions of the first seven weary days. Then, on the last day, the baron rose to the rostrum and presented Item Eight—the resurrection of the Olympic Games! Some people say the delegates were too woozy from the previous night's wine to realize what Item Eight was about. Others say the enervating length of discussion on the other seven items had drained everyone so thoroughly that Item Eight would have carried no matter what it advocated—just so adjournment followed. Still others insist that the wily baron had packed that hall of the Sorbonne with friends of Item Eight. Perhaps it does not matter why the resolution passed.

The fact is that the delegates—from France and Russia and the United States and England, Greece, Belgium, Sweden, Spain and Italy—leaped up and applauded Item Eight. They stamped their feet. They shouted, and they voted unanimously to exhume the Olympic Games. And the first Olympiad, they decided, should be held in 1896 in Athens, the second in Paris in 1900.

Word spread quickly back to Paris that there was trouble in Athens. The government of Greece really did not see how it could *afford* the Olympic Games. The glories that were Greece were no more. The treasury was near bankruptcy. Greece in the nineteenth century was a rocky, unforgiving land in large part. The majority of the people were not the beautiful athletic beings who graced antique urns and statuary, but tough wiry peasants who fought the barren ground like beasts in order to win survival. Athens was a plain little town of 130,000 people. When citizens first learned that they had to host the Olympic Games, they were appalled. A newspaper editor ran a worried editorial, saying he was alarmed that "foreign visitors will come and see only the nakedness of our land."

The baron hurried off to Athens himself to try to raise morale and put things in their proper order. He had an emergency meeting with the prime minister, but to no avail. The prime minister would not bend. There simply was not enough money in the Greek treasury to finance a luxury like the Olympic Games. The baron used all his political skills, even blatant blackmail. He carried with him—and frequently brandished—a letter from a powerful friend in Budapest, saying that the Hungarian government would be delighted to sponsor the Olympics of 1896 if Athens failed. The baron wrote a wicked little note to the Athenian newspaper *Asty* in which he said, "We have a proverb which says that the word 'impossible' is not French. Someone told me this morning that the word is Greek, but I didn't believe him."

When he was unable to persuade or coerce the prime minister, the baron declared that he must see the king. Upon discovering King George was not in the capitol, Coubertin arranged an audience with Crown Prince Constantine. And here, it is agreed by Olympic historians, the baron did something very wise. He did not speak a paean to ancient Greece and the sagacity of Aristotle and the splendor of Olympia and the immortality of so much that occurred there. Instead, the baron simply told the prince that the world held great admiration

69

for the Greece of the nineteenth century. He spoke about the magnificent courage displayed by modern Greeks in breaking the iron collar of Turkish rule, and he talked of the little country's grim and unyielding capacity for self-pride and self-salvation after long decades of alien rule—"when the world no longer knew there were any Greeks."

The prince sat entranced, and the baron cried, "It is in *this* Greece that I believe."

Transported perhaps by Coubertin's eloquence, young Constantine replied, "And I, sir, believe in *your* Olympics."

So it was done. Though Greece was a democracy and the royal family had no legal access to government coffers, the king and his sons and Coubertin organized a public fund-raising campaign which ultimately produced 300,000 drachmas ($36,000). The government issued a special commemorative Olympic stamp which netted another 400,000 drachmas. But still more—much, much more—had to be found to restore the once-splendid Panathenaean Stadium of Herodes Atticus. It had fallen to ruin and was little but a stony, bramble-choked ravine. The Greeks knew where to turn for philanthropy. There was a rich and generous merchant of Alexandria, George Averoff, a man as wealthy as Croesus and Onassis combined and already renowned for his public gifts.

There were two Averoff brothers—Anastassios, the elder, and George. Their name originally was Apostolakas, but Anastassios migrated to Russia and changed it to Averoff for business reasons. He became extremely rich through various forms of commerce and investment, contributed vast sums of money to the Russian Army during the Napoleonic Wars and was well known and respected by powerful financiers throughout the world. His brother, George Apostolakas, was born in 1818 in Greece, went to Egypt to seek his fortune and, in view of the high reputation of his brother's name, had changed his name to Averoff also. George became rich dealing in Egyptian cotton, wheat and gold thread. His greatest coup occurred in 1861 during the U.S. Civil War, when he purchased the entire cotton crop of Egypt and sold it in Europe at huge markup since the American South could export almost nothing because of the Union blockade at sea.

George Averoff remained a bachelor and lived a simple Spartan life, yet his celebrity in the late nineteenth century was perhaps even greater than that of Aristotle Onassis today. For George Averoff was a philanthropist of incredible generosity. He donated millions of drachmas for educational institutions, including Athens Polytechnic University and the Greek Army's equivalent of West Point. He built the Athens prison, which was named after him. When George Averoff died in 1899, he left much of his fortune to the state; among other things, the government purchased the first cruiser Greece ever had and named it after him. Today it is a naval museum.

But of course, the most obvious monument to this shrewd commodities merchant is the Olympic Stadium in Athens.

George Averoff donated all the money for the stadium, 920,000 drachmas ($184,000). It was a gleaming white pile of Pentelic marble, with seats for 50,000. And at its entrance there rose a statue of the cotton merchant Averoff. At the opening ceremonies of the first modern Olympic Games, the crown prince gave a stirring speech in praise of the merchant. Then he pulled the cord which removed the Greek flag veiling Averoff's statue, and the crowds roared: "Long live the Crown Prince! Long live Averoff! God bless Greece!"

Baron de Coubertin was much in evidence during those first Games. He wrote in an official report his analysis of what the new Olympics meant: "Their revival is not owing to a spontaneous dream, but it is the logical consequence of the great cosmopolitan tendencies of our times. . . . Men have begun to lead less isolated existences, different races have learnt to know, to understand each other better and by comparing their powers and achievements in the fields of art, industry and science, a noble rivalry has sprung up amongst them, urging them on to greater accomplishments."

He wanted no mistakes made about the origins of the new Games: "As for myself," he wrote, "I hereby assert once more my claims for being sole author of the whole project."

Nevertheless, the marble statue that would stand for all time before the Athenaic Stadium, monument to the movement the baron had begun, was that of a cotton merchant from Alexandria. Not an athlete and not a Greek god and not a small French baron but a rich businessman. And when they had returned to France afterward, the baron's wife asked him the cruelest question: "Why was it that not one time did they mention your name at any ceremonies?"

Baron de Coubertin's loyal nephew, Geoffrey de Navacelle, said recently: "The Bible says that one is never a prophet in his own land, and my uncle was never understood by the French."

The Olympics of 1900, which might have been the baron's own personal triumph with or without a marble statue, became his crown of thorns. It was to be held in conjunction with the Paris World Exposition. Full of himself and buoyed by worldwide acceptance of his Games, the baron exuberantly suggested to the exposition organizers that a giant replica of Mount Olympus be erected in the center of Paris. This met with disdain. Then, when the baron began busily trying to put together the Olympics himself, he was shunted off, and his ideas were labeled "shabby and undignified."

It was only a few weeks before the exposition was to open that the organizing committee realized that the Olympics was in chaos and hurriedly put the baron back in charge. He could salvage very little at that late hour.

The next time Paris had an Olympics was in 1924, and it was a far better production than 1900. When it was finished, the Baron de Coubertin resigned as president of the IOC, saying, "My work is done." He never attended another Olympics, although three more were held before he died.

During his life he was given medals and decorations from many countries, but never anything from France that he felt he could accept. He was offered a Legion of Merit, but he refused it on the grounds that he believed only military men should have it. Upon his death, his nephew recalled, "The family immediately received telegrams from all over the world, from all the leaders—from Hitler, Mussolini, the Mikado even. The French government's telegram came twenty-four hours later."

A few years ago, Charles de Gaulle arranged for the baron's body to be moved to the Panthéon, where France buries her famous men. The baron could have shared his tomb with the likes of Voltaire, Rousseau, Zola and Hugo. But his family refused because they thought it would be against his last will and testament. And so his bones still lie in Lausanne, and his heart still rests in the marble column in front of the sanctuary where the Olympic flame flickers at Olympia.

The doughty baron was, obviously, the major influence on the modern Olympics; they would not be at all were it not for him. But for the last twenty years, his kingly position as presi-

73

dent of the International Olympic Committee has been held by a man who is perhaps even more zealous in his devotion to the Olympic Games than the baron ever was. And though the heart of Avery Brundage may never rest in Olympia when he is dead, it has certainly been unalterably captured by the Olympic ideal while he is alive.

4. A Carp That Tastes Like Rabbit

THE scene is the Holiday Inn in Luxembourg one afternoon in the fall of 1971. The International Olympic Committee is in convention there, and its members are about to leave the hotel for special ceremonies downtown which will begin at 4 P.M. sharp. It is not far from the Holiday Inn, but one must use the conveyances available, and there is an army bus waiting outside, courtesy of the Luxembourg government. Many members of the IOC get aboard the bus. The sheikh from Lebanon and the rajah from Pakistan and the baron from Spain and, eventually, the exiled King Constantine of Greece seat themselves on the bus. When the bus lumbers away from the hotel, it is about 3:30 P.M. They will be there in plenty of time for the formalities.

About 3:40 P.M. a fine, shiny car pulls up to the front of the hotel, and the duke himself— Duke Jean of Luxembourg— leaves the hotel, walks to the car and slides into the driver's seat. He waits for a moment while a single motorcycle pulls out in front of him as an escort; then he drives away to the appointed place.

Now it is after 3:50 and time is very short. A chauffeured limousine is waiting at the hotel with the motor purring. There is a dignified flurry at the hotel door, and Avery Brundage, president of the IOC for nearly twenty years, emerges alone and enters a rear door of his limousine. It is 3:55 P.M., and it will require a very quick, very direct route to make it to the ceremonies, in time. But then four policemen on motorcycles wheel into place, one at each fender. Their sirens shriek, and Avery Brundage is off. Of course, he has time to spare, for he is traveling in the style to which he has become accustomed as president of the IOC.

A bystander, slightly awed by it all, says jokingly to a Holiday Inn bellman, "Who was that? The Pope?"

And the bellman replies quite seriously, "Yes."

He is an old man now, eighty-four years, but he has kept his spine straight, his stomach flat, his handshake dry and powerful. If there were the horns of calluses in his palms, they could be the hands of a plowman. But there are no calluses, because he made himself a millionaire half a century ago, and he is used to handling pieces of paper or telephones in his work, not plows. He still has the shoulders of a blacksmith; though they are a bit bowed now, they bob with vigor when he walks.

Avery Brundage has always moved with that special briskness and authority of a man carrying a clear conscience, sinless and convinced of his blessings. There is something close to radiance in his face on occasion. True, it is a light beaming from far off, from another time when the works of Horatio Alger were considered profound, when ethics could not be conditional and when compromise was a word applied to acts of moral laxity. Perhaps the kind of anachronistic zeal and moral fiber which illuminates the steely eyes of Avery Brundage is best characterized in his own quote about his own favorite sport, heel-and-toe walking.

"*That* was a beautiful event," said Mr. Brundage, "and I excelled in it. It puts an enormous strain on nearly every muscle in the body. It is the closest a man can come to the pangs of childbirth. The great difficulty was in judging it. The judges would have to keep running alongside and lie down with their noses almost on the cinder track to make sure you always had one foot in contact with the ground. The judges didn't like their part of it, and they have dropped the event from most programs. I think it's too bad. Why, after I did half a mile of heel-and-toe walking, sometimes I could hardly stand up."

Though there is still much vigor in Avery Brundage, it does not always flow in a strong, steady current. His voice is husky and quite strong and rich at times, but then it will slowly fade, as if it were a deep color gradually being bleached. His voice sounds at those times as if it were coming from a place much farther away than Avery Brundage is sitting. On occasion, his voice simply stops altogether, and there is silence for many seconds. The eyes of Mr. Brundage seem fixed behind his ascetic metal-framed spectacles; there is a suspicion of tears even. But then he will blink and begin to speak again. Usually he picks up exactly where he left off and does not drop a sentence. But sometimes he will begin speaking about something quite different from his subject when he stopped.

Knowledgeable business people estimate that Avery Brundage is worth $25,000,000. It is said that he spends $50,000 of his own money each year in pursuit of his duties toward the Olympic Games. One does not ask a man like Avery Brundage about such matters, for it would be a nearly barbaric violation of manners. However, he once volunteered almost nonchalantly: "You didn't have to be a wizard to make a fortune during the Depression. All you had to do was buy stocks and bonds in depressed corporations for a few cents on the dollar and then wait. I was just lucky."

He was once very poor. He was born in 1887 in Detroit. His father walked out when he was quite young, and even though Avery Brundage sold newspapers to help his mother buy bread for the family, there was not enough money. He was sent to Chicago to live with relatives, and eventually he worked his way through the University of Illinois, graduating in the class of 1909. On the Illinois campus he was a big man, a track star, a fraternity leader, a writer for the literary magazine, *The Scribbler*. One of his contributions to *The Scribbler* was titled "The Football Field as a Sifter of Men": "No better place than a football field could be chosen to test out a man. Here a fellow is stripped of most of the finer little things contributed by ages of civilization, and his virgin nature is exposed to the hot fire of battle. It is man against man, and there is no more thorough mode of exposing one's true self. . . ."

Avery Brundage exposed his own true virgin nature to an excruciating assortment of track competitions that made football seem like a parlor game. Although the heel-and-toe walk and high jumping and putting the shot were his specialties, he eventually became addicted to the exalted tortures of the pentathlon and the decathlon and, worst of all, to the masochist's delight which Brundage fondly calls "the old American All-Around."

The American All-Around was a frenzied, strenuous series of ten events, all of which had to be performed in a single afternoon with no more than five minutes between each event. (An Olympic decathlon is a piece of cake by comparison if for no other reason than that its events are sprawled in relative leisure over two full days.) In 1914, when he was twenty-six years old, Avery Brundage appeared in Birmingham, Alabama, to compete in the American All-Around championships, a stocky, iron-muscled fellow with the grim, messianic face of a missionary. He was unbeatable in 1914, and in 1916, and in 1918; he won the U.S. championship all three years. No one equaled his consistency. He was canonized by sportswriters as "The Champion of Champions." In 1919, at the fairly ripe age of thirty-two, he retired from the old American All-Around.

Brundage's best performances, although none were records, were noteworthy: He ran the 100-yard dash in 10 seconds flat; high jumped 5 feet 11 inches; put the 6-pound shot 42 feet; ran the high hurdles in 16 seconds; broad jumped 21 feet 7 inches; pole vaulted 10 feet $\frac{2}{10}$ inch; threw the 56-pound weight 29 feet 4 inches; walked 880 yards in 3 minutes $3\frac{3}{4}$ seconds; threw the hammer 125 feet $2\frac{1}{2}$ inches; and ran the mile in 5 minutes 17 seconds.

Of course, nothing Avery Brundage did—or could do—equaled the athletic genius of his contemporary, the Indian Jim Thorpe. In Brundage's only attempt at Olympic competition, which took place in Stockholm in 1912, he was entered in the pentathlon and the decathlon. The austere Brundage was known as "Old Ironsides" because of his spartan capacity for endurance; he had none of the rippling grace and little of the lithe natural ability of Thorpe. While Jim Thorpe was winning gold medals in everything he entered in Stockholm, Avery Brundage finished a creditable fifth in the pentathlon, then fell to fifteenth in the decathlon when he dropped out after completing eight events.

Brundage was only an athlete then and had nothing to do with the disqualification of Thorpe for professionalism, which followed the 1912 Games and cost Thorpe his medals. Years and years later, when Jim Thorpe was a bleak and tragic drunk bereft of dignity, various sentimental sportswriters or officials would periodically plead with Brundage, then president of the USOC and the AAU, to initiate actions to return Thorpe's Olympic medals to him. Avery Brundage would not bend. He said, "Jim Thorpe was the greatest athlete of our time. Why does he need medals to prove it?"

The source of Avery Brundage's wealth and (ultimately) his influence is the Avery Brundage Construction Company, which he founded in time to take advantage of the explosive building boom in Chicago in the 1920's. The Avery Brundage Construction Company built many of those stolid brick piles in the Loop and up the North Shore, buildings all characterless but strong enough to stand against the bitter gales off Lake Michigan and the savage blast of winter blizzards coming to Chicago from Canada.

For quite a number of years, Avery Brundage owned the LaSalle Hotel, which was built in 1909. Though it has been modernized, it still has the feel of a dowdy period palace. Mr. Brundage has his office in the LaSalle Hotel, a dim and forgettable three-room suite on the eighteenth floor, painted and carpeted and sparsely decorated as if for transients. There is a secretary in the first room, then Mr. Brundage's assistant, then Mr. Brundage's office at the corner. This is the seat of power of the Olympic movement, the one that is "a twentieth-century religion." There are two windows, darkly draped, which look down on parking ramps and neon signs climbing up the sooty sides of buildings. The room is small; there is a bookcase with a few expensive coffee-table-sized volumes and a couple of vases. Avery Brundage owns a collection of Oriental art valued at $40,000,000, but it is housed in its own wing of the San Francisco Art Museum. Nothing tasteful or memorable appears on the walls of his office. Well, there are two paper posters advertising the 1972 Summer and Winter Games, but souvenir buyers at Munich and Sapporo could purchase both for a couple of dollars.

It is unprepossessing, verging on the shabby. One simply cannot put it out of his mind: Avery Brundage's office is a hotel room. If the desk were removed and the bookcase taken out and the Olympic posters taken down, this room would have a bed with a brown metal headboard and a small brown dresser. If Avery Brundage were not occupying the room, there would probably be a traveling salesman from Toledo, Ohio, or Mason City, Iowa, stretched out in shirt sleeves atop the bedspread. He would be wearing black shoes with white socks, and his necktie would be loose. He would be paying, perhaps, $13.50 a day for the room.

Over the years, Avery Brundage has made hundreds of speeches and uttered millions of words, always in the manner of a man who cares not a whit where the chips may fall. Here are a few of his quotes which have served to endear him to a few people and made him anathema to many, many more:

Avery Brundage once said, "In fifty years of sports I have never known or heard of a single athlete who was too poor to participate in the Olympic Games."

Avery Brundage once said: "If in certain countries there are people who are too poor to play (which is doubtful), let the government raise their standards of living until they have some leisure time instead of asking us to lower our amateur standards. After all, we of amateur sport cannot be expected to reconstruct society."

Avery Brundage once said (after a bitter exchange over his 1933 decision to disqualify the incomparable Mildred "Babe" Didrikson from amateur competition): "You know, the ancient Greeks kept women out of their athletic games. They wouldn't even let them on the sidelines. I'm not so sure but what they were right."

Avery Brundage once said, "I'm a hundred and ten percent American and an old-fashioned Republican. People like me haven't had anybody to vote for since Hoover and Coolidge."

In discussing the flagrance of nonamateurism among Olympic skiers, Avery Brundage said: "As long as they make those boys and girls compete seven or eight months a year, they have to be paid. They must eat. If they don't get money above the table, it'll have to come from below. I don't know how they can control it—maybe they should give skiers painting lessons and then buy all their pictures from them. . . ."

Avery Brundage said in 1958 before the seventy-first convention of the Amateur Athletic Union: "I've heard a lot of talk about subsidies for athletes. You cannot make a champion with a subsidy. I was in Russia again two or three years ago, and it was shortly after the world's gymnastics championships in Rome where the Russians had taken practically all the medals. I said to some Russians that if this sort of thing continued, no one would want to play with them. They said, you can't blame us for wanting to win, can you? I said, no, provided you follow the regulations. They said, we have 800,000 trained gymnasts in the Soviet Union. You must believe we have some good ones. I do believe that."

More than a decade later Mr. Brundage was asked why the IOC continued to ignore the apparent inequities between fully state-subsidized Iron Curtain athletes and many Western "amateurs" who have no such permanent support for their training.

He said, "I have been offered no proof, no documentation that would require action against Iron Curtain athletes. You must have *proof*, you know, and that is hard to come by."

The essence of Avery Brundage's obsession with amateurism in the Olympics is rooted in his own puritanical interpretation of the work ethic—the devout and venerable conviction that man's intrinsic worth is measured in productive *work*. Sport is a toy. Sport did not lay bricks for the Avery Brundage Construction Company, and sport did not buy Avery Brundage's art collection. It is offensive to the self-made man in Avery Brundage that people are willing to employ themselves at something so fanciful, so unproductive as a vehicle of *fun*. They are grasshoppers frolicking all fall while he and other work-righteous people are sturdy ants that deserve to prosper and to thrive. Nearly twenty-five years ago, he summarized his views this way, and they have not changed at all:

"Sport is a pastime and a diversion—it is play; and play, according to the dictionary, is action for amusement—opposed to work—free, spontaneous, joyous—for recreation. The minute it becomes any more than this, it is business or work and not sport. Sport is purely incidental and should not be allowed to interfere with the main business of life.

"It is an avocation and not a vocation."

When he speaks of professional sports (which he does not appear to enjoy doing since, whenever he does so, he looks as if he had just bitten a live mouse), Mr. Brundage dismisses them abruptly: "They are not sports at all but a segment of the entertainment game—show biz you'd call 'em." ("Show biz" is uttered with a startling sneer.)

In his world, definitions are unmistakable, delineations clearcut. "It's simply black and white, a verity is a verity," he says.

"An amateur does not rely on sports for his livelihood. The word is just what it implies—a lover, from the Latin word *amator*. An amateur engages in sport for the love of the game. Only love. The devotion of the true amateur athlete is the same devotion that makes an artist starve in his garret rather than commercialize his work. If a man has the ability to succeed in another field, he has no business taking part in professional athletics."

A subject which stirs almost as much acid and ire in Mr. Brundage as the thought of strong grown men collecting a salary for playing games is that of college athletic scholarships. Mr. Brundage habitually refers to college football players as "trained seals" because he feels that many of them do not play only for love. He feels that the massive national network of recruiting and enticement to bring athletes to a certain college by buying them a free education is a "flagrant dishonesty." "Why should an educational institution have to *hire* its students?" he demands, aghast at the preposterousness of such an idea.

In 1966, he spoke to a college audience in Hayward, California, and he said: "Do you think for one little minute, ladies and gentlemen, that our civilization and by that I refer to the manner in which we conduct our affairs, our business and, above all, our politics, has not been affected by the exposure for the last fifty years of millions of our youths in their most formative years to this disgraceful fraud . . . ?"

Avery Brundage is adamant and evangelistic on the subject; he is convinced that when it comes to the Olympic ideals, the United States is the most corrupt nation in the world. At Hayward, he said: "Other countries have hailed and adopted the ideas of the Olympic Movement proclaimed by Coubertin, have instituted national programs of physical training, and competitive sport for its moral, social, aesthetic, spiritual and educational values, but in the United States' educational institutions, commercialization of the sport program has killed most all of the benefits and led to deplorable conditions. . . . The enemies we have made with our shifting foreign policies are now saying we cannot even play without being paid, that even in sport we are guilty of double dealing, that we are a nation of dollar chasers where gold is God."

In the summer of 1971, at twilight of a Sunday evening in that uninspired office of his, Mr. Brundage said sadly, "The word 'amateur' is misused in the United States more than anywhere else in the world. We say that an amateur is somebody who's not good enough to be a professional. That's absurd, but it says more about us than anything else I can think of."

Avery Brundage won a libel suit in France in 1959, and he said it was a "great victory for amateurism." It was a bitter, angry case. An assistant editor of the magazine *Le Miroir des Sports*, which is ordinarily a well-mannered publication, wrote a column of swinging vitriolic prose on December 29, 1958. The piece was titled "The Olympic Flag Is the Symbol of a Lie." The editor was André Chassaignon, a feisty little former soccer player, and he plainly saw the state of affairs in the Olympic movement as an outrage.

"The man who delivers the Olympic oath in Rome in 1960 will lie in the name of every athlete in the world," wrote Chassaignon. "He will lie because the IOC makes him lie. And the IOC with Brundage at its head, will know he's lying—as John Landy [the Australian miler] lied in 1956, as all of Landy's predecessors lied.

"Why do they lie?" asked Chassaignon. "Because nearly all of the so-called Olympic 'amateurs' in the world today are not amateurs at all, but hypocritical professionals!"

Chassaignon was only warming up. He went on with a pointed little fable. "Do you recall the charming tale of Gorneflot? He was the hero of a novel by Alexandre Dumas who, during Lent, bought a rabbit and had it baptized as a carp so he wouldn't break the rules of abstinence.

"Well, rabbits baptized as carp or professionals camouflaged as amateurs—it's all the same. Monsieur Brundage plays the role of Gorneflot. He sits down before a rabbit stew and says, 'My, what a delicious carp. . . .' "

And Chassaignon went on: "What do *you* call a man who exercises no other profession than foot racing and exercises it ten hours a day? Avery Brundage calls him an amateur. We call him a professional. . . . The IOC refuses to admit the truth because the truth troubles them. They know better than anyone that their definition of an amateur is devoid of all substance and honesty. The scandal of the IOC is much more grave because it strikes at young men who are supposed to serve as the model of youths the world over! *Unhappiness to him who scandalizes children!* There's a phrase on which the leaders of the IOC should well meditate!"

Right after Christmas, 1958, Avery Brundage filed suit for defamation of character. This caused headlines in France, and *Le Miroir des Sports* broke all its previous sales records. Chassaignon became an immediate celebrity among Frenchmen who had long scorned the grumpy idealism of Avery Brundage.

When the suit was at last heard in September, 1959, the trial lasted but one day. The judge ruled the article had been "defamatory and incriminating" and he ordered the magazine to default 100,000 francs to Mr. Brundage. Chassaignon did not show up at the magazine office for a little while, and when he did, he said that the suit didn't matter too much to him because the magazine had paid the money. Avery Brundage framed a one-franc note from the settlement and hung it for a time in his office.

Perhaps any argument over amateurism in the Olympics is merely an exercise in verbal existentialism, because today Olympic amateurism is mostly a metaphysical wish or an infinity of semantic shadings. Certainly the men who compete as "Olympic amateurs" doubt that in recent years there have been any such beings in existence.

Parry O'Brien is broad of shoulder and of widening girth; he is forty now, a mortgage banker in Los Angeles following his sterling career as the world's best shot putter. He was a four-time Olympian and won gold medals in 1952 and 1956, a silver medal in 1960, and he finished fourth in 1964. He was in Mexico City as a visitor in 1968, and he has known several hundred Olympic athletes in his time.

One day in the summer of 1971 at lunch in a Beverly Hills restaurant, Parry O'Brien was sipping a Virgin Mary (meaning sans vodka), and he was asked if his gold medals had ever been of any material use to him. O'Brien's eyes narrowed and seemed to take on the same dim chill that a poor risk mortgagee might have evoked. "A dime and an Olympic gold medal could not get you around a block," said Parry O'Brien.

The next question to Mr. O'Brien was what he thought about amateurism in the Olympic Games, and Mr. O'Brien said matter-of-factly that athletes habitually accept appearance money as an "honorarium" and that other sub rosa payments had been made by promoters for years. Parry O'Brien said, "I have never known a name Olympic athlete who was an amateur."

Michel Jazy, thirty-five, of Paris, is a flamboyant fellow who tools around the city in a white Mercedes and dresses in memorable sports clothes which he designs himself. He is a publicity man for Perrier Mineral Water and for Le Coq Sportif, and he broadcasts sometimes for Radio Luxembourg. He is blond, very handsome, and he had an unforgettably graceful stride when he ran the 1,500-meter run in the Olympics of 1956 and 1960 and 1964. His television image was superb. Unfortunately, he won just one Olympic medal—a silver one from Rome. Still, he knew the Games.

"I did not run only for money," said Michel Jazy. "No, I would have run without pay. But, yes, I was a professional like everybody else. In America your professionals go to college for scholarships. In the Eastern countries they are in the military. In Scandinavia they are firemen. Of course, the money I received was not much. If I had made much, I would not have retired from running at the age of thirty. But even without money, I would have continued to run because, in spirit, I was a real amateur."

Don Schollander, twenty-five, the Yale graduate who won five gold medals and a silver for swimming in 1964 and 1968, is now one of the two athlete members of the U.S. Olympic Committee (the other is Bill Toomey). Schollander is a polished and intelligent fellow, and he espouses a line that one might call the New Left in Olympic thinking. "The IOC must set up rules that are more lax," he said. "Avery is the last surviving amateur; I didn't have a scholarship at Yale, but I certainly could not qualify as an amateur. I trained far more time than the rules allowed.

"The only sensible, the only *fair* thing to do is open the Olympics to everyone—for outright professionals and everyone. Certainly, you'd have to control it. You couldn't have a guy winning the hundred meters, then standing up and saying into a microphone, 'I drink Gordon's Gin—you all go out and buy it too.' You couldn't have guys running with a Sears, Roebuck emblem on their shirts, but the point of the Olympics is to bring people together. Why not do it? We've found that there is no viable way to control amateurism, so let's stop pretending."

Schollander said: "After Munich this summer, I'm going to organize a meeting of all the athletes who competed—and a lot who have retired. It will be absolutely international. Call it a union, if you want—that's what I'd liken it to. And the point will be to get the athletes in on the administration, the policy-making of the Olympics. We must restructure the IOC. We must open it up for everyone. It doesn't matter if a man makes money at sports; he's not a leper, he's not an outcast, he's an athlete and his essential motivations aren't all that different from the so-called amateurs."

In 1968 Harold and Olga Connolly wrote for pay an article for the Associated Press, and it was titled "Why Amateurism Is Dead." It said, among other things, that there is no longer any such being as an amateur athlete. Then, in some kind of ironic agony of conscience, the Connollys immediately donated their check to a Mexican orphanage because—well, because they wanted to protect their Olympic status as *amateurs* even though they had just pronounced the entire genus dead.

To compound the irony, they needed the money. There are few Olympians in this world who enjoy less the look or the life-style of being subsidized than Harold and Olga Connolly. They formerly lived on Kelmore Street in Culver City, California, which is an inlet of the endless sea of suburban banality that laps at cloverleafs of the L.A. freeway system. They are naught but a schoolteacher and his wife, struggling with almost aching good cheer through these lean years when he is getting his master's degree and she is working and their four children (aged five to twelve) are growing.

Hal is now forty-one, Olga thirty-nine, and it is sixteen years since their East-West Olympic romance leaped across the chasms of the cold war and became headlines in every newspaper in the free world. He was from Boston, she the lovely Olga Fikotova of Prague, Czechoslovakia. They met in 1956 at the Olympics in Melbourne. Hal won a gold medal in the hammer throw, Olga won one in the discus; then they wooed and won each other. In 1957 Hal more or less stormed the bastions of Czech bureaucracy, and after a great deal of trouble received permission to wed Olga in Prague. When they did, the New York *Times* ran an editorial which said: "The H-bomb overhangs us like a cloud of doom. The subway during rush hours is almost impossible to endure. But Olga and Harold are in love and the world does not say no to them."

The Connollys have competed in every Olympics since 1956 as members of the U.S. team, and both of them were in training to make the 1972 Games. One evening recently they talked spiritedly about it all—and nothing could seem farther from the pageantry and panorama of an Olympic gold medal ceremony than the living room of their home—tiny, cluttered, rented, perhaps nearly threadbare, but overwhelmed and illuminated by the energies of the Connollys and their four children. Olga is very tall, but not bulky or thick as the idea of a woman discus thrower might suggest. She moves with feminine grace. Her face is nearly beautiful, with black-brown eyes and fine brunette hair and a bright, quick smile. She is nicely articulate in conversational English and has written a book, *The Five Rings of Destiny*, about her marriage.

She said, "This will be our fifth Olympics, and we are competing because we love the Games, not because of medals. We have so many friends. We are so at home there. More than winning another medal, it's the idea of helping others break the ice and become friends. There's a greatness about the Olympics that is never really fully understood; it's the only place the whole world gets together; it surpasses the United Nations."

Olga Connolly went to the plastic-topped dining table where her youngest, Nina, was eating a hot dog, delicately cut the food and gently dabbed a napkin at the child's face. Then she left the room for a moment and returned carrying a four-foot iron bar which she hefted with ease in a couple of quick calisthenics. Even doing that, she looked feminine, motherly. She said, "I carry this bar in the station wagon with me all the time so I can work out whenever the mood strikes me. I get distracted easily, so I must do what I can when I can. Hal is never bothered by anything. For weeks he was training with a dead rattlesnake right in front of his ring. He didn't even notice it."

Harold Connolly is a big-chested fellow and bulky through the thighs and hips, with heavy shoulders. His left arm is withered, a profound handicap in making the two-handed hammer throw, but he held the world record from 1956 to 1965. On this evening, the Connollys were going to dinner at a restaurant with visitors, but Hal sat at the table next to Nina and quickly wolfed down two hot dogs. He saw the surprise register on the faces of his dinner companions, and he chuckled, "I'm trying to put on forty pounds. I compete best when I'm around two hundred and fifty."

Olga giggled, "Hal is really quite something to go out with at two hundred and fifty, a great barrel. But he loses weight as fast as he gains it." Connolly said, "Well, either I gain it or we don't go to the Games. We have made a pledge to each other that if one doesn't make the team, neither of us will go. And if we both make it, we won't go unless we can take the children with us."

Later, at the restaurant, Olga said, "This is our first time out for dinner in fifteen months, and perhaps we will go fifteen months more before we do it again. We must save to keep up our training and also to have some money for the children to join us in Munich if we make the team."

Then, over steaks in a Beverly Hills restaurant, they talked in tandem about the follies and the facts of amateurism in the American Olympics program.

HAL: "I know I wouldn't want to be paid for my athletics; if you were paid, you'd be shipped here and there like so much cattle. But I'm not against some sort of subsidization. You know, our guys are over in Europe this summer so they can make enough money to help them train next year for the Olympics. They'll bring home anywhere from three to fifteen thousand dollars from a summer on the European circuit. You can clear three thousand dollars in four, five weeks. Sure, there's satisfaction in doing this on your own, but it is also very frustrating."

OLGA: "Government subsidy would be a good thing, I think. It's anathema to the U.S. committee, but their whole attitude is so foolish and really insulting to athletes that this is only one facet of their thinking. They're ignorant and shallow, not mean in their attitudes. But the Olympic Committee always refers to the U.S. team as *boys* and *girls*. There is a TV ad on right now —send your *boys* and *girls* to the Winter Olympics. We are *not* boys and girls; in Czechoslovakia you win a medal and you are made a 'Master of Sports'—not a *boy*, but a master."

HAL: "Do you know that when a man makes the U.S. Olympic team, he has to pay for his own passport and medical exam? That doesn't happen anywhere else. I lived in Europe, and they took care of me as an athlete. In Finland they take care of athletes with free massages and physicals. Al Oerter [Olympic champion discus thrower in 1956, 1960, 1964 and 1968] could have made thousands of dollars in Europe."

OLGA: "I took it upon myself to go and see Avery Brundage. I told him, Mr. Brundage, you are a socialist; you hate commercialization, but subsidization is okay. He was nice, and he asked me what would be *my* remedy for defining an amateur, and I told him he should call a summit conference of all the top athletes in the world and ask them to come up with an outline of an amateur which would be accepted by everyone. Athletes have a feel for honesty, I told him. He said it was an interesting idea, but that the publicity over it—all the stories kicking around the controversy—would probably kill it before it did any good."

HAL: "The fact is that under Rule 26 [the IOC's bylaw defining Olympic eligibility] I don't know *any* amateur. A true amateur would have to pay his own way to the competition. It's funny, but the only real amateurs I know of are the guys who compete over forty in those masters' meets."

OLGA: "Well, we don't want any charity—they can keep it. But it is ludicrous now. Bill Schroeder, who runs the Helms Hall of Fame, had a funny but very interesting idea. He said there's only one way to have a U.S. Olympic training camp, and that's to have the whole team spend two or three hours a day in a cannery. You see? We'd spend our time growing strawberries, then can it and call it American Jam and sell it, and then we could afford an American training camp and everyone would be honest. But I have a better idea. I'm going out selling Amways soap—it's an ecology product. This will finance the Connolly family training for the Olympics. I spent thirty-three dollars for the initial kit—I tried the soap on our car, it's pretty darned good. So. From selling the soap, I need to make three hundred dollars a month. We have a five-thousand-dollar inheritance from relatives. I now make eighty-four hundred dollars and Hal gets four thousand from part-time teaching at UCLA—he could get more at night school, but he can't teach at night and still train. He must train at night, you know. So I've got to sell this Amways soap. It's like a little boy selling papers so he can go to camp. Well, next week I'm going to start by going to some airlines or hotel chains and saying, 'Please buy my soap so I can go to the Olympic Games.' That's the American way. Now, if I could just find Howard Hughes, I know he'll help because it's a superior product, I know that, great for cleaning jet engines."

HAL: "She's a great saleswoman. And the soap comes in red, white and blue packages. Who could resist?"

A scene which is perhaps more Olympian than anything Avery Brundage has ever envisioned occurred a couple of years ago in the Connollys' tiny, green-shingled rented house in Culver City. The visitor to the Connollys then was Romuald Klim, the great Russian hammer thrower who had defeated Harold twice in the Olympics. On that night the schoolteacher from Boston and his wife from Prague and their good friend, the Soviet hero from Moscow, sat together on the worn and inexpensive furniture. "My little Nina was climbing all over Klim, and he was laughing," recalled Olga Connolly. "And we were eating hot dogs off paper plates, and there we were watching our little old television together—we were watching the first Americans walk on the moon."

5. The Bluest-Blooded Club

THE seventy-four members of the International Olympic Committee are not celebrated for having a close or constant rapport with the Klims and the Connollys and the Michel Jazys of this world. Although the IOC lays down all rules, all policies, all bylaws and all eligibility procedures for Olympic competition, its members have the aloof air of just having come down from some elegant attic where the real world does not penetrate. The IOC is utterly autonomous in all that it does, self-perpetuating, accustomed to operating in star-chamber privacy. The IOC is, without question, the most exclusive, blue-ribbon, blue-blooded club in the world. It may even be the wealthiest. There are some who insist it is definitely the most aged, but that is probably not true, for the average age of IOC members is fifty-four.

Nevertheless, there is a clear—and proper—assumption among Olympians that the IOC is not constituted of run-of-the-mill fellows.

"If you took a poll, you'd find that the favorite sports of

the IOC members are yachting, fencing and equestrian—the high society sports," said Arthur Lentz of the U.S. Olympic Committee. "Also some shooting. You rarely find a member who is very interested in track and field. They are not athletes, as a rule. It's like the Jockey Club—can you think of any members there who have ridden in a horse race?

"IOC members usually fit one or more of three qualifications—they are men of extreme wealth, of high governmental or social position or of royal birth."

Besides Avery Brundage, there are three vice-presidents on the executive committee. One is jolly Lord Killanin, fifty-eight, a beefy peer from Ireland who was once a journalist for the London Daily Mail; one is the self-effacing Jonkheer Herman Van Karnebeek, sixty-eight, of Holland, who is on the board of Esso Netherlands and Heineken Breweries; and one is the suave Count Jean de Beaumont, sixty-eight, of France, whose family can be traced back to 1191 and the First Crusade and whose financial holdings in Rivaud & Company (his father-in-law's firm) make him one of his country's richest men.

To point up the extreme cosmopolitanism and aristocratic mien of the IOC, here are thumbnail sketches of a few more members:

• Sir Adetokunbo Ademola, sixty-six, of Nigeria, was the eldest child of his highness Ademola, who was Yorubaland's wealthiest and most influential ruler in the early twentieth century. Sir Adetokunbo, knighted by Queen Elizabeth, was the first Nigerian to be a chief justice.

• Rajah Bhalindra Singh, fifty-three, of India, whose father was Maharajah Bhupindar Singh of Pattiala, has been on the IOC since he was twenty-six years old. Unlike most Indian royalty, the rajah has never been keen on playing polo or shooting tigers.

• Hadj Mohamed Benjelloun, sixty-one, of Morocco, is enormously wealthy because his father owned sixty acres of stony real estate in the late nineteenth century and some of those acres are now the city of Casablanca.

• Syed Wajid Ali Shah, sixty, of Pakistan, has a magnificent white mustache and lives in Punjab. He is chairman of two companies, managing director of a third, executive director of a fourth and a director of three others.

• Sheikh Gabriel Gamayel, sixty-six, of Lebanon, comes from a line of sheikhs which dates back 200 years. He is a pharmacist by profession, but perhaps not by necessity. Each summer he moves from his winter town house to his summer house, a 500-year-old treasure palace on the mountain of Bikfaya.

Titles and ancient family ties abound on the IOC. There are also the Grand Duke Jean, fifty-one, of Luxembourg; Greece's exiled King Constantine, thirty-two (youngest man on the IOC); Spain's Baron Pedro de Ybarra y Mac-Mahon, fifty-nine; Indonesia's Buwono IX the Sultan of Jogjakarta, sixty; His Royal Highness Prince François-Joseph of Liechtenstein, sixty-six; England's Lord Duke of Pavenham, sixty-six; Belgium's Prince Alexandre de Merode, thirty-eight; Prince Gholam Reza Pahlavi, forty-nine, of Iran; Prince Tsoneyoshi Takeda, sixty-three, of Japan.

Two titled members of the IOC have won medals in the Olympics. One is King Constantine, who captured a gold medal in the Dragon Class yachting in 1960. The other is the sixth marquess of Exeter, now sixty-seven, the former Lord Burghley who won a gold medal for England in the 400-meter hurdles in 1928. After that he became a Knight of the Garter, governor of Bermuda, parliamentary secretary of the Ministry of Supply and a Member of Parliament from Peterborough. His title dates to 1571, and one of his major interests is maintaining his family's exquisite manor—Burghley House—in Lincolnshire, England.

A down-to-earth good fellow, Lord Burghley recalls his Olympic triumph with refined relish. "Whether you win or lose matters a great deal these days," he said, "and we did want to win very much then, too. But it simply wasn't the end of the world if you didn't. Before the Games of '28, I thought I'd do well to finish third, but after the trial heats, I knew I might have a chance. And in the finals I remember that I thought, 'I'll have a bash at that last hurdle and remember to stretch for it and not shuffle.' When I won I thought, 'How splendid!' People were naturally very pleased." Lord Burghley became lame after his hipbone was removed during an operation a few years ago. Indomitable as usual, he had the bone mounted as an ornament on the hood of his Rolls-Royce.

The bulk of the IOC is made up not of titled gentlemen, but rather of wealthy statesmen and well-groomed capitalists. The exceptions include a handful of Iron Curtain representatives such as Constantin Andrianov, sixty-two, a blocky, moody Russian who bears a startling resemblance to Nikita Khrushchev. Andrianov strolls alone a lot, pudgy hands tucked together at his back. Though he is a member of the IOC executive committee, Comrade Andrianov speaks only Russian and alone of the members needs a constant translator. Everyone else meets the requirement that each member must speak either English or French.

Despite their backgrounds, when members of the IOC get together, they still resemble a freshly barbered convention of wealthy Masons from Ypsilanti, Michigan. They are simply a well-groomed but nondescript crowd of blue suits and gray hair. Thus, Douglas Fergusson Roby, seventy-four, a stocky, gray-haired, well-groomed but nondescript Mason from Ypsilanti,

Michigan, fits in nicely with the dukes and rajahs. Once a star football player at the University of Michigan (class of '23) and a Phi Delta Theta in good standing, Doug Roby became wealthy working for the American Metal Products Company. He had ascended to the position of chairman of the board when he retired in 1960. He has been a member of the International Olympic Committee since 1952, and he is proud of his association.

"Some of my best friends are on the IOC. It's probably the bluest-blooded club in the world, but there's no selfishness. It's not like business associates. The IOC is a comfortable bunch of people."

Speaking of their "comfortable bunch of people," Doug Roby explained, "We just don't want to get into the mess of democracy in the IOC. The Russians wanted to democratize it by adding the presidents of all one hundred and twenty-nine national Olympic committees and the presidents of all twenty-seven sports federations [those international governing bodies which regulate the various separate sports such as skiing, table tennis, track and field, etc.]. Well, we have one body of seventy-plus now, and it's too unwieldy, so what would we do with more than two hundred members? The Soviet proposal was made so they could get control of the IOC—mostly because there'd be a whole slew of African countries let in, and the Russians would have had them in their bloc.

"We only want the kind of members who will follow our principles. There is no rule that any country has to be represented. There is no such thing as a vacancy that must be filled on the IOC. We are always looking for good men, but we have a nominating committee that screens them very, very carefully. Yes, there have been men censured, I suppose—at least a few I know disappeared without fuss and no one really wondered why. We knew. To be a member, you must have spare time and some money and an amateur sports background. But you can't be, say, president of the New York Yankees and be a member. That wouldn't do. You have to take an oath that you will always protect the principles of the IOC.

"You couldn't be on the IOC unless you were fairly wealthy because I'd say the average IOC member spends three to five thousand dollars a year. It is true the IOC is made up of old men. I've been on for twenty years, and I was a relatively young fellow at fifty-three when I made it.

"It sounds weird for an American to say it, I suppose, but this undemocratic organization has worked all right so far. It may not work any other way with all the pressures on us. Now the acid test comes after Munich when Avery steps down.

"Personally, I think Avery should have gotten out years ago. He has stayed too long, and he will leave a terrific void because he hasn't groomed anyone to replace him. There is no obvious successor. Well, let's see—I respect De Beaumont, he's from the Olympic founder's country, a man of means but maybe a little eccentric. Then again I hear that Baron de Coubertin was a little eccentric, too. Oh, the baron's ideals were fine, but his private life was a little eccentric. Andrianov couldn't be it because he only speaks Russian, and that would be bad for the IOC image. It's beyond Lord Burghley, beyond him physically. And the Dutchman has only been on the IOC for seven or eight years. I really don't know who it will be. It will have to be a strong man to overcome the geographical struggles. I'm afraid we'll have to reorganize the whole IOC sometime soon."

Thus, uneasiness pervades the International Olympic Committee, the specter of imminent and unavoidable change can be felt just beyond the horizon. It is not unlike watching a black cloud sweep across the sun, knowing for certain that there will be a change in the weather, but not being sure at all if that change will bring sweet rain or thunderbolts and floods. The departure of Avery Brundage from Olympic affairs in the fall of 1972 will lead to abrupt and possibly traumatic changes to both the Olympic establishment and its establishmentarians. When Mr. Brundage moves aside, it will be as if a mountain had fallen down. No man has been so much the keystone—and the alter ego—to the Olympic Games as he for the past two decades.

The Olympic establishment may never see an individual quite so strong again. Perhaps it shouldn't. Yet this stubborn, stiff-necked old millionaire has given much of himself and though he should have bent far more before the winds of change blowing in the world outside the Olympics, he rarely compromised his principles. One can admire the strength of his stance more than the substance of his views.

Yet he has built his Olympic career on some sound ideals. For as Bill Toomey, the decathlon champion, said: "I don't think Avery Brundage knows it or would ever admit it if he did know it, but he is really a lot like the kids of today. He is against commercialism and materialism and doing things simply for the sake of profit. He is really an idealist—a wonderful, hardheaded old idealist. If he were sixty-five years younger, he'd probably be a hippie."

Part III

Olympiads and Olympians: A Chronology

To the world, Olympic heroes tend to stay suspended in amber at their moment of victory. There they are, flushed with youth, exalted by triumph, crystallized in time like a work of art—afloat above a crossbar. Perhaps our own intimations of death are held at bay by the image of other mortals preserved as eternally young. Perhaps that is the essence of the Olympics —a single, intense, splendidly theatrical instant of triumph shared by competitor and spectator alike. There are the medals stamped from precious metal, hymns and flags and transcendant applause —it is so fleeting, yet so beautiful that it can only be called perfect.

But of course, there is always more.

Our memories of them may not admit it, but Olympians carry no identifying characteristics once the victories are won and the medals given out. There is no "Olympic ideal" in the lives of athletes after they've won, no constant momentum generated by the acclaim, no patterns spun from gold. There is almost nothing predictable—except that their lives are never the same once an Olympic medal is won.

This is true, if for no other reason, because they were once famous as Olympians and they are never really forgotten in their own lifetimes. It is also true because many of them feel that they will never again reach such a pinnacle as the Olympic victory pedestal. This may sound inspiring, but it is also sad, for most Olympic contestants are very young to reach their life's peak, and they have a long time to live in anticlimax.

In a way, what happens to Olympic winners after the Olympics may do as much to define the Games of the twentieth century as anything else. There is no mythology here; these are some of the idols of our modern Olympics viewed long after the instant of triumph. You will find that their feet are made neither of gold nor of clay—only flesh.

To provide a historical setting around their Olympic heroics as well as their post-Olympic careers—and to give bolder emphasis to the ever-changing, ever costlier, ever more complex phenomenon of the Olympics—I have combined the portraits of Olympians with a chronology of the modern Olympiads.

Most Olympic chronologies are horrifyingly fact-filled, inclusive of reams of statistical records concerning which athlete won which athletic event in precisely how many seconds, feet or points. This particular chronology includes precious little of this type of information. The emphasis here is more on the offbeat and the trivial—artibrary and antic—which I think define the Olympic Games and their growth better than mere results of athletic contests.

1896

Held in Athens from April 6 to April 15. Unseasonably cold. Snowed once. 285 athletes from 13 countries competed. Amazingly well organized. Esthetic success as well. Athletically mediocre to poor: not a single world record broken. George I, King of Greece. Guglielmo Marconi received first patent for wireless this year. Wilhelm Roentgen discovered X rays year before. Curies discovered radium two years later. William Jennings Bryan delivered "Cross of Gold" speech at Democratic convention.

Spiridon Loues, Water Carrier, Deceased

This is an official description of one of the unforgettable moments in modern Olympic history: the finish of the first modern marathon in Athens:

After a few minutes which seemed centuries a movement is noticed at the entrance of the stadium. The officers and the members of the committee hasten thither. Finally a man wearing white, sun-burnt, and covered in perspiration, is seen to enter. It is Loues, the victor in the marathon race.

He arrives running on the right side of the arena, most fatigued, but not to exhaustion, followed by the members of the Committee and the ephors [magistrates] who cheer him. The Crown Prince and Prince George run with him, one on each side. The king, when the runner reaches his place in the Sphendone and bows to his greeting, gets up and waves his nautical cap for a long time in deep emotion. Some of the aides-de-camp rush forward, embrace the runner and kiss him. The two princes, who were joined by Prince Nicholas, lift the victor in triumph. The foreign officials applaud with emotion. . . . The air echoes with shouts of victory, hats are thrown into the air, handkerchiefs wave as also small Greek flags, up to then hidden, are now unfolded.

The victory of Spiridon Loues, then twenty-four years old, was the mightiest triumph of the '96 Games, for until then Greece had won no gold medals in its own Olympics. He was only a poor water carrier from the village of Amarousion; his job involved hauling large containers of water on the back of a mule over the crude roads between his village and Athens (the Greek capital had no water depot of its own then). Twice daily, Loues covered the nine-mile route, jogging steadily at the flanks of his mule, because he could not ride with the water loaded on. Of course, it was this endless running that conditioned him for his stunning Olympic victory.

Few men have had the promise of such rewards rained on them for a single accomplishment. As he left the stadium, the path of Spiridon Loues was littered with watches and watch chains and valuable cigar cases. Men rushed up to him and offered to give him whatever things of value they had. A tailor said he would make his suits for all time; a barber promised him a lifetime of shaves; a restaurateur swore that Loues could eat free forever. One man offered him 25,000 drachmas ($3,000), and another wanted to give him 100 drachmas a month for life. Loues said no. He wanted to preserve his amateur status. Later King George I asked the little water carrier if he had any special wish, and Loues replied without hesitation: "Yes, a cart and a horse so I won't have to run after my mule anymore." It was done. Spiridon Loues went back to being a water carrier soon after the Games. There is no record that he ever collected any of the avalanche of lifelong rewards he was promised in the immediate afterglow of triumph. The marathon of 1896 was the first and last important race Spiridon Loues ever ran. In 1930, Otto Szymiczek, longtime coach of Greek distance runners, met Loues, who was then married and the father of three grown sons and two daughters. Spiridon Loues seemed unhappy. He had been besieged by family problems. He lived a narrow, frugal life, working as a guard on the farms around Amarousion, a job given to him by the community after progress ended his job as a water carrier. Otto Szymiczek began taking Spiridon Loues with him to help coach runners and to help raise morale on the Greek team. But the old runner was often morose. He told Szymiczek that he wished he had asked the king for more than a horse and cart back in those golden days of fame.

Spiridon Loues was a guest of honor at the Berlin Olympics in 1936, and when the Germans asked him if he missed anything from Greece, he said, "Yes, some retsina" the traditional Greek resinated dry wine. The following day the Nazis flew in a case of his favorite wine from Athens. In 1943, Spiridon Loues, winner of the first Olympic marathon, died in Amarousion. He was a poor and unhappy man. His beloved Greece was a defeated nation, occupied by troops of Nazi Germany.

The journalism of the Olympics has served to make Olympians considerably larger than life, far more interesting in newsprint than they are in reality. From the first Olympiad, the fourth estate was busy doing its damnedest to help the Olympics transcend mere mortal facts and become the stuff of a penny-dreadful romance.

Rufus B. Richardson covered the Games for *Scribner's*

Magazine and wrote an article in the issue of September, 1896. He said:

> It is difficult to ascertain just what Loues has been doing since the race. A cycle of myths is already growing up about him. It is not uninteresting to be present at this genesis of myths in which the newspapers play a considerable part. It was reported of Loues that he declined all gifts offered him, and declared that all he wished was the royal clemency for his brother, who was in prison. But since he has asserted in print that he has no brother in prison, and since others have asserted for him that he has no brother at all, that myth is for the present disposed of as far as Athens is concerned; but who can stop a fiction that is gone out into all the earth?
>
> The same may be said of another story published here in the papers in regard to Garrett [Robert Garrett of Princeton University] to the effect that after his victory in putting the shot he sent home to Princeton this telegram, 'Guskos conquered Europe, but I conquered the world.' A newspaper man subsequently confessed that this telegram was a fiction of his, but he took great pride in it; for he said it was what Garrett ought to have sent.

Sir George Robertson,
Government Official, Retired

Those were gentler, simpler days than now, and even though the machinery of myth was churning to build the Games into the "sacred" plastic spectacular they have come to be, the Athens Games were truly competitions among individuals rather than nations and ideologies. The athletes were considerably more casual than the rigidly conditioned Olympians of today have come to be.

A strapping young Englishman named George Stuart

Robertson first learned of the events to be held in Athens while he was strolling along the Strand in London during the winter of 1896. A small sign was posted in the corner of the window of a shop owned by the travel agent Thomas Cook, and the young fellow stopped to read it. He saw that it urged passersby to drop their cares and book passage for Greece that March in order to view and, perhaps for the extraordinarily spry, to participate in the first Olympic Games of the modern era.

George Robertson, a whimsical though brilliant student at Oxford, decided that he would go to Athens to compete as an Olympian. Many years later, when he had lived to be ninety-one years old, a wrinkled, twinkling, wise old soul who was widely celebrated for his tart critiques of art and who had been knighted in 1928 for loyal service to the British government, Sir George Robertson reminisced about his decision: "Oh, it all seemed a bit of a lark. The Greek classics were my proper field at Oxford, so I could hardly resist a go at the Olympics, could I?"

By boat and by train, he journeyed to Athens. There he met the King of Greece, George I, of whom he recalled, "Nice chap. Sense of humor. Poor fellow. Assassinated at Salonika, wasn't he?" He also met the king's three sons. They were shouldering much of the responsibility for the Games, and George Robertson thought this a sensible arrangement: "It's always a good idea to have princes running your Olympics. Then, there can be no arguments, can there?"

In Athens, he also met Baron Pierre de Coubertin. The baron has been all but canonized since, but Sir George could only remember of him, "Funny little man, the baron."

George Robertson was a hammer thrower at Oxford ("a proper hammer with a wooden handle and a leaden head, not some confounded ball on a string like they throw now"). Alas,

111

the Olympics of 1896 had no competition for hammer throwers, so he entered the shot put, where he finished fourth, and the discus throw, where he finished sixth. All things considered, George Robertson found the Games nicely tasteful. "There wasn't any prancing about with banners and nonsense like that," he said. "I suppose we had some kind of Olympic fire. I don't remember it if we did."

He won no medals, but at the closing ceremonies George Robertson bounded to his feet at a secret sign from King George I and loudly recited to the crowd an ode in Aeolic Greek, which he had composed himself. The local committee had refused him permission to read his ode, but young Robertson had conspired with the king to allow him time to do it. "Oh, the king was awfully bucked by it all," recalled George Robertson. Yes, the king was bucked enough so that he gave George Robertson an olive branch and a laurel wreath and a pin which he took from his own tie. The pin was encrusted with sapphires and diamonds.

Two weeks after his arrival in Athens, George Robertson returned to London. He found he had spent $11 in Greece as a contestant in the first modern Olympic Games. "Oh, it was all a huge joke; it was a splendid lark," recalled Sir George. He chuckled at the thought.

It is an endless and perhaps witless pursuit to wonder what might have been had the heroes of old performed with the benefit of the technical miracles of now. How would Charlie Paddock or Paavo Nurmi or Jesse Owens have run on a Tartan Track? How would Johnny Weissmuller have swum in a modern "fast" pool? How high would Cornelius Warmerdam have vaulted with a fiber glass pole? There can be no definitive answer to how modern technology might have affected contests of yore—except in the case of Gardner Williams, the swimmer who traveled to Athens with the Boston Athletic Association team.

Here the answer is not in doubt. Had Gardner Williams been swimming with the technological aids now available at the Munich Games of 1972, God knows well that a gold medal would be his. For among the electric myriad of gimmicks to aid athletes at the XX Olympiad there is precisely Gardner Williams' need—"a small warm-up pool where competitors can get used to the water temperature (twenty-six and twenty-seven degrees Centigrade) of the competition pool before the start."

Now, Gardner Williams was a magnificent swimmer. He had won many sprints in American pools before he went to Athens. He was properly confident he would win the gold medal in the 100-meter free style which was to be held in the Bay of Zea on the Mediterranean Sea. Ah, but for the lack of a "warm-up pool" his confidence was all for naught. The writer-runner Thomas Curtis was there that day in 1896 to record Gardner Williams' vain quest for glory:

> He journeyed to Piraeus on the day of the first swimming competition. He was blissfully ignorant that even the Mediterranean is bitterly cold in the month of April. He had travelled 5,000 miles for this event, and as he posed with the others on the edge of the float, waiting for the gun, his spirit thrilled with patriotism and determination. At the crack of the pistol, the contestants dived head first into the icy water. In a split second his head reappeared. "*Jesu Christo!* I'm freezing!" he cried. With that shriek of astonished frenzy, he lashed back to the float. For him the Olympics were over."

The American team did well in Athens, otherwise. They had had their problems in getting there, however. Ellery H. Clark

113

won the broad jump and the high jump at Athens, and in his published recollections of the I Olympiad, he wrote about the American team's trip to Europe on the German steamship *Fulda*:

> Our first thought, of course, was to keep in good condition during the voyage, and to accomplish this we at once cast about us for the best means of getting our daily exercise. The captain, after a single glance at our spiked shoes, promptly forbade their use upon his much-prized decks, yet rubber-soled gymnasium shoes did nearly as well, and every afternoon we put on our running clothes and practiced sprinting, hurdling and jumping on the lower deck. My own speciality—the high jump—was rendered particularly interesting by the pitching and rolling of the vessel. It all depended upon whether you left the deck at the moment when the vessel was bound up or down. If the former, about two feet was the limit you might attain; if the latter, there came the glorious sensation of flying through space; a world's record appeared to be surpassed with ease, and one's only fear was of overstaying one's time in the air, and landing, not on the decks again, but in the furrow of the wake astern.

The Americans' welcome in Athens was impressive.

> The streets were thronged with people [wrote Clark]. There was a brass band of many pieces welcoming us insistently, overwhelmingly. Banners—blue and gold for the Boston Athletic Association, orange and black for Princeton—were waving above the crowd; we found ourselves engulfed and marched away—we knew not whither. . . . It was at some building of governmental significance that we finally arrived. Our welcome was magnificent. There were speeches in Greek, cordial, we had no doubt, lengthy, we were certain. There was champagne—much of it—and until we were able to explain the reason for our abstinence, international

complications threatened. Even then, I think our hosts scarcely understood. Training? What did that signify? A strange word. Come, a glass of wine, to pledge friendship. No? Very well, then, so be it. Strange people, these Americans!

One fellow in Athens who had no such problems with training and wine was a certain dashing citizen of France. Ironically, Baron de Coubertin had been able to persuade only a few of his countrymen to journey to Athens to participate in the baptism of the baron's beloved new Games. Still if there had to be but a handful of Frenchmen, it would be hard to improve on the charming and unforgettable theatrics of this particular Olympian.

The opening ceremonies were over and the new Pentelic marble stadium in Athens echoed with the murmur of the crowd. The king and queen waited expectantly on their velvet-cushioned marble chairs in the royal box. The first events of the first modern Olympiad—the preliminary heats in the 100-meter dash—were about to begin. The contestants soberly arranged themselves along the starting line. There were two Greeks, a German, an Englishman, the American Thomas Curtis from Princeton and the Frenchman. He seemed all atwitter even though he had taken several swigs of red wine only moments before he lined up. Many years later, Thomas Curtis wrote of these moments:

> As we stood on our marks, I found myself next to the Frenchman, a short, stocky man. He, at that moment, was busily engaged in pulling on a pair of white kid gloves, and having some difficulty in doing so before the starting pistol. Excited as I was, I had to ask him why he wanted the gloves.
> "Aha!" he answered, "zat is because I run before ze Keeng!"

With white gloves flashing, the Frenchman ran a showy but slow race before the king. He failed to qualify for the finals.

> Later after the heat was run [wrote Thomas Curtis] I asked the French fellow in what other events he was entered. He was in only two. "Ze cent metre and ze marathon." To me this was a curious combination. He went on to explain his method of training: "One day I ron a leetle way vairy queek. Ze next day, I ron a long way, vairy slow."
> I remember the last day of the Games. The marathon had been run. All the other runners who finished had completed the race. The King and Queen had left, and the stadium was about to be locked up for the night. And then, all alone, the little Frenchman came jogging into the stadium running "vairy slow" and passed in front of the empty thrones of the royal box, wearing his little white gloves, even though the King was not there to see them.

Ah, so our hero won no medals, but let history record that his white gloves were the first of a long line of artifacts used in public demonstrations of personal advocacy at the Olympic Games. Seventy-two years later, in Mexico City, the gloves would be black.

1900

Held in Paris from July 2 to July 22. 1066 athletes from 15 countries competed. Slipshod affair. French hosts considered sports events insignificant element of International Exposition. The Seul Programme Officiel *contained* no mention of word "Olympics"; events listed beneath this heading:

République Française
Exposition Universelle de 1900
CHAMPIONNATS INTERNATIONAUX
Course À Pied & Concours Athlétiques Amateurs
Organisés Par
L'UNION DES SOCIÉTÉS FRANÇAISES DE SPORTS ATHLÉTIQUES

Carry Nation began hatchet-swinging saloon raids in Kansas during this year. Galveston, Texas, tidal wave killed 5,000. Avery Brundage was twelve years old; Charles de Gaulle was ten.

There was no cinder track for these Games because the French refused to chew up the fresh green turf in their beloved park Pré Catalan. A 500-meter oval was sketched in lightly upon the undulating grass surface. Discus throwers and hammer throwers sometimes watched sadly as their best efforts disappeared into a grove of trees. There were shrubs and weeds growing at the base of the running hurdles. The crowds in Paris rarely exceeded 1,000 people for any event.

American competitors, dressed in college or athletic club uniforms, impressed the French. One reporter wrote, "The natty college costumes of the Americans were a decided contrast to the homemade attire of some of the best European athletes, who, instead of donning a sweater or bathrobe after the trials, walked about in straw hats and overcoats."

However sporty they may have looked, the U.S. entrants were operating on a shoestring. For example, Amos Alonzo Stagg had to borrow $2,500 from friends to transport a few

117

fellows from the University of Chicago track team to the Olympics in Paris. Other college teams paid their own way, as did the New York Athletic Club.

There was trouble in Paris from the start. For one thing, the Americans were appalled when the French announced that some of the events would actually be held on Sunday. Amos Alonzo Stagg nearly had a tantrum over such sacrilege: "Everybody here feels it is a contemptible trick! Not a single American university would have sent a team had it not been definitely announced that the Games would not be held on a Sunday. Even at this late date, it is likely that the American teams will unitedly refuse to compete if the French officials persist in carrying out what seems to us a very nasty piece of business."

As it turned out some Americans did not mind violating the Sabbath. They won some medals on Sunday. They won quite a number more on the weekdays, too—including a gold medal in the Olympic tug-of-war. The American teams won no medals at all in Olympic croquet, Olympic bowling on the green, Olympic still fishing in the Seine or Olympic pigeon flying.

Perhaps they would have done better if they had been *positively* aware that they were competing in the II Olympiad of the modern Games. According to the flamboyant Charles H. Sherrill, then director of the New York Athletic Club entries and later an ambassador to Turkey under Calvin Coolidge, no Americans knew that they were participating in anything but a rather shoddy French track meet until they received their medals and found the word "Olympic" in the inscriptions.

The organizers of the II Olympiad had made a superficial attempt to be efficient and businesslike. They had, for example, given a questionnaire to all participants which asked probing questions—such as: "Were you reared as an infant naturally or artificially? What is the color of your beard? How strong was your grandfather?" The French attention to detail did not go far beyond that questionnaire. Once the never-on-Sunday controversy blew over, there was still the sour affair of the marathon race. The possibility arose that dirty tricks had been perpetrated in favor of the home team.

The route for the marathon had been changed drastically—and suddenly—not long after foreign entries had familiarized themselves with the original, uncomplicated course between Paris and Versailles. The new marathon was to be run four times around a track, then off along a difficult and circuitous trail through the streets of Paris and back to the track. As luck would have it, French marathon runners finished first, second and third.

Or was it luck alone?

The winner was a fellow named Michel Teato, a baker boy who had strengthened his legs by running about Paris delivering fresh bread. It was duly noted by skeptics after Teato's surprising triumph that a baker boy familiar with the bread routes of Paris might have also known the marathon course better than people who did not deliver bread there. Of the three U.S. runners in the race, A. L. Newton of the New York Athletic Club did the best. He finished fifth—approximately an hour behind Teato.

This was strange, said Newton later, for he recalled that he had loped past the French contingent about halfway through the race and that he was never overtaken again to his knowledge until he arrived at the finish line to find the three winning Frenchmen and a Swede named Fast cooling their heels. It was also considered a surprise that although much of the course led through great areas covered with mud and water, none of the first four participants was soiled.

1904

Held in St. Louis, Missouri, from August 29 to September 7. 496 athletes from 11 countries attended, but great majority American. An Olympics best forgotten. Held in conjunction with hundredth anniversary of Louisiana Purchase and St. Louis World's Fair. Spawned song "Meet Me in St. Louis, Louis," which probably was best thing spawned. New York subway ribbon-cutting ceremonies occurred in October. 1,030 people died as steamer General Slocum *burned at Hell Gate, New York. Population of St. Louis 600,000. Russo-Japanese war began.*

Emil Breitkreutz, Surveyor, Retired

Now eighty-eight years old, Emil Breitkreutz was a lean and fleet-footed lad in 1904, and he won the bronze medal in the 800-meter run in that III Olympiad. He later became a surveyor for the Bureau of Power and Water in Los Angeles and worked there for many years until he retired in 1948. A longtime resident of San Marino, California, Emil Breitkreutz is still a familiar figure at West Coast track meets. Recently, Emil Breitkreutz spoke drily about the Games of '04:

"The Olympics didn't amount to much then. They were only a little tiny part of the big show in St. Louis. There was not a lot of international flavor to the Games. It was largely a meet between American athletic clubs. I ran for the Milwaukee AC, and I never gave any real thought to the idea that I was representing the United States of America.

"Well, *everything* was different then. We never trained ourselves as hard as the boys do now. When I used to work out in my hometown of Wausau, Wisconsin, the insane asylum was about a mile from our house. I used to run over the dirt road to the asylum, around it and back home several times each week. It was about two and a half miles in all, I guess. I'd run alone, for the pleasure of it, you know. My father used to worry that the guards at the asylum, seeing a fellow in white shorts and white shirt running away, might think it was an inmate making a getaway. But it never happened—I mean, the guards never chased me."

Mr. Breitkreutz chuckled, thought for a moment, then said, "No, sir, the Olympics didn't amount to much then. Of course, as time went on, they got to be a big thing around the world. Then winning my bronze medal meant quite a lot more. Never in terms of money, of course."

Many YMCA and novice competitions were held in conjunction with the St. Louis Games, and there was lots of confusion. At one point an Olympic 800-meter runner, Johannes Runge of Germany, leaped off the starting line in his specialty, ran a strong race, finished first easily, only to discover that he had mistakenly competed in a handicap 800-meter run. Spent and sweating and panting from that effort, Runge immediately joined a crowd of Olympians waiting to start the real 800-meter race. He made an impressive opening sprint, then faded and finished fifth—which was still fairly miraculous.

Attendance averaged 10,000 at the Olympics, and Americans monopolized events to an embarrassing fare-thee-well. The United States won seventy-seven medals presented for recognized Olympic events. This was exactly seventy medals more than the runner-up country, Cuba.

121

The St. Louis *Post-Dispatch* gave the Olympics a true hometown drumbeater's treatment. In a preview story, the paper said, "The Olympian Games proper, lasting an entire week, will be not only greater than those at Athens and Paris, but doubtless the greatest to be held for years to come." A few days after the Games began and Ray Ewry of Texas already had two of the four gold medals he would win for running and standing jumps, the *Post-Dispatch* featured this enthusiastic headline:

GREAT WORK DONE BY ATHLETES
IN THE STADIUM EVENTS
Record-Smashing Was a Matter of Daily
Occurrence and Came To Be Accepted As
a Matter of Course.

TEXAS MAN PROMISES
TO BE FAMOUS JUMPER
Showed Skill and Speed in His Work, and
Gets High Mark Even Against the World
Champions Whom He Met.

Along with all the good news and pictures of the Olympics on that day, the paper also printed this shirttail filler paragraph on the sports page:

He traveled in a sleeping car;
The lights were low and dim;
He had an upper berth, and so
The thing closed up on him.
His arm got caught and tightly squeezed,
Don't ask if he was calm;
But this I'll say, that now he has
A berth-mark on his arm.

The 1904 marathon was a farce. The day dawned ablaze, a typical St. Louis summer oven. At the start of the race, a troop of men on horseback went galloping off to clear the course for the runners. Then came the competitors, accompanied by a raucous, excited corps of trainers and coaches on bicycles, all shouting instructions. Then came a fleet of doctors and nurses in fuming automobiles and clattering buggies to administer to the stricken. One reporter said, "The roads were so lined with vehicles that the runners had to constantly dodge the horses and wagons. So dense were the dust clouds on the road that frequently the runners could not be seen by the automobiles following them."

Most popular runner was a small Cuban mailman named Felix Carvajal, who started the race in a long-sleeved shirt, black street trousers cut at the knee and black oxfords with leather soles and heels. Felix jogged along near the lead, chatting in Spanish with spectators who could understand nothing that he said. At last he stopped and indicated to some picnickers that he would like them to give him a peach. They refused, so he simply grabbed two and ran off, munching. Later Felix climbed an orchard fence and ate a few green apples. Then he continued to run along, well at the head of the pack. At last, as had to happen, the peaches and the green apples caught up with Felix Carvajal. He was forced to lie down by the road until his stomach cramps subsided. He somehow recovered and continued to pound along in his low-cut leather shoes and finished an astonishing fourth.

There was also Fred Lorz of New York. Despite the dazzling heat, he set a killing pace early in the race. About halfway, he broke down and staggered off the course in agony, nearly unconscious. He waved groggily to other runners as they passed by. Eventually he felt well enough to get up and accept a ride

123

in a passing doctor's car. The automobile cruised past all the contestants until, about five miles from the finish, the radiator boiled over and the car broke down in the heat. Feeling quite frisky now, Lorz bounded out of the car and jogged easily the remaining distance to the finish line—far ahead of all other competitors. The crowd in the grandstand roared. Officials rushed to his side and pumped his hand and slapped his back. Everyone assumed he had won, of course. For some reason, Fred Lorz found this amusing, and he went along with the joke until Alice Roosevelt, daughter of the President, was about to hand him a trophy for winning the marathon. At that point, Fred Lorz laughed and told the truth. No one else laughed. The Amateur Athletic Union suspended him for life. A few months later some of his friends convinced the AAU that though Lorz's prank was tasteless, it was harmless, and he was reinstated. In 1905 Fred Lorz won the Boston marathon.

The St. Louis winner, Thomas Hicks of Boston, later admitted he had been fed consistent doses of the drug strychnine throughout the race to numb his pain and exhaustion. This was not illegal at the time.

Of all the grand and foolish things that have come to pass in the name of the Olympic Games, the Anthropology Days events at St. Louis should live long in infamy as the most ridiculous. This exhibition was to pit costumed members of "the uncivilized tribes" against each other—Pygmies and Moros and Cocopa Indians and Sioux and Ainu and Patagonians and so forth. They were to participate in archery contests, pole climbing, tug-of-war, and even in a mud fight. Whatever might have been expected from all this, the Fair sponsors (all presumably offspring of "civilized tribes") were profoundly unimpressed with what happened. The final report on Anthropology

Days in the official history of the St. Louis World's Fair was stern and disapproving:

> The only disappointing features in the series of events [during the entire Fair] were those in which the uncivilized tribes participated. The world had heard of the marvelous qualities of the Indian as a runner and of his splendid power of endurance. It had read much of the talent of the Kaffir, of the great remarkable athletic feats of the Filipinos, and of the great agility and muscular strength of the giant Patagonians.
>
> All these traditions were dashed. In actual competition the representatives of the savage and uncivilized tribes proved themselves inferior athletes, greatly overrated. Doctor W. J. McGee, Chief of the Department of Anthropology, attributed the poor performances of the savages to the fact that they had not been shown or educated.
>
> An Americanized Sioux Indian won the hundred yard dash in remarkably slow time, and an African Pygmy in the same event made a record that can be beaten by any twelve-year-old American school boy. The giant Patagonians entered the sixteen-pound shot putting contest. Their best performance was so ridiculously poor that it astonished all who witnessed it. Every high school championship has been won with a better record. In the running broad jump the best record was made by an Americanized Siouz Indian but it was not equal to Ray Ewry's running broad-jump record.
>
> The Patagonian could throw the shot only ten and a half feet. [Olympic champion] John Flanagan's score exceeded the combined throws of three Patagonians.

When the Games of '04 were over and the last Patagonian had gone home, Baron de Coubertin sighed and summoned his stiffest aristocrat's upper lip: "In no place but America," he said, "would one have dared to place such events on a program, but to Americans everything is permissible, their youthful exuberance calling certainly for the indulgence of the ancient Greek ancestors."

Two years later a semiofficial Olympics was held in Athens, and once again, the Greeks did a splendid job both organizationally and esthetically. The event was entirely free of snafu and bad feeling.

Matt Halpin, coach of the U.S. contingent in Athens, reported for the New York *Evening Mail* the opening Olympic ceremonies:

> Before the King and Queen of Greece, all the other available royalty and more than 60,000 people, the Olympic Games at Athens were formally opened yesterday with ceremonies sufficiently impressive for the coronation of some great monarch. We paraded—900 athletes from all over the world—and a grand march it was. I headed our bunch, carrying the American flag, and we got a louder hand all around the track than any other group. When I dipped the Stars and Stripes passing the royal box, the King staked me to a smile that made me feel that I belonged. . . . [Then] the Crown Prince Constantine handed out a line of guff to King George, after which George climbed down out of the swell imperial layout and contributed his spiel, which opened the games. . . .

The Greeks were still excited over memories of Spiridon Loues stunning marathon victory in 1896; everyone in Athens closed his shop on the day of the '06 race. Once again, there were stirring promises of immediate rewards to a Greek winner —a large statue of Hermes, a loaf of bread every day for a year, a free lunch for five every Sunday for a year. Of the seventy-three starters in the race, no fewer than thirty-seven were Greeks. But, alas, none had Loues' stamina or his speed. The winner was 115-pound William Sherring of Canada, who represented the Shamrock Athletic Club of Hamilton, Ontario. He ran with a giant shamrock on his chest, and though he could not qualify for the rewards offered to a Greek winner, he did receive a free goat in Greece and a free house when he returned to Canada.

In retrospect, it was this small, successful, but unofficial Olympics that saved the Games for the rest of the twentieth century. The Olympics of 1900 and 1904 had been fiascoes of the first order. And the Games of 1908 were to be even worse in their way. Had it not been for Athens '06, the world might well have been tempted to wash its hands of the Olympic Games. They seemed to breed nothing but ill will and bad tempers wherever they went—a far, *far* cry from the baron's dream of making sport a force for world peace.

1908

Held in London from July 13 to July 25. 2,059 athletes from 22 countries attended. Bitterness prevailed. King Edward VII and Queen Alexandra reigned over British Empire on which sun never set. Year later Robert Peary reached North Pole, on sixth attempt accompanied by Matthew Henson, a black man, and four Eskimos. Year earlier, Standard Oil of Indiana fined $29,240,000 by Judge Kenesaw Mountain Landis for accepting freight rebates. All Chelsea, Massachusetts, destroyed by fire.

These Games were to have been held in Rome, but the eruption of Mount Vesuvius in 1906 obliterated several towns and put a heavy financial load on the Italian government. The Olympics were switched to England, where there was an eruption of quite a different kind.

The Games of 1908 featured a very nasty feud between Americans and Englishmen that apparently began when the U.S. team arrived at the stadium in London, gazed around and suddenly realized that, within the full fluttering forest of flags on display, Old Glory was nowhere to be seen. As it turned out, the Swedes had no flag there either, and they quit the Games, and the Finns had none either, but they simply marched (albeit grimly) anyway.

The Americans did not let the matter pass so easily. The British claimed that they simply had not been able to turn up a Stars and Stripes suitable for flying at the stadium. This explanation did not soothe the angry Yanks. When the opening ceremonial parade commenced, the American shot putter Martin Sheridan was leading the United States forces, carrying a particularly large and brilliant flag. Flag-bearers from all other nations obeyed the gentle protocol of the day by dipping their flags in tribute to the head of state, King Edward, as they passed his seat of honor. Not the Americans.

The burly, hot-tempered Sheridan muttered, "This flag dips to no earthly king." The crowd gasped, but Sheridan held his flag erect when he stomped past the king.

Perhaps in the heat of that bitter week, such an arrogant and insulting act could be forgiven. The fact is the American flag has never again been dipped in honor to another head of state. Not in sixty years. At Mexico City in 1968, Harold Connolly, the veteran hammer thrower, was asked by the USOC to carry the flag in the opening parade. Connolly, a burly fellow whose principles are every bit as unyielding as Martin Sheridan's, replied, "I'd be honored, but I may as well tell you, I'm going to dip it when I pass the president of Mexico."

Harold Connolly was not allowed to carry the flag that day, and the protest begun in 1908 continues without letup.

Anger over the flags was not the only point of contention in London. The American hurdler Forrest Smithson, a divinity student, was so enraged that some races were being held on Sunday that he ran his specialty, the 110-meter hurdles, with a Bible in his left hand. He won and set a new world record.

Then there was the matter of the marathon, which Irving Berlin more or less immortalized in his song. After Dorando Pietri was disqualified for receiving aid from the staunchly anti-American British officials, the United States' Johnny Hayes was given the gold medal. There was never an official protest about it, but later revelations have proved that Hayes, too, should have been disqualified. He was in no way an amateur athlete.

All during his track career, sportswriters habitually referred to Hayes as a shipping clerk at Bloomingdale's department store in New York. When he was declared winner of the Olympic marathon, the store displayed his photograph everywhere and proudly announced that their favorite clerk had actually trained for his victory by running about the roof of the store during his lunch hour. Bloomingdale's also announced it was promoting Hayes from shipping clerk to head of the sports department.

All this proved to be sheer department store flackery.

Hayes was never promoted by Bloomingdale's. He never ran around on the roof. Indeed, he never really worked for Bloomingdale's, though the store did pay him under the table so he could afford to train full time on a track outside New York. This had been arranged by the Irish-American Athletic Club. Once the Olympics was over, both Hayes and Dorando Pietri became professionals, unabashed and openly. In a match race in Madison Square Garden, the Italian won by sixty yards.

129

Besides the upheaval over flags, the Sabbath and the marathon, London saw the only walkover race in Olympic history, yet another nasty bit of business. In the 400-meter run there were four finalists, an Englishman and three Americans. Papers all over England warned that the Yankee gang would probably be out to crowd Lieutenant Wyndham Halswelle clean off the track. Sure enough, coming into the last 100 meters, all four runners were bunched. British officials along the track began crying, "Foul! Foul!" A judge rushed onto the track and grabbed J. B. Taylor, an American, in midstride. Another judge scurried to the finish line and cut the tape himself before the other two Americans could break it in victory. Then the judges deliberated. They called the race void and ruled the Yank J. C. Carpenter disqualified for fouling Halswelle.

Of course, the Americans thought they had been judged wrongly. "The race was as fair as any ever run," said James E. Sullivan, a United States Olympic official. The *Times* of London disagreed:

> It certainly seemed as if the Americans had run the race on a definite and carefully thought-out plan. It was not as if Carpenter, the one who forced Halswelle to run wide and elbowed him severely as he tried to pass him, had himself taken a wide curve at the bend and then run straight on. He appeared rather to run diagonally, crossing in front of the Englishman so that he was obliged to lose several yards. . . . This is a fair and impartial account of what happened.

To protest Carpenter's disqualification, the other Americans refused to run the race again, and Wyndham Halswelle briskly strolled around the 400 meters all by himself to win a gold medal for not-so-merry old England.

Edward T. Cook, Farmer, Retired

He is a crisp old soul, with bright blue eyes and a good strong nose and the social voltage of a man easily fifty years younger. At eighty-four, Edward Tiffin Cook, Sr., of Chillicothe, Ohio, still looks as if he might—just possibly—pick up his old bamboo pole and break into a sprint and fling himself over some crossbar way up there. But, no, it has been sixty-four years now, *sixty-four years*, since Edward Cook was an Olympic champion. In London, he tied for first in the pole vault at the then astronautic height of 12 feet 2½ inches, a world record.

The man he tied was A. C. Gilbert, then a young Yale man who was working his way through college as a magician. Gilbert later became famous and monumentally rich by his invention of the Erector Set, which was perhaps the best-selling toy in the world during the first half of the twentieth century. "Oh, I didn't know Gilbert well," said Edward Cook. "Knew he was a Yale man. Yes, knew later about Erector Sets. He's dead now. They say we tied, and so I guess that's the way it was. It was kind of funny, the British called it a pole jump, not a pole vault. We didn't have jump-offs in those days, but I had fewer misses at my jumps than Gilbert did. I guess I'd have won under today's rules. Doesn't matter much now, though, does it?

"Strange things happened. This Gilbert took a hatchet during the competition and was out digging a hole in the dirt at the base of the crossbar. To get his pole in, you know. The officials made him go out and fill it in. Tamp it down. But he still rammed his pole in to help. We weren't allowed to dig holes, but he did it anyway. I was lucky because I hadn't been practicing with a hole."

131

Edward Cook now lives in a charming white brick house, shuttered in black and fenced with black wrought iron, a couple of blocks from downtown Chillicothe. About 10 miles out of town is the old family homestead—Willow Branch—an eleven-room farmhouse set on 1,100 lovely wooded rolling acres that have been owned by Cooks since 1797; Thomas Jefferson's name appears on the deed. Edward Cook began his track career after watching one of his older brothers compete in the first high school track meet ever held in Chillicothe. "My brother Spencer entered something that day, a race I guess, and they had a prize for first, which was a sweater, and a prize for second, which was a five-pound box of candy. Spencer didn't care a hoot about the sweater, but he wanted that box of candy, so he ran second and got it. That looked good to me, too, so I started practicing track as soon as I got back to the farm that afternoon."

Edward Cook became a schoolboy phenomenon around the Midwest, then went to Cornell, where he was a broad jumper (he did 23 feet 5 inches), as well as pole vaulter (he broke his own world record at 13 feet a year or two after the Olympics).

The bitter events at the London Olympics are dim memories for Edward Cook. "Oh, yeah, I remember something about the flag business; I guess maybe the British *did* forget to fly the American flag. I don't remember why. And, yeah, I can see us now at the opening ceremonies walking into the stadium—who was that dummy who led us in? He was carrying the flag and failed to dip it. I remember that, yeah, I remember that. It was a light thing, though, nothing really.

"But I remember Sir Thomas Lipton entertained us on his yacht, the *Erin*, and the ambassador to the Court of St. James's gave us a party and had lots of girls for the boys to use. And I remember the lord mayor of London gave us a big party. Oh, yeah, and another thing, this Sir Arthur Conan Doyle gave our Olympic team an invitation to his big country home, one he'd just built. Six of us went out, I remember. I don't know what the reason was that the British and Americans were fussing so much. Maybe the British didn't have any use for us because we were winning too much."

Edward Cook's blue eyes sparkled. "Oh, you know, I got a *lot* of recognition from the Olympics," he said. "A *lot* of real pleasure and fame. But no fortune. Oh, no, no fortune. It came out of the ground out here on the farm. Yeah, I was back on the farm a couple years after the Olympics. I had no desire to compete anymore; I was past my peak. I quit Cornell and came home. Corn was twenty-five cents a bushel. I farmed for quite a while, but things really got tough. The corn was so cheap. Finally I took a job over at Oakwood School in Dayton in the late twenties as football coach and director of athletics. But I quit in 1941 and came back here to Chillicothe.

"You know, I lost my gold Olympic medal over there in Dayton. We used to come back to the farm every summer, and somebody broke in our house in Dayton and stole it right out of the house. That made me feel bad for a while. But I've still got the certificate."

Paul Anspach, Lawyer, Retired

Paul Anspach is ninety and physically sound except for being a little bit deaf. Over four Olympiads beginning in 1908, he won two gold, two silver and two bronze medals as a Belgian fencer. He is to be an honored guest at the Munich Games because he

133

is the oldest living gold medal winner. When someone inquired of M. Anspach to what he attributed the secret of his long life, he replied, "I do not know whether one has good health because one practices sport or whether, as I rather suspect, one does sport because one has the privilege of good health. Anyway, sport may maintain health, but it must not disturb the regularity of one's life. I have never deprived myself of anything. I have smoked since 1914. I have smoked quite a lot."

A wealthy lawyer, whose grandfather was governor of the National Bank of Belgium, M. Anspach lost all but one of his Olympic medals in 1940 when the Gestapo ransacked his apartment and imprisoned him. M. Anspach has always stuck to the letter of the law of amateurism. Once after he had competed in an open fencing tournament at Nice, he finished third—a place which earned a nonamateur the cash reward of 1,200 gold francs, a tidy sum at the time. Rather than compromise his principles, M. Anspach coldly rejected the cash, hurried back to Belgium, and purchased a fine piece of art. Then he sent the bill—which was precisely 1,200 francs—to the organizers of the tournament in Nice, and they paid.

1912

Held in Stockholm from July 6 to July 15. 2,541 athletes from 28 countries participated. Generally judged one of finest Games in modern era. King Gustav V reigned in Sweden. Titanic went down with 1,503 victims. Robert F.

Scott found South Pole. Year later Sixteenth Amendment passed, allowing U.S. Congress to levy income tax.

Dan Ferris, eighty-two, secretary emeritus of the AAU, has been to every Olympic Games since 1912. He recalled the Games in Stockholm recently: "The Swedes did a great job, a perfect job. It was by far the best Olympics yet. The U.S. team went over on the SS *Finland*. A cork track was put down on the deck so the track team could practice in spikes. We stopped in Antwerp for two days to get coal and then went on to Stockholm. We were the biggest ship ever to enter the harbor there. We lived on the ship, and it was an ideal way to travel because the whole team got to know each other. The way they travel now the swimmers get to know only swimmers, the equestrians only equestrians, et cetera.

"This was, of course, Jim Thorpe's Olympics. He had had great publicity, and all the Swedes knew him. On the last day of the Games after he had won the decathlon, he and some of his cronies decided to celebrate. They stopped off for some drinks, and Jim Thorpe imbibed too freely. When he got back to the boat, he started running around kicking at the doors and yelling, 'I'm a horse! I'm a horse!' In the midst of all this confusion, King Gustav sent a cutter out to our boat to pick up Thorpe. We had to tell them Jim Thorpe was not on board, that he was in town someplace."

A few months after the Stockholm Olympics, the Indian Jim Thorpe was officially disgraced forever in the annals of the Games (if never in the hearts of genuine fans). Thorpe had, of course, won both the pentathlon and the decathlon, a Herculean performance. But soon after a newspaper in Massachusetts spread the word that Thorpe had been paid a few dollars for playing baseball with a team in the Piedmont League. This was

135

a scandal of major proportion since Jim Thorpe had already been labeled the world's greatest athlete. Dan Ferris recalled Thorpe's plight: "As soon as the story broke, we wrote to Carlisle College, where Thorpe had gone, and he admitted it; he never tried to hide the fact he got money. We had no choice but to declare him a professional. We sent his medals back to Sweden and his trophies to the IOC office in Lausanne. You see, besides the gold medals, he had got a silver model of a Viking ship for winning the pentathlon and a bronze bust of King Gustav for the decathlon. These trophies were never awarded again, and they have been in the IOC museum in Lausanne all these years. . . ."

The gold medals were then awarded to the two men who finished second to Jim Thorpe—Hugo Wieslander, eighty-one, of Sweden, for the decathlon, and Ferdinand Bie, a Norwegian doctor who died in 1961, for the pentathlon. Wieslander was critically ill late in 1971 and could answer no questions about his feelings over having Jim Thorpe's medal all these years. But a friend, Sven Laftman, eighty-three, who has been for years a Swedish Olympic official and who competed in 1908, said, "Hugo has never felt just right about having the medal. A year ago he told me, 'Thorpe was the best man in the field. I wasn't. He should have the medal.' Hugo tried to find Jim Thorpe five or six years ago so he could give back the medal, but he told me, 'No one knew where Thorpe was, so I kept the medal. . . .' "

Jim Thorpe had died a penniless drunk in a trailer in Lomita, California, in 1953.

Dr. Bie, as it turned out, became Norway's first gold medal winner when he was given Thorpe's tarnished bauble for the pentathlon. He often told his friends, "It is not pure gold. I do not consider it the first prize. That belonged to Jim Thorpe. . . ."

But Ferdinand Bie never saw Jim Thorpe after they competed against each other in 1912, and he never tried to return the medal.

Ralph Craig, Civil Servant, Retired

Ralph Craig, eighty-two and feisty, won two gold medals in the 100-meter and 200-meter sprints in 1912, then competed again thirty-six years later in the Olympics as a yachtsman. His Dragon Class boat finished eleventh. A former New York civil servant, Mr. Craig lives in a retirement apartment in Alexandria, Virginia, where there are photographs hung of him in his youth. He was a handsome, erect young man with a thick shock of brown hair. Now he is stooped, walks with a cane, wears a hearing aid, has prismlike spectacles, speaks in a shaky voice. But he is sharp as a tack when he talks, and he is no withered flower to interview. Here is a part of an interview with him in the spring of 1971:

Q: "Mr. Craig, what has it meant to you to be an Olympic medal winner?"

A: "That's an obtuse question."

Q: "Didn't your medals mean anything?"

A: "Sure they do. Hm. I've never been asked that question before. Well, they've given me a greater span of friendship all over the world. It gives you an entré into things and an ease of meeting new people. Of course, it depends on the individual once you get in the door."

Q: "Where do you keep your medals?"

A: "My wife put one on a chain. Hm. At least I have two, so I can leave one to my son and one to my daughter."

Q: "Is it true that in the hundred-meter race in Stockholm that you had seven false starts?"

A: "Leave out the word 'you.'"

Q: "Is it true that in the hundred-meter race in Stockholm there were seven false starts?"

A: "There were seven false starts, and I made one of them. Another American who had competed in the Paris Games—those 1900 Games were kind of horrendous, you know—he told me if you ever get to the Olympics, if anyone moves a muscle, you go too. Don Lippincott and I ran the whole hundred meters on one false start. The foreign officials were totally incompetent, and I was afraid not to keep running even though they fired the recall gun. I was told, don't take a chance—*go!*—so I did. They did fire the recall gun, but I didn't believe it. At the end of the event—after all the false starts finally stopped—they put up the flags. I looked up, and the one on the highest pole was for me. They gave the medals at the end of the Games. We all marched in, and the King of Sweden gave us the gold medals. I remember Jim Thorpe lined up in front of me, and he came back with this big bust of the King of Sweden. He said, 'What the hell do I do with this goddamn thing?' Well, hm, I'm not sure he said 'goddamn.' The King of Sweden didn't do his homework; he put the wreaths on wrong. I went up twice, and he said to me, 'What, you again?' The second time I went up, he got the wreath on right."

With a remarkably blind eye toward the weather vane of world politics, the International Olympic Committee selected Berlin to host the 1916 Olympics. Of course the Kaiser's armies had started World War I long before the Games were to be held. Operating by the same dim lights, the IOC unerringly selected Tokyo as site of the 1940 Games, which also had to be canceled because of the militaristic tendencies of the Olympic host nation.

1920

Held in Antwerp from August 14 to August 29. 2,606 athletes from 29 countries attended. A gloomy Games; specter of World War I hung too near. King Albert ruled Belgium. League of Nations began in January. Nicola Sacco, twenty-nine, and Bartolomeo Vanzetti, thirty-two, arrested in April for killing two in Braintree, Massachusetts, payroll holdup.

Belgium had only a year to prepare for the Games. There was little interest in festivals of any kind, for most of Europe was still in mourning after the carnage of the war. Although the Belgian government managed to construct a new 30,000-seat stadium, almost no one came. Tickets were only thirty cents apiece, but attendance never rose above 10,000 until schoolchildren were dismissed from classes and allowed into the Games for nothing.

Mrs. Alice Lord Landon, sixty-eight, was a diver at the Olympics in Antwerp. She won no medals, but on the interminable boat trip over she did meet her husband, Richard, who won the gold medal in the high jump. They live in suburban Lynbrook, New York, and he is recovering from a heart attack. Mrs. Landon is a round and bubbly lady, graying and looking perhaps as if she has never had anything more strenuous on her mind than finding a nice way to arrange an armful of irises for a centerpiece. This is deceptive, for besides being an Olympic diver, Mrs. Landon was the first woman to swim Long Island Sound from Rye to Oyster Bay. She was thirteen. The press, however, would not believe her, claiming she had gone partway in a row boat. So Mrs. Landon did it a second time while skeptical reporters watched.

The Games of 1920 were not a festive affair. "Poor Antwerp wasn't really ready for something like the Olympics," recalled Mrs. Landon. "We had cornhusk mattresses, and the women lived in a YWCA hostess house; the boys were in a horrible school barracks.

"The swimming and diving competition was held in part of the old moat that used to surround the city in ancient times. It was the clammiest, darkest place, and the water was frigid. It was so cold the coaches had to pull swimmers out of the water. The water was absolutely still, no ripples at all. It looked bottomless and black, and from the high board it looked like you were diving into a hole all the way to the center of the earth. It terrified me, and I did terribly."

Antwerp was the first year a U.S. women's team competed (there had been official Olympic swimming competition for women in 1912, but no Americans went). "There were fifteen of us," recalled Mrs. Landon, "and two hundred and fifty men on the boat going over. Oh, it was marvelous for us, although many men were not very pleased that we were going.

"The IOC had decreed for the Games that all women's bathing suits had to have sleeves to the elbow and pants to the knee. Well, at that time the California swim suit had come in. It was made of wool, but it looked like suits do today, more or less. We told the IOC that we didn't have suits with sleeves and pants anymore. They said we could not compete without them, and they said we had to stop and pick some up in England.

"Well! They loaded those black things on board, and we were all hysterical. They were thin as paper. They were the most indecent things you ever saw. You could see right through them. Oh, we laughed and laughed over them. But of course, we refused to wear them and ended up in our California suits."

Dan Ferris of the AAU was along for the Antwerp Games, of course. He recalled, "There was not time to raise money for the team because of the war. And to get us over there, the government gave us this great rusty old army transport, the *Princess Matoika*. Oh, it was a terrible, terrible ship. When we arrived to board, they had just taken off the bodies of 1,800 war dead from Europe. When the team filed up the gangplank, the caskets were sitting there on the docks, lines and lines of coffins. It was a shocking way to start.

"The athletes were quartered down in the hold. The smell of formaldehyde was dreadful. What a black hole that was for them. The athletes had to sleep in triple-decker bunks that hung on chains. The place was infested with rats. The athletes used to throw bottles at the rats. It was terrible, but we had to go this way because we had no money. No money at all."

Paavo Nurmi, Recluse

He is a legend, and the major newspapers of Finland and of the world have his obituary already written and set in columns of cold lead type and waiting on steel trays in composing rooms to be pulled out when he dies. Most have had the type set for years. Perhaps they will not even know for sure when he does die, for Paavo Nurmi is a recluse, and he communicates with almost no one. He is seventy-five years old, and his heart, once perhaps as steady (at forty beats per minute) and as strong as any heart on earth, is feeble and uncertain.

Paavo Nurmi, the most celebrated long-distance runner of the twentieth century, can no longer get about without a cane.

141

He suffered a massive coronary failure about five years ago and others more recently. In Helsinki, where he lives in an apartment building which he owns himself, Nurmi is considered to be a miser, a sour and penny-pinching fellow who made a fortune with wily real estate investments and with his store, the Paavo Nurmi shop, which deals in sporting goods. He was certainly worshiped and envied, but perhaps rarely loved, as often happens to efficient and ascetic self-contained men.

Beginning at Antwerp in 1920, Paavo Nurmi won more gold medals in track than any Olympian ever. He won nine. He also won three silver medals. He entered only twelve Olympic races in all. No one ever monopolized his sport more, no one was more celebrated and lionized, more the heart of a cult, than Paavo Nurmi in his heyday, the twenties. He was born in 1897 on the nails of poverty in Turku, a cold rural settlement that was the former capital of Finland. His father died when Paavo was twelve, and his mother went out to do laundry. The boy, eldest of five children, became an errand runner, pushing a heavy wheelbarrow through the streets of Turku.

He began running in the black pine forests around the town and practiced by chasing the mail train. He soon became so intense about his running that people avoided him because, where he had been taciturn to the point of glumness before, now he did nothing but talk—about nothing but running. "It was the replacement for his father," said an old friend. "Running was Nurmi's attempt at finding real life." His formal education continued only through elementary school; he became a machine shop worker and then went through Finland's compulsory military service, where he was a weapons fitter.

He never stopped his running—but he never stopped educating himself either, for there was a monkish quality to him, and he developed a thorough cultivation of his mind, though he never shared it. He loved classical music and attended concerts often. And always alone. He was married for only one year, then divorced, and neither he nor his wife has remarried. He communicates with his one son rarely, and only a nurse stays in his home regularly. When he is seen now, on occasional shuffling cane-propped walks through Sibelius Park across from his apartment house, he is alone.

Paavo Nurmi won his first gold medals in the 10,000-meter run and two cross-country events in Antwerp, then picked up five more in the 1,500-meter, the 5,000-meter, the 3,000-meter team race and two cross-country races in Paris 1924, then one more in the 10,000-meter run in Amsterdam, 1928. Over ten seasons Nurmi reached every world record in his distances—including 1 mile, 2 miles, 3 miles, 4 miles, 5 miles, 6 miles, 1,500 meters, 2,000 meters, 3,000 meters, 5,000 meters, 10,000 meters, and 20,000 meters. He also ran farther in one hour than anyone had before him—11 miles 1,648 yards. He was said to have brought home thousands of dollars, his first big jackpot, after a trip to the United States in 1925, and there was an investigation into the purity of his amateurism. He was exonerated.

Nevertheless, he was offended in the United States because he felt he was being exploited as a kind of carnival freak, an exhibit to be gaped and gawked at. Word had spread that his secret of retaining power as the Phantom Finn came from eating black bread and fish. One day a reporter noted that Nurmi was lunching on meat and rolls, and he said, "What, no black bread and fish today?" And Nurmi turned a scornful eye on him and said, "No black bread and fish *any* day. Why should I eat things like that?"

For nearly all his life, for well over fifty years, Paavo Nurmi has been a hero, always with people nudging each other and staring as he walked by. A statue was erected in his likeness in a park in Helsinki when he was just twenty-six years old. A friend recently sat shaking his head and said with a kind of melancholy awe, "Just think, for forty-eight years Nurmi has had to look at his own statue—what would that do to a man?" In 1932, when Nurmi was declared ineligible because he was a professional, Finland nearly went into mourning, for it meant he could not run in Los Angeles for yet one more gold medal—the marathon, the only Olympic long-distance victory he did not have. It was well known that the Swedish track federation under the presidency of J. Sigfrid Edström had demanded that Nurmi be disqualified. So furious were the Finns that their track federation refused to let Finnish runners compete against the Swedes for years, and the Finnish Railways Administration even canceled a large order for railroad wagons which was to have been placed with the Swedish firm which Edström headed.

In 1952 at the Helsinki Olympics, Nurmi, the rich hermit, astonished everyone by appearing suddenly in Helsinki Stadium to run the final lap carrying the torch to light the Olympic flame. He had trained hard for that single lap, and his powerful flowing stride was unmistakable. The crowd responded to him slowly, with a wave of sound that began as a low rumble, then rose to a horrendous thunder. The national teams, assembled in tight formations on the infield, broke ranks and began to rush closer to the track to see the legend as he ran. Even the glowering Russians of those frigid cold war days stood at the edge of the track and cheered Paavo Nurmi. He showed no emotion then, as he had never allowed himself a smile or an embrace when he competed as a young man. Many people wondered why the reclusive, aging Finn had chosen to fly this one more time, and the consensus was that it was, in great part, an act of revenge: Nurmi knew that his nemesis and his betrayer, J. Sigfrid Edström, would be in the stadium for his last Olympics as president of the International Olympic Committee.

Nurmi's reputation for stinginess is legend in Finland, and thus the people were surprised recently when it became known that Paavo Nurmi was renting one of his many Helsinki apartments at half the normal cost. Apartments in Helsinki are extremely hard to find. People were all the more surprised that Nurmi was doing it for Ville Ritola, an aged and sick man now, who, in 1928, defeated Nurmi in the 5,000-meter run. The two had never liked each other, and Ritola had only recently returned to Finland after spending most of his life in the United States.

A few years ago, after his first nearly fatal heart attack, Paavo Nurmi arranged to leave his wealth (valued at about a quarter of a million dollars) to a foundation that supported heart research. It seemed logical enough, for long ago Nurmi had made it known that no penny of his would ever go to support sports in Finland, since he was convinced that far too much of those funds was wasted or leaked away by stuffed shirt officials and useless bureaucrats.

When he announced his bequest for heart research, Nurmi reluctantly agreed to hold a brief conversation with reporters. His face was pallid and old, but his replies were tart and typically hard. A reporter asked, "When you ran Finland onto the map of the world, did you feel you were doing it to bring fame to a country unknown by others?"

"No," said Nurmi. "I ran for myself, never for Finland."

"Not even in the Olympics?"

"Not even then. Above all, not then. At the Olympics, Paavo Nurmi mattered more than ever."

Paolo Ignazio Maria Thaon di Revel, Count

He is tall, erect, dignified, plainly an aristocrat at eighty-four and his life has been the antithesis to that of the grim Finn Nurmi. His illustrious family first received its letters of nobility in 1617, and they have served Italy for many generations as admirals, warriors and statesmen. Count Paolo's father was the Italian counsel in Piraeus in 1896 when the first Olympics was held in Greece, and the count, then eight years old, clearly remembers the victory of Spiridon Loues in the marathon there. He himself served as Mussolini's Minister of Finance, Treasury and State Participations for eight years. Count Paolo was a member of the IOC from 1932 to 1964, and he is still an honorary member. He has a great Roman nose, and his eyes, very light blue, twinkle when he speaks. Count Paolo won a gold medal for fencing in Antwerp.

"When I was young, sport was a privilege for the elite," he said. "Now it is the privilege of the mass, of millions of people. Coubertin made rules for a small select crowd. The rules should be revised. Avery Brundage is too much a Coubertin. I'm quite certain that if the baron were alive, he would change those rules. The Olympics have become an enormous affair with mastodonic expense. And they are necessarily political. Yes, Coubertin's idea was not to mix politics and sports, but in modern times politics does enter. Whether you like it or not, it enters."

The count is very rich, with large agricultural holdings in Sardinia, many business interests in Turin where he lives; and for ten years he was president of Rome's gas company. He is a satisfied man. "My life has been divided into statesmanship, business and sports, and I would begin all over again, taking the high moments at the altars and the moments in the dust. The IOC was like a family once; now it is extended and enlarged. The Bolsheviks have been amalgamated very easily along with the kings and shahs and princes. The IOC is really antiracist. It's funny, if you think of it. When Jesse Owens won in Berlin, it was an American victory. Today it would be a black victory."

1924

Held in Paris from July 5 to July 27. 3,092 athletes from 44 countries participated. Better than 1900 fiasco. Gaston Doumergue President of France. First woman governor in United States, Nellie Tayloe Ross of Wyoming, elected. Year earlier Beer Hall Putsch in Munich led by Adolf Hitler. Year later Scopes trial on teaching Darwin's theories of evolution in Dayton, Tennessee.

The 1924 Games were scheduled for Amsterdam, but Baron de Coubertin had decided to step down as IOC president and asked that Paris be the host city. He surrounded himself with royalty at the opening ceremonies—including the Prince of Wales, the Crown Prince of Rumania, the Regent of Abyssinia and the President of France. Crowds ranged up to 60,000.

Benjamin Spock, later America's No. 1 baby doctor-author-radical, rowed No. 7 for the Yale crew, which won gold medals. For once, most of the American team did not have a glittering array of complaints about accommodations; they sailed aboard the SS *America* and stayed at an estate at scenic Rocquencourt on the Seine once owned by Prince Joachim Murat, who was an aide to Napoleon. There were eleven concrete barracks for the athletes. The officials stayed at the mansion, of course. Dr. Spock was not entirely enthralled with the food. "Our first breakfast was a little wizened orange, one croissant and one curl of butter," he recalled. "But the meals improved."

During their first night at Rocquencourt, the Americans were roused from bed by a huge fire in the village. A dozen homes were destroyed in the blaze while the U.S. athletes pitched in on bucket brigades and rescue missions to help. One Frenchman died in the fires. American team members raised $200 among themselves and gave it to his widow.

The U.S. team had its own athlete-chaplain, the Reverend Ralph Spearow, a pole vaulter from Oregon, who conducted Sunday services while the team was away from home.

The Finnish team was magnificent, with seven gold medals in distance runs (courtesy of Paavo Nurmi and Ville Ritola), plus victories in the javelin, the pentathlon and the marathon. A reporter for the New York *World* considered this remarkable record by the Finns and wrote: "Every person in that country goes through, day after day, the ordeal of talking in Finnish. After that, why should one be surprised at anything Finns accomplish?"

John Weissmuller, Movie Star

Perhaps second only to Sonja Henie and her $47,500,000 in the Olympic income sweepstakes would be John Weissmuller, now sixty-seven years old. He earned several million dollars during his unforgettable career as Tarzan and Jungle Jim. One day in the spring of 1971, around noon in a bar in Fort Lauderdale, Florida, Johnny Weissmuller sipped a Bloody Mary. Tourists kept glancing sideways at him. Johnny Weissmuller is a huge friendly man. He stands out in a crowd. This day he was wearing an electric blue suit. His hair, still worn at Tarzan length though he has not played that part in a movie for years, is dyed a remarkable, sad color. It is something between the orange of a clown's wig and the red of a squirrel's tail. His voice is high-pitched and even squeaky, although it is said he can still occasionally rattle the crockery in a restaurant by unleashing a splendid long pent-up OOOOOooooooeeEEEEEAAAAAA-HHHHHH! as if he were gliding far above the diners on a vine. His face is beaten, tanned, rucked with pouches and seams and an old man's parched riverbed of wrinkles. Startlingly, his smile is fresh and boyish.

In 1924 Johnny Weissmuller won three gold medals, and in 1928 he won two, all in individual swimming events. He once held fifty-one world records. They all have been broken now. It is deeply disturbing to Johnny Weissmuller that none of his marks remain. At times when he is troubled about this, he will telephone Buck Dawson, the manager of the Swimming Hall of Fame in Fort Lauderdale. During those conversations, Buck Dawson can be heard saying soothingly into the phone: "*Everyone* knows you're the greatest swimmer the world ever saw, Johnny. No one even *heard* of these kids who break your records, Johnny. Don't worry. They only know *you*—Johnny Weissmuller, the world's greatest swimmer."

In the bar with people furtively watching every move he made, Johnny Weissmuller spoke of the days when he was an Olympian: "Bill Bachrach was my coach. His brother was a lawyer in the Leopold and Loeb murder case. With Bachrach you *better* darn well be a champion. He was a giant, weighed three hundred pounds. He once kicked me in the stomach to make a point. Once in Hollywood, when I was doing Tarzan, we wondered if an elephant could swim in deep water. We pushed in a little elephant—a thousand pounds or so—and he swam just like a dog. He had his trunk up in the air. The director decided I ought to swim with the elephant, and I did. Once the elephant gave me a helluva kick in the rib cage, and I darned near sank to the bottom. That kick reminded me of Bachrach. . . .

"Bachrach was like a father to me. I lost my dad when I was fourteen. I had nothing. I had to work as a bellboy and go to school at night to make it. When Bachrach and I would go to meets, we were supposed to get eight dollars, nine dollars a day from the AAU. Bachrach got around that. He'd tell a meet promoter, 'Listen, I'll get Johnny to break a record for you. It'll get lotsa publicity for your pool. Then you give me a hundred dollars.' They'd wonder if that wouldn't make me a pro, but Bachrach'd say, 'No, you're giving the one hundred dollars to me. I'm the pro, not Johnny.' With the one hundred dollars we'd eat steaks instead of mush and sleep in hotel suites instead of cots in a dormitory. . . .

"I was in training for the 1932 Olympics when I was offered a five-year five-hundred-dollar-a-week contract with BVD swimming suits. Bachrach said, 'Sign, John.' I signed. I'd go around to swimming shows and tell people, 'You swim faster in our suits because the stripes go up and down.' One day I was in L.A., and they asked me to do a screen test for Tarzan. I ran around in a loincloth—little bitty thing—and I climbed a tree and picked up this girl and carried her around. I ate lunch in the studio cafeteria. I couldn't believe it. I saw Greta Garbo, Gable, Mickey Rooney, Wallie Beery, Marie Dressler, Doug Fairbanks —Doug Fairbanks, *senior*. He was my idol. There were a hundred and fifty Tarzans trying out. I went back to selling BVD suits and then I got a wire: COME BACK. YOU'RE TARZAN.

"When I got to Hollywood, the producer told me my name was too long to fit on a marquee. 'Shorten it,' he said. The director said to the producer, 'Don't you know who this is? This is the greatest swimmer in the history of the world.' So the producer said, 'Okay, keep your name. We'll write some swimming into the picture.' That's how fast your life changes."

Johnny Weissmuller has had five wives. He does not have a good business head. "My trouble," he said sadly, "is that I believe everybody. I sign the paper where they tell me to sign." The millions he earned were spent long ago. Johnny moved to

150

Florida from California in the 1960's. "A friend of mine in Fort Lauderdale gave me a condominium free. I asked him why and he said, 'I figure your name is going to help fill it up.' It happened. It filled up in two years, and he told me I had to move out. But by then I had some other good connections in Florida." In 1971 Johnny Weissmuller opened what he hoped would be a tourist attraction called Tarzanland in central Florida.

Harold Abrahams, Barrister, Retired

Harold Abrahams is seventy-one years old, a dignified, retired London lawyer, a staunch fellow still, who is chairman of the British Amateur Athletic Board. In the 1924 Olympics Harold Abrahams won the 100-meter dash, defeating an impressive group of sprinters, including the immortal Charlie Paddock, who was then considered the world's fastest human. Harold Abrahams was a burly, ebullient competitor who made no secret of the fact that he trained on cigars and Guinness ale. Had he scored his victory in a later day, it would have created an uproar all over England. As it was, the *Times* of London carried only this curt report: "In the final, H. M. Abrahams, who won, could do no more than equal the Olympic record."

Over the years since his triumph, Harold Abrahams has thought about the motives that spurred him to win. "The medal had a bearing on my career, of course. I was a celebrity. I remember when I was a barrister appearing in a case after the Olympics that Lord Justice Banks remarked of my presentation: 'Mr. Abrahams, as one would have expected, covered a great deal of ground in a very short space of time.' People knew me through my victory, but that was not the reason I tried to win.

"No, my brothers [Sir Sidney Abrahams and Sir Adolphe Abrahams] were both well-known athletes. Eventually, I

151

wanted to show I could do better than they. When I won, there wasn't any great surge of patriotism in me, though I *was* pleased for Britain.

"But another reason why I hardened myself to win was that there was a certain amount of anti-Semitism about in those days. When I was at school at Repton and at Cambridge University, too, looking back now I may have exaggerated the whole thing at the time. Certainly, I didn't run in the Olympics to win for all of the Jews. I ran for myself. But I felt I had become something of an outsider, you know. That may have helped. . . ."

Harold Abrahams spoke with nostalgia of those days when the Olympics had not yet become a worldwide industry. "It was all so different then. When we won, there was hardly any fuss. There was no victory ceremony that I recall. I remember years later on the telly I was interviewed about my victory and I said, 'The proudest moment of my life was when the Union Jack went up!' But you know, in fact, I don't believe there was a flag raising at all in Paris. I don't think I was even interviewed at *all* by any journalist after I won. Oh, maybe someone from our team gave me a clap on the back. I recall there was some handclapping when I went in to dinner with the team that night.

"When did I get my medal? Well, it was about a month later. I was home in London. It came by post."

1928

Held in Amsterdam from July 28 to August 12. 3,015 athletes from 46 countries participated. First time women allowed to compete in track and field. Queen Wilhelmina ruled the Netherlands. The dirigible Graf Zeppelin *wafted from Friedrichshafen, Germany, to Lakehurst, New Jersey. Stalin issued first five-year plan. First all-talking picture,* Lights of New York, *opened on Broadway.*

The ingenuousness of the Olympics of Harold Abrahams' recollection was rapidly fading away to be replaced by new intensity and new motives. By 1928 some early hints of the nationalistic chauvinism that would rise within the Olympics began to turn up. By 1928, the Olympic movement began to take on the organizational overtones of a huge corporation—particularly in the United States. The American track team sent to Amsterdam had a manager, three assistant managers, a head coach, ten assistant coaches, a trainer and five assistant trainers. The president of the U.S. Olympic Committee was General Douglas A. MacArthur, and he firmly declared the team to be in such "superb condition for this great test" that "Americans can rest serene and assured."

Alas, the men's track team proved to be far from superb. The only U.S. runner to win an individual gold medal was Ray Barbuti in the 400-meter run. People muttered that it was a blow to the nation's pride. It was said that the team was fat and overconfident and overcoached. Nevertheless, when all the points were added up, the United States had scored better than any other country. And in his report following the Olympics, General MacArthur left few purple phrases unturned in arguing that American chauvinism had been well served in Amsterdam.

"Nothing is more synonymous of our national success than is our national success in athletics," he wrote. "The team proved itself a worthy successor of its brilliant predecessors." MacArthur soared almost out of control when he described some of the specific American victories: "The resistless onrush of that matchless California Eight as it swirled and crashed down

153

the placid waters of the Sloten; that indomitable will for victory which marked the deathless rush of Barbuti; that sparkling combination of speed and grace by Elizabeth Robinson which might have rivaled even Artemis herself on the heights of Olympus."

If any skeptics still doubted that the United States had bred less than an assortment of its own gods and goddesses to send to Amsterdam, the general let it be known they were wrong. "The American team," he wrote, "worthily represented the best traditions of American sportsmanship and chivalry. Imperturbable in defeat, modest in victory, its conduct typified fair play, courtesy and courage. It was worthy in victory, it was supreme in defeat. . . ."

MacArthur also reported that the total cost of sending this legion of paragons to the Olympics was $290,000.

The American team lived aboard the same ship in which they sailed to Amsterdam. Counting the return trip (a rough voyage during which even the horses got seasick), United States Olympians spent forty-two days on that boat. At the end of the trip, the USOC medical officer, Dr. J. Herbert Lawson, reported: "We found an exaggerated condition of nervous tension with increases of minor ailments in a number of cases due to insufficient rest, worry, close confinement on the boat and the uncontrollable heat and noise, especially at night, which was occasioned in part by the number of non-competitors on board and the breaking of training by those who finished in the early competitions."

Morale was very low because of these conditions, but A. C. Gilbert of Erector Set fame, the USOC's morale and recreation officer for the trip, reported that the Olympians had much enjoyed the program of activities which included bridge, dancing, movies, a masquerade ball, a vaudeville show, a Monte

Carlo night with phony money and other games such as a cracker-eating contest, blindfolded men hitting crackers off opponents' heads with a rolled newspaper and transferring beans with a straw.

Ulysses J. DesJardins, Pool Entrepreneur

Ulysses J. "Pete" DesJardins, sixty-four, won gold medals in both springboard and tower diving in 1928. He now lives in Miami and is in the swimming pool business. "I didn't mind the boat so much," he recalled. "Eleanor Holm and I were sweethearts. General MacArthur said to me on the boat, I hope you're not getting serious. He was a fine guy. We danced and sang on the boat. Eleanor would sing 'Ding Dong Daddy from Dumas,' the big song of the day. Going over, we had a tough training table, but coming back, I stuffed myself on creamed strawberries and I gained ten pounds.

"The Olympic pool in Amsterdam was next to a railroad siding. When you were diving, you could hear the whistles blowing and trains switching on the tracks, but it didn't bother me. The pool did have a big crack in the bottom, though. The water kept leaking out, so they had to keep filling it up at the exact rate it ran out the crack. We were real eager then. We'd get up at five A.M. to practice. It was dark, and we had to take the boat to shore, then go over cobblestones in a bus to get to the stadium. We'd get there at six A.M., climb the fence and practice. Oh, yes, we were eager.

"A funny thing—no, a sad thing happened after the tower diving. They declared an Egyptian—Farid Simaika—the winner and me second. They started playing the Egyptian national anthem and everything; then they had to interrupt it. I had gone

155

to the boat to shave, thinking I was second, when this girl came running up the gangplank yelling, 'Pete won, Pete won!' They had to lower the Egyptian flag and apologize to Simaika and everything. They'd made a mistake—he had won in total points, but I had won first place from four of the five judges, so I got the gold and he didn't."

If the diving provided the most confused situation at Amsterdam, then the single sculls competition on the waters of the Sloten Canal provided the most charming drama of the Games.

The great Australian sculler Henry R. "Bobby" Pearce was poised for his quarterfinals race against Saurin of France. The gun cracked. The waters broke into turbulence as Pearce and Saurin began their desperate strokes. Suddenly a small flock of ducks glided out of the sky, braked their flight and set down upon the canal—directly in Bobby Pearce's course. The Australian saw them, smiled grimly, then rested his oars briefly and watched over his shoulder as the ducks paddled serenely out of his path. Then he picked up the stroke at a furious pace and beat Saurin by twenty lengths, setting a new Olympic record at the same time. Bobby Pearce won the gold in 1928 and again in 1932 before he turned professional, but the story of Bobby Pearce's *noblesse oblige* toward the ducks is perhaps more treasured in Australia than his victories.

Jules Ladoumegue, Misanthrope

From the days when he was a pale and suspicious waif, a quick-witted orphan who traveled with a band of gypsies along the dirt roads and vineyards of France, he was always a professional runner. He ran races for his bread at the Sunday country fairs, and if he did not win, he did not eat. "Ah, of course, the authorities reproached me about that later," he recalled with typical bitterness. "I was twelve years old then, and what did I win? A bottle of wine. A piece of steak. Yet they reproached me."

Forty years ago, Jules Ladoumegue, now sixty-five, was celebrated as the finest middle-distance runner on earth, the holder of six world records, the winner of a silver medal in the 1,500-meter run at Amsterdam in 1928. In 1931 French officials accused him of taking money to race and banned him for life. Since then, Jules Ladoumegue has felt cheated and forsaken. "I have become a misanthrope," he said.

Jules Ladoumegue lives in a small apartment on the seventh floor of a building across the Bois de Boulogne from Paris. He is alone there with a cat and a dog. The place has a shabby feeling to it, but it is full of sunbeams and fresh air on a nice day, and there is a harpsichord standing upon the threadbare scarlet carpet. There are many trophies displayed, including his silver Olympics medal. Like so many aging athletes, Ladoumegue seems to consider his still lithe, lean body a kind of trophy too. His movements are almost ostentatiously brisk, and he stood very erect, posed and said, "Look, look. I am not a gram more now than when I was running. I still run every morning in the park with my dog. All the dogs in the quarter follow me. They know who I am."

Ladoumegue persists in emphasizing the bitter flavors in his life. "The one thing that makes me so sad," he said, "is that I will have left nothing. A poet leaves something. A writer leaves something. A musician leaves something. But a champion? A champion leaves nothing. For me life is cruel. Maybe for a Kennedy or a Rothschild it is easier. But for me, I prefer the cruel life to the easy life. An orphan has no choice. They made a film

157

out of the life of Jim Thorpe. With Burt Lancaster. It was a terrible film. They should do a film on my life. It's so human."

He sat, very erect, on a soiled, sun-dappled armchair, and he spoke of people he recalled as old friends: Charlie Chaplin, Jacques Brel, Gary Cooper. He remembered that in 1932 he sailed for the United States aboard the *Ile de France* to cover the Los Angeles Olympics for a French newspaper. Among the passengers were Greta Garbo and Gary Cooper. Ladoumegue waved his arms as he recalled the scene: "We docked in New York, and there were thousands there. Journalists, photographers. They were there for me—the holder of six world titles—not for Garbo, not for Cooper. Ah, but during the night a French journalist spread the word that I was bad, that I had been disqualified. The next day there was nothing in the newspapers about me. *Nothing!* No one paid attention to me at all in America—except the gangsters. Like Al Capone."

Ladoumegue wrote a book in 1939 called *Dans Ma Foulée*, and it won the Grand Prix for Sports Literature. "Ah, I was not lucky. The night I won the Grand Prix the publishing house went bankrupt; I'm marked by things like that. People accused me of not writing the book, but I did write it. Because I am a poor orphan, they do not think I can write. But I received fine qualities from God. Of course, I didn't sell many copies. If I had smoked marijuana or been a homosexual, I would have sold thousands. *Thousands!* But I told the truth. I told how when I grew up, I ran with horses, and it was the horses who taught me how to be a champion at running. The world is rotten."

Ladoumegue said he lunched with Joseph Stalin after winning a race in Russia. "Stalin himself gave me my trophy"—he indicated a glass bowl with silver trimmings stamped with Russian characters which spelled Stalin's name—"and he was so impressed with my patriotism he insisted on having me to lunch."

Once in a locker room in Berlin in 1930, a strange thing happened. "I had competed and returned to my locker. I saw a little man lurking among the lockers. I knew he wasn't an athlete; he was too small. I thought he might be a masseur or something and I said nothing." Years later, in 1939, Ladoumegue was again in Berlin, long ago disqualified as a runner and now performing with a vaudeville troupe. After one performance, he was asked to play a special matinee the next day. When he returned to the music hall, he was suddenly whisked into a limousine and driven to a hideaway where he entered a salon to be greeted by Adolf Hitler, Josef Goebbels and Hermann Göring. "Ah, we dined," he said, "and Hitler said to me, 'Do you remember that man hiding in your locker room? That was me, hiding from the police. I have never forgotten you.'"

Eerie tales of the famous and the dead roll through Ladoumegue's conversation in an unending ghostly procession. The self-proclaimed misanthrope seems to find pleasure in his memories, if not in his fate. His recollections transport him beyond bitterness. None seems to illuminate the shadows around this old man as much as his rapturous recollection of the Olympic Games forty-four years ago. "The Olympics was something symbolic. It is no longer so for the young, no longer a symbol. But for us it was something to be an Olympian. We were one of a race apart. When you were chosen to be in the Olympics, you could consider yourself to be in the elite—spiritually and athletically.

"The Olympics—ah, they are so very beautiful. The *belles histoires*, something from Greece, something so noble. And the ceremony, the opening ceremony. It was like something that seems to rise from the ground and carries you high into the sky. It is as if you were just born, and you can do nothing but remain very still, very calm, very happy. I have seen many things in my life, many things in the war, and I have cried many times in my life. But when the runner carries the flame into the stadium, and the birds are freed and all the flags of the world are flying, I cry. I must cry. Even your Lieutenant Calley, a beast like that, would have to cry when the Olympic Games begin."

As he was preparing to run the 1,500-meter event, he was very heavily favored to win the gold medal. Suddenly he was gripped with "an immense fear, because it was so terrible to be the favorite.

"I went to a church, I could do nothing else. I had discovered an old church in Amsterdam in the Gothic style, grand and dark down among the pews and high among the buttresses. There was no one there, no priest even. I walked to the altar, and I put my running shoes, my running shorts, my jersey on the altar. Then I knelt to say a prayer. Then I changed into my running uniform, and I stayed in that dark church until it was time to run."

When Ladoumegue lost the race to the Finn Harry E. Larva, his world collapsed, and his life could not be the same again. "I wanted so much to bring an Olympic victory to my country, to the country of Coubertin. It was a brutal defeat. I saw myself as the winner. I had fire in my heart. And then I fainted. I am a patriot—I am not a Frenchman of the First Republic, the Second Republic, the Third, Fourth or Fifth. For me, France is the school where I was brought up, my church, all that. I fought in the war for that. . . .

"When I saw the Finnish flag being raised, I cried and cried on the podium. . . ." His face was radiant in the recollection, but then it turned sour.

"After my defeat, the false intellectuals jumped on me like vultures. 'He cannot be an Olympic champion,' they said. 'He doesn't have the class.' They said if I had been educated, I would have been an Olympic champion.

"What they don't know is that I was all alone, running against those others. I burned myself out running against the second favorite. At the end, with three meters to go, I was passed, and after the finish I fainted.

"Life changed after that, mainly because of the meanness of people. I didn't have the right to lose, they said."

He shrugged. "The Olympics is not everything. The Games don't stop an athlete. The Olympic flame dies. The athletes remain. An athlete is like a gypsy. He travels with his own truth." He paused.

"Well, I was an orphan when I began. I was strong. I became a champion, and then I was disqualified for life. For nothing. I became an orphan again. They had adored me, all over the world. But now I was again a public orphan. I went to war; I came back and then came to be what I am now—nothing."

Ladoumegue, who once held six world records, glanced at his trophies; then he petted his dog. "If I die tomorrow, I will die in the hospital alone, I have no money. I am just like Jim Thorpe."

1932

Held in Los Angeles from July 30 to August 14. 1,980 athletes from 37 countries participated. First really spectacular of modern Games. 1,000,000 people paid $2,000,000 to attend. Stadium held 105,000, had thirty miles of seats, cost $1,700,000. Track pronounced fastest in world. Made of *crushed peat. Charles Lindbergh's baby kidnapped. Pope Pius XI ordered electric heating in Vatican palaces. Depression— apple sellers, breadlines, Hoovervilles.*

President Herbert Hoover did not attend the Olympics— the first time the head of government of a host nation did not show up. He sent Vice President Charles Curtis instead, just as Dwight Eisenhower sent Veep Richard Nixon in 1960 when the Winter Olympics were held at Squaw Valley—the *second* (and only other) time a government head did not attend an Olympics in his own country.

The Los Angeles Olympics were a typically flamboyant California production, and they set the pattern for the vastly expensive, lavishly ornate facilities that were to come. No one was more instrumental in establishing the form and the sub- stance of the Los Angeles Games than the garrulous Zack Farmer, a former cowboy, who worked twelve years to get the Olympics to Los Angeles as chairman of the local committee. He recalled: "Hell, Chicago tried to steal the Games from us as late as two years before they started. They told the IOC we were going to flop out here, that the climate was too hot. West- brook Pegler was with the Chicago Tribune Syndicate, and he was sent to blow us out of the water. Of course, I admit we were a noisy, blatant damn town that annoyed everybody in the country, I'll admit that.

"But we weathered all storms. I treated those International Olympic Committeemen like men, not diplomats. You take those guys and put your feet under the table with 'em and lift a mug of beer and, by God, you've made *friends*."

L.A.'s Olympic Village, which covered 250 acres and housed all the male athletes, was the talk of the Games. "Oh, there was resistance to it at first," said Zack Farmer. "You have no idea of the resistance, because these different countries were afraid of political and racial differences; they were afraid of the idea. They all squawked they had training secrets and didn't want to live close together. They said, by God, we don't believe you can ever discipline the American public to leave that Village alone and give us privacy. They said Americans are known as the most undisciplined goddamn people in the whole world. Oh, we got privacy for those athletes, all right. We fenced it all in and put cowboys on riding the fences. Those Europeans used to love to watch those cowboys lassoing any SOB who tried to climb over the fence.

"That Village was the marvel of the Games. They wrote books about it in Europe afterwards. We damn near had to drive the athletes out to get them to go home after the Games. It was the most grand and pathetic thing you ever saw, those big hulks practically cried. They *loved* it.

"We built especially designed Olympic houses—two rooms with a shower between and a wardrobe. Two beds and a little porch out front. It was made of composition board built on templets—ten-by-twenty-four feet without the porch. We built them and set them up for one hundred and sixty-five dollars apiece. Why, we could put those houses up, plumbing and all, in one hour and fifteen minutes.

"After our show we sold our Olympic houses—they were portable—to auto courts, construction companies. We salvaged everything for one hundred cents on the dollar. Well, everything but the paved street. You can't sell a paved street."

There were some remarkable individual athletic feats performed in Los Angeles. The magnificent Mildred "Babe" Didrikson won gold medals in the javelin and the 80-meter hurdles, setting world records in both events, then took a silver in the high jump after officials ruled she had dived over the crossbar, an illegal jump then. There were six women's track and field events held in Los Angeles, and in all, six world records were broken. Men competed in twenty-two separate track and field events; Olympic records were shattered in nineteen of them, and world records were broken in seven.

Beyond that, there were a couple of memorable individual performances that perhaps did not catch a lot of headlines at the time. Attilio Pavesi of Italy won the 100-kilometer bicycle race. On his handlebars he had a bowl of soup and a bucket of water. In a bib hanging from his shoulders were a dozen bananas, cinnamon buns, jam, cheese sandwiches and spaghetti. Around his neck were two spare tires.

No one ever bettered the performance of the Swedish wrestler Ivar Johansson, sixty-eight, in 1932. He won two gold medals in two different classes—the regular middleweight and Greco-Roman welterweight—in the same Olympics. He is a retired policeman in Norrköping, and his cheeks are ruddy as a boy's, and if he were not stone bald with a white fringe of hair about his pate, he would seem to be in his forties. While Ivar was a cop, his main job was arresting drunks, he recalled. "Our crime rate never amounted to much."

As for his feat in Los Angeles, he said, "At one o'clock one afternoon I finished the middleweight competition, and I was the champion all right. I did not, however, go to get my gold medal; one of our leaders did that for me. Me? I went to the *bastu* [sauna], and I did gymnastics in there until I could not stand it anymore. Oh, it was so hot. Then I came out and lay on a table while the trainer wrapped me in sheets and blankets. When my sweat stopped running, I got into a bathtub and turned the water hotter and hotter. I stayed in the tub about twenty minutes, then back into the *bastu*, the blankets, then the tub, then the *bastu*. I did this for three hours. And my cheeks became sunken.

"I weighed seventy-seven kilos [169 pounds] when I started, and in three hours I lost five kilos [11 pounds]. I was spitting cotton, but I didn't dare take even a sip of water for fear of gaining a hectogram. The next morning, before the matches, I was two hectograms too heavy [7 ounces] and I went back to the *bastu* to try and make the weigh-in at ten o'clock."

In half an hour he lost 10 5/10 ounces and made it, but he also had to stay at that weight for four days. "I could only rinse my mouth with water—not swallow. I chewed some lean meat. I watched other wrestlers walking by with juicy pears and apples and grapes, and I *hated* them. I thought I would not live—but of course I did, and of course I won."

Buster Crabbe, Actor

He is still a good-looking man, but the smooth baby-faced look of Flash Gordon is long gone. Nor is his blue-eyed and blond interpretation of Tarzan really there anymore. His dark glasses are bifocals, and there is gray in his hair; his face is craggy now, sharp and seamed, but Clarence Linden "Buster" Crabbe, sixty-four, is definitely a matinee idol—albeit one who has slipped toward sunset—and it is certainly fitting that he made his reputation in the Olympics held closest to Hollywood.

Buster Crabbe is an outgoing man, modest and warm, eager to talk about his sports love, swimming. "Duke Kahanamoku was the first major Olympic swimmer, no doubt about that. People couldn't believe the times he was swimming until he won the Olympics in 1912. He won then and again in 1920 and barely lost to Weissmuller in 1924, then didn't race in 1928—

but he made the U.S. team in water polo in 1932. He was forty-two years old. Duke was my god. He was a great sport. In Hawaii he wouldn't embarrass local champions; he could beat them by the length of the pool, but he'd always make it look close."

Buster Crabbe made the U.S. swimming team in 1928, went to Amsterdam and won a bronze medal in the 1,500-meter. Then, in 1932, he won a gold medal in Los Angeles. Amsterdam was a great disappointment, but memorable. "For some reason we couldn't practice in the Olympic pool and had to go to Utrecht. There were little fish in the pool there, and they got in our suits. I think the water was pumped in right out of the canals; it wasn't even strained. I'll never forget those fish.

"In Los Angeles, I used to drop by the little house in the Village where the Japanese lived because I wanted to see what they ate. God, it was raw eggs with rice. Then there was the famed oxygen incident. A well-known American coach who shall remain nameless was convinced the Japanese were doped, that they were getting some kind of stimulation from drugs. They were winning everything. And when they got out of the pool, they'd have these bright-red marks on their faces. This is what made him so suspicious. But do you know what it was? They'd been sniffing oxygen, and the marks were from their oxygen masks—legal as hell."

Buster Crabbe's career made an abrupt and profoundly profitable turn because of the 1932 Olympics. "Paramount Pictures came over and asked about fifteen athletes to try out for Tarzan. It was interesting; we got to see the studio, and it only cost me a day. They took pictures from the waist up facing forward, and they shot profiles, and they had me pose throwing a spear. Then I had some screen tests, and I got the part—I became the seventh Tarzan. It came down to John McCartney and

Randolph Scott—Randy was too skinny, they said—and myself. I was making eight dollars a week in a stockroom trying to put myself through law school, so I was happy to take the part. It got frustrating, though. I'd been to law school, and I could speak English, and here I was, King of the Jungle, grunting stuff like 'Me Kasbah.' It took me a long time to live down the part. I got typed.

"I kind of backed into the Flash Gordon thing. I read the comic strip, and I happened to be on the set when they were casting, so a producer asked me to do Flash. At first I thought, Gosh, no one's going to sit still for this thing—Flash in a rocket ship taking off for Mars and Dale saying a thousand times, 'Look *out*, Flash!'

"But this was 1936. It became the most expensive serial ever made—cost seven hundred and fifty thousand dollars when most of them were a hundred thousand dollars. It turned out to be a big moneymaker. Only one other movie made more money for the studio.

"The big trouble was they had to bleach my hair for the part. I always believed in taking my hat off in elevators, but when I was playing Flash, my hat stayed on the old bleached head. I also played Buck Rogers, but my favorite part was the TV series *Captain Gallant*, because my son Cuffy was with me in it."

Cuffy now stands six feet three inches and weighs 280 pounds. Buster Crabbe's acting career has changed, too, being little more than bit parts for quite a while, except for an ad-lib Western called *Comeback Trail*, released last fall. Buster has been a stockbroker and sold swimming pools and run a boys' camp near Lake Saranac in the Adirondacks and directed the swimming program at the Concord Hotel in the Catskills over the years. He has also appeared in TV commercials selling a body T-shirt. He is in good shape for modeling; he won the three events in the over sixty class and set three age group records before joining the winning relay team in the Senior Sports International meet in Los Angeles in the summer of 1971.

Takeichi Nishi, Cavalryman, Deceased

Takeichi Nishi was a splendid horseman; he cut a dashing and polished figure among the Hollywood crowd in 1932, and he counted Mary Pickford and Douglas Fairbanks, Sr., and Will Rogers as his friends. He was only a lieutenant in the Japanese cavalry, but he was a baron, wellborn, a man with a gracious and powerful social presence. The widow of Baron Nishi is a gentle pretty gray-haired woman who lives in a small apartment filled with his memorabilia in Tokyo's fashionable Azabu district. Recently she recalled that Douglas Fairbanks, Sr., once said, "One Baron Nishi is worth ten diplomats." She also remembered that a Los Angeles restaurant owner had written after the 1932 Olympics to tell her that since her husband had won his gold medal there in the equestrian *Prix des Nations* event, the restaurant was full of people who wanted to order sukiyaki.

Baron Nishi, who his widow estimated was gone from home about thirteen years of the twenty they were married, once sent her a postcard from Los Angeles that said, "I'm being very popular here. Bye-bye." She laughed over that, and then in an ancient (and perhaps not so fashionable) style of Japanese female resignation, she said, "My husband had many pretty girlfriends. So I believe he was popular, and I never would divorce him."

She recalled that Baron Nishi had been despondent after the

Japanese attack on Pearl Harbor, but that he had said, "I have many friends in the United States, but I must go to war, for I am first a soldier and second a friend." Most Japanese soldiers leave a lock of their hair when they go off to fight, but the Baron Nishi cut the mane from his horse and left that and his favorite boots instead.

There are many stories about the baron's death, said his widow. It happened in caves off the beach at Iwo Jima, where the Japanese troops were battling advancing U.S. marines. As one story goes, a marine knew of the baron—then a lieutenant colonel—through his Olympic exploits, and knowing he was in command of troops in that section of the island, the marine shouted, "Come out of the caves, Colonel Nishi. You're too fine a horseman to die in there." Of course, the baron would not surrender. Mrs. Nishi has talked to Japanese soldiers who came to tell her that they saw him make a valiant stand and that they saw his body after he fell.

"Oh, he could not surrender," she said. "To surrender is disgrace, and to surrender and leave his men behind is an even bigger disgrace." She said she is very proud of her husband and that she has been told that there is a plaque on a rock along the sandy beach at Iwo Jima which marks the place where the great Olympic horseman died.

Juan Carlos Zabala, Masseur

"If I had a hundred lives, I would do it a hundred times." In the Los Angeles Games of 1932, the Argentinian Juan Carlos Zabala won the marathon, and though he is now sixty, a dignified-looking, stocky gray-haired fellow who dresses in tweedy good taste while making his daily visits around Buenos Aires as

169

a professional masseur, Zabala remembers the event as if it were yesterday. "At the starting gun, I thought of my country. My idea was to put my rivals to a psychological test. I did this by making a false start, which was annulled, to see what their reaction would be. The second time I started correctly. I had an obligation with my fellow countrymen, and I did not want to let them down. Having been orphaned as a baby, I suppose I wanted to be a leader. I had promised to come back to Argentina the winner, and I did. Otherwise, I suppose I would not have come back at all."

Juan Zabala is wealthy now, owner of much valuable land in Benavidez, just outside Buenos Aires on the Pan American Highway. He has a large, California-style bungalow there, a fine garden filled with flowers and lovely cactus, a small stone studio built for his elder daughter, who is a painter, and a nursery stocked with 800 leghorn hens for his son, who is studying agronomy. He has blueprints in hand for building still another such chicken nursery on his property, plus a kidney-shaped pool for his son to cultivate exotic aquatic plants, plus yet two other houses for his son and younger daughter to live in. Juan Carlos Zabala also owns several horses and has begun breeding polo ponies on another section of his land.

His wealth, he said, is directly related to his track career of the 1930's. "In fact, I suppose the Olympic Games had little effect on my life," he said. "I was simply the first South American to win a marathon. But when I came back, I had a lot of money—some from an inheritance in Europe, and some from my own winnings betting on myself. I always bet on myself, and sometimes I gave a handicap. In one race before the Los Angeles Olympics, I ran in a race organized by the New York *Times*, and I wore very narrow leather-soled shoes. They made me lose. They started to disintegrate with the heat, and my trainer pulled me out of the race when he saw that my feet were bleeding. Of course, I did not win money in that race."

Zabala ran consistently in Europe in the thirties, got a diploma in physical education and medical massage in Germany in 1934, lost the marathon at Berlin in 1936, then was caught by the war in the Sudetenland and did not get out of Germany until 1941. He quit racing then. "With the beginning of the war, I could not conceive of practicing sports while humanity was destroying itself," said Juan Zabala. "I had Jewish friends in Germany who were disappearing everyday into concentration camps. Who could run?"

Back in Buenos Aires, Zabala bought a town house in Buenos Aires, plus twenty-five acres of land in Benavidez. Then in 1955 he was forced to flee the country because of rumors that he had spoken against the dictatorship of Juan Perón. He moved his family to New York, waited until Perón was overthrown, then returned in 1959. He found his Buenos Aires house a shambles, looted by vandals, and he eventually lost the house in a court fight.

But he is happy again now. Each morning he leaves his home at sunrise carrying his black masseur's case, takes a microbus to his practice, and works the day through, usually returning home well after ten o'clock at night. "Ah," said Juan Zabala, "why do I have what I have and other sports figures— the majority of them—have so little? I had too much luck. That is all it amounts to—sometimes life denies to many what it gives to a very few. I was among the chosen ones as regards health and money."

Not long ago, Juan Zabala suggested to other Argentine Olympic competitors that they form a cooperative to protect

171

them against financial troubles as they grew old. He suggested they build homes and a hospital for aging Argentine Olympians. He was ridiculed for making such a proposal.

1936

Held in Berlin from August 1 to August 16. 4,069 athletes from 49 countries participated. Modern history's most unforgettable, most controversial, most spectacular, most overtly political Games. Adolf Hitler was Chancellor of Germany. King Edward VIII abdicated throne of England for Baltimore divorcée Wallis Warfield. Ethiopian Emperor Haile Selassie fled his country as Italian troops advanced; Mussolini announced annexation of Ethiopia as Italian territory. Spanish Civil War began.

When Adolf Hitler's regime gained control of the German government on January 30, 1933, one question which arose almost immediately was whether or not the Nazis would proceed with the Olympic Games of 1936. There was good reason to assume the Führer might simply cancel out, for when the International Olympic Committee made the award to Berlin in 1931, there had been a furious outcry among Nazi youth and sports organizations. To them, the idea of competing against "inferior non-Aryans" was a gross insult, a racial slur of the first magnitude.

Indeed, on the campuses of eighteen German universities something called the Fighting Organization Against the Olympic Games was established, and the notorious anti-Jewish newspaper *Der Stürmer* denounced the Games as "an infamous festival dominated by the Jews."

Besides this rather fierce reluctance among Nazi youth, there was the dismal fact that Germany had done poorly in the 1932 Olympics in Los Angeles, which was not really good advertising for a society built on claims of racial superiority. Only four gold medals were returned to the fatherland from Los Angeles: one by the four-oared shell with coxswain, one by a weight lifter, one by a bantamweight wrestler, and the fourth by an obscure writer of a poem titled *"Am Kangehenzonga"* which was entered in the now long-forgotten cultural competitions that struggled for notice for many years.

There was also a question of whether the Third Reich could afford the costs of a Berlin Olympics. And surely the most valid argument raised by Nazis against having an Olympics was that it was more than likely that an innocent world nosing around Germany would unearth sinister secrets: that rearmament, though still camouflaged, was under way and that a systematic program of repression and persecution against Jews and political opponents had begun.

Thus, the Nazis stalled and argued among themselves for nine months. Finally, on October 30, 1933, Hitler decided to override the objections of such exalted Nazis as SS leader Heinrich Himmler and Foreign Minister Baron Konstanin von Neurath. Hitler chose to go along with his propaganda genius, Josef Goebbels, who argued that the Games would show the world that Nazism was both efficient and peacefully inclined. Hitler announced that the Games would be held in Berlin, beginning August 1, 1936. And once this was announced, the Germans swung into action with a vengeance; they ended up spending $30,000,000, far more than any other Olympics had previously cost, and they made the Games into an unforgettable showcase for Nazism. They put up a new 100,000-seat track and field, stadium, six gymnasiums, a swimming stadium and many smaller arenas. They installed closed circuit television for crowds who could not attend the events in person and a radio network that reached forty-one countries. Their press facilities were immense—the first Telex was used; a zeppelin was on hand to transport newsreel film out of Germany. They had photofinish equipment, electronic timing devices and a magnificent lighting system for breathtaking nocturnal dance-and-calisthenic performances.

The Olympic Village, built for quick clandestine conversion to a military barracks as soon as the Games ended, was remarkable. More than 3,700 male athletes from forty-nine nations lived there in handsome brick-and-stucco cottages—really sound buildings which made the tiny bungalows used in Los Angeles' Village look like privies. Indeed, to make certain no one missed the contrast between U.S.- and German-made housing, Nazi propaganda experts had bought one of the L.A. bungalows and put it on display in their Village.

Berlin was awash in a flood of military uniforms. Jackboots cracked everywhere, and the warrior's livery of the Hitler Youth, the NSKK, the SS, as well as the full-dress regalia of Wehrmacht, Navy and Luftwaffe troops, all but swamped the civilian crowds. Yet in the euphoria of the spectacle, with grand forests of flags rising everywhere and brass bands in full serenade at every corner, it was apparently easy to overlook the specter of German militarism.

The swastika, substituted for the old black, white and red flag of Germany before the Games, flew over all like abstract black vultures. The Nazi salute was given by nearly every German at every opportunity. The deep thundering roars—

"Sieg Heil! Sieg Heil!"—in Olympic Stadium sounded like the detonation of a thousand cannon.

The question of Nazi anti-Semitism was far more prevalent than that of German militarism to most people. The Germans had attempted to shine up their image by selecting the fencer Helene Mayer, who was partly Jewish, as a member of the German team. She had already won a gold medal in 1928, so it was certainly not a sacrifice in quality. Still, the selection was made only after pressure from the IOC and some Americans. Miss Mayer was living in Los Angeles at the time she was chosen. She won a silver medal in Berlin, and as she stood upon the platform, Helene Mayer snapped a Nazi salute toward the Führer, an act which brought a roar from the crowd, most of whom were well aware of the significance of her being a Jew. After the Olympics she emigrated to the United States again. She eked out a meager living as a language teacher, and when the war ended, she returned to Germany and married. She died of cancer in 1961.

In an attempt to blunt the criticism over anti-Semitism, the Germans also invited Palestine to enter the Olympics; the invitation was declined. None of this quite managed to still the furor in the United States over whether an American team should even be sent to Germany. The dispute was almost as fierce and as divisive as Vietnam came to be, particularly after September, 1935, when Hitler issued his Nuremberg Laws, depriving Jews of their German citizenship and their civil rights.

As early as 1933, Avery Brundage, then president of the U.S. Olympic Committee, was asked about German anti-Semitism. He said: "Frankly I don't think we have any business to meddle in this question. We are a sports group pledged to promote clean competition and sportsmanship. When we let politics, racial questions, religious or social disputes creep into our actions, we're in for trouble."

The New York *Times* replied in an editorial: "When Nazis deliberately and arrogantly offend against our common humanity, sport does not transcend all political and racial considerations."

A sort of hysteria seemed to set in as the Games drew closer. Brundage and the USOC became more and more rigid —and ultimately more rabid—about going to the Games. Brundage released an official USOC brochure which argued that "the persecution of minority peoples is as old as history" and that "the customs of other nations are not our business." He compared the American team members who wanted to go to Germany to "the Minute Men of Concord and the troops of George Washington at Valley Forge." As more opponents of the Olympic Committee began rising all over the country, the statements from the USOC transcended all sense of morality.

Brundage said: "Certain Jews must now understand that they cannot use these Games as a weapon in their boycott against the Nazis."

Frederick W. Rubien, secretary of the USOC, said: "Germans are not discriminating against Jews in their Olympic tryouts. The Jews are eliminated because they are not good enough as athletes. Why, there are not a dozen Jews in the world of Olympic caliber."

General Charles H. Sherrill, a member of the USOC and the IOC, said: "It does not concern me one bit the way the Jews in Germany are being treated, any more than lynchings in the South of our own country."

Things could scarcely get worse than that. But the U.S. team went to Germany, and Avery Brundage has always been convinced that there was no other proper thing to do. In 1937

Mr. Brundage appeared in Madison Square Garden as principal speaker for the pro-Nazi American-German Bund. He had not changed his mind then: "No nation since ancient Greece has displayed a more truly national public interest in the Olympic spirit than you find in Germany. We can learn much from Germany. . . . We, too, if we wish to preserve our institutions must stamp out Communism. We, too, must take steps to arrest the decline of patriotism." (Mr. Brundage resigned from the America First Committee on December 8, 1941, the day the United States declared war on Germany.)

In the summer of 1971, in his office in Chicago, he had not changed his mind. "The Berlin Games were the finest in modern history. I will accept no disputes over that fact," he said.

In the beginning, there were six sprinters from the United States in Berlin. Four of them did run on the 400-meter relay team, and two did not. The United States relay team won gold medals, beating the Italian team by 15 yards and setting a world record. Ever since, there has been a bitter dispute over the makeup of that team. Many angry charges have been cast about, accusing people of everything from regional favoritism to personal partiality to white racism to cold and calculated anti-Semitism. Perhaps the controversy would have burned itself to ashes and blown away within a few months of the Berlin Games—except for a strange and unsettling string of coincidental facts:

The two sprinters who did not run were Marty Glickman and Sam Stoller. They were also the only Jews on the U.S. track team. They were also the *only* members of the team who did not compete in *any* events in Berlin.

What really happened? When a man tries to re-create the truth, he can bring it to light only along with his own distortions and his own desires, his own fantasies and insights. As it was in *Rashomon*, so it was in Berlin, 1936.

Besides Marty Glickman and Sam Stoller, there were the four members of the medal-winning relay team—Jesse Owens (for whom the relay meant his fourth gold medal), Ralph Metcalfe, Frank Wykoff and Foy Draper. Also deeply involved were the United States team's coach, Lawson Robertson of the University of Pennsylvania, and his assistant, Dean Cromwell of the University of Southern California. They made the final decisions about which runners to use. They both are dead now and can no longer testify. And so is Foy Draper, who was killed in World War II.

Glickman, Owens, Metcalfe, Wykoff and Stoller all are alive, and here is what each recalls to be the truth of the events that transpired before and after the 400-meter relay:

• Marty Glickman, fifty-four, is a short, round, balding fellow who does not now in any way resemble a world-class sprinter. He is a professional broadcaster in New York City. He announces the races at the Yonkers trotting track, has done play-by-play of the New York Giants football games for many years, does the Mets games and has his own radio sports programs. Marty Glickman said:

"Four or five days before the race, Coach Robertson and Dean Cromwell said we were going to have a trial race between Foy Draper, Sam Stoller and me to keep us in shape and to see in what order we'd run the relay. Stoller finished first, I was second and Draper was third. Then the morning of the relay we had this surprise meeting of the sprinters in this bedroom at the Olympic Village. Robertson got up, walked around a little and said he had heard the Germans were hiding their best sprinters, keeping them under wraps. He looked worried. He said Stoller and myself were out because we couldn't take any chances on losing. Jesse Owens spoke up and said, 'Look, Coach, I've had enough. I've already won three medals. I don't want to run the relay. Let Marty and Sam run.' Robertson said, 'Nothing doing, Jesse, you will run.' "

Marty Glickman paused, shook his head at the memory, then said, "Well, I was only eighteen, but I was brash and I said, 'Coach, this is ridiculous. You don't hide world-class sprinters; they have to race to get experience. Any American relay team you pick will win by fifteen yards—*any* of our runners, the milers or the hurdlers could run against the Germans or anyone else and win by fifteen yards.'

"Then I said, 'If you drop us, there's going to be a helluva furor—we're the only two Jews on the track team.'

"Robertson said, 'We'll take our chances on that.'

"Sam Stoller spoke up then and asked what about the trial race where Foy Draper finished last, and Robertson said Draper had more experience than we did. Well, everyone in the room was raising hell by now. Everyone was terribly upset and talking. Except Ralph Metcalfe. He didn't say anything. Ralph had never won a gold medal, so he didn't say anything. . . ."

As for the motives behind his being left off the relay team, Marty Glickman said, "There were several things. Frank Wykoff and Draper were both from USC, and that was probably part of it since Cromwell wanted his own boys to run. Also, Avery Brundage and Dean Cromwell were members of the America First Committee. They were Nazi sympathizers.

"The Germans had been terribly embarrassed by the success of our black athletes. To save the Germans from further embarrassment, they didn't want to have the only two Jewish boys on the team win something, too. That was a lot of it. . . ."

• Jesse Owens recalled things this way:

ALL THAT GLITTERS IS NOT GOLD

"In the time trials in Berlin Stoller and Glickman were winning. Maybe that should have been the main consideration. But Draper and Wykoff were from USC, of course, and Dean Cromwell was their coach. Sam Stoller was from Michigan and Marty Glickman was from Syracuse. I remember we had a team meeting the morning before the race and I stood up and said, 'I've already got three medals, I don't need any more. I'd like to relinquish my place to Sam Stoller.' It didn't work that way, of course, but frankly I doubt that the Jewish factor was the deciding issue. The Germans didn't give a damn about who won then. Probably if Glickman and Stoller had been from USC, they'd have run the relay. . . ."

• Ralph H. Metcalfe, sixty-two, is a Democratic Congressman from Illinois's First District. He is a longtime patron of and a well-oiled cog in Mayor Richard Daley's Chicago political machine. Ralph Metcalfe served faithfully under Daley for years on the City Council of Chicago, then in 1970 was elected to fill the Congressional seat vacated by the death of William Dawson. Dawson was black, and so is Ralph Metcalfe, one of thirteen blacks in the Ninety-second Congress. Representative Metcalfe is graying and has a neat mustache. He is a cautiously polished fellow in his conversation, yet fairly ebullient, and he ultimately gives the impression of being outspoken when perhaps he is really only being a politician. He had won a silver and a bronze medal in the 1932 Los Angeles Olympics. Congressman Metcalfe lost the 100-meter race to Eddie Tolan by an eyelash according to the angle of the photofinish camera ("I'll never believe I really lost"), and he finished third in the 200-meter race, even though it was discovered later that he had run seven feet more around the curve than other contestants owing to an official's measuring error at the starting line. "I'd been told sportsmen never complain," he says now. "I did not open my mouth then. But in 1936 I did protest."

As the Congressman remembered the meeting in Berlin before the relay: "I protested quite loudly when the coaches left off Stoller and Glickman, but Dean Cromwell wanted Draper and Wykoff. And no one could persuade him otherwise. Certainly I should have run because I was not competing in any other events besides the hundred [where he won a silver medal behind Owens]. I also had the fastest finish. Jesse is one of my best friends. I'm glad he won four medals, but he already had three when the relay meeting was held. But he didn't say a word that I recall. I guess he wanted Number Four that bad. We ran in a strange order—Jesse was leadoff, though he had a notoriously slow start; then I was second, then Draper, then Wykoff. Wykoff should have been first, and I had the best finish. It's the only race I ever ran where I was mad.

"Of course, I'm convinced it was the Jewish thing that was behind it. Glickman and Stoller should have run."

• Frank Wykoff, sixty-two, was the superintendent of schools in Carpinteria, California, when he made the 1936 Olympic team. He had already run on the '28 and '32 teams and had won gold medals on relay teams both years. Recently, after many years as an administrative subaltern in the Los Angeles public school system, Frank Wykoff retired. He is a soft-spoken fellow, rather gentle but weary-looking, as if he had perhaps carried the weight of a public school bureaucracy around on his back too long. He remembered the events in Berlin this way:

"Originally it was definitely supposed to be Marty Glickman, Sam Stoller, Ralph Metcalfe and myself. Then the night before the race they announced that Jesse Owens insisted on

going for four medals. Then I heard Metcalfe was not going to
run, that Sam Stoller would. I felt very bad. The four of us—
Glickman, Stoller, Metcalfe and I—had been working well together. We could have set the record, too. Easily. In fact, we
were the only four sprinters who actually practiced as a relay
team. No one else had even done any baton passing. I felt
very bad about all of it. Down in my heart, I think it was done
the way it was because of the Jewish thing. I'm sorry, but I
believe that."

• Sam Stoller, fifty-six, is an executive for a radio-TV station
in Roanoke, Virginia. After his failure to make the relay team,
Stoller was so stricken that he swore he would never race again.
He held to that oath for about a month, and eventually he won
the NCAA 100-yard dash championship. Because of his fame
in track he met the comedian Joe E. Brown, had a screen test
and wound up appearing in thirteen movies—including one
with Carole Lombard and another with Mae West. During his
weeks in Berlin Sam Stoller kept a diary. Here are some pertinent excerpts:

Aug. 4—Coach Robertson approached me at the stadium
and said, "Sam, your baton practice has been excellent, and
you ran a very fine race yesterday. You needn't worry.
You're running in the relay. Had you taken third as Draper
did, you would not have run. As it is, I'll have to break the
news slowly to Foy." . . . Well, it is interesting to note that
Foy Draper, realizing that he may be off the relay because
of his poor showing, confidentially told me to get together
with all the white boys and protest against running the relay
with Negroes. I told him that I didn't like the idea. . . .

Aug. 6—Here it is Thursday and the coaches have
worked with our relay team only once. . . . However, I've
been assured of running because of my winning the time
trial. . . .

Aug. 8—This is the one day in my life that I'll remember to my dying days. [This was the morning Stoller was told he would not race; it was also his twenty-first birthday.]

Aug. 18—I've finally regained my composure. The most humiliating episode in my life has worn off enough so that I can once more think, eat and sleep properly. The night before the race Jesse Owens came up to me and said, "Well, Sam, Robertson just told me that the relay tomorrow is Owens, Metcalfe, Stoller and Wykoff." I felt pretty good knowing that I was to run. However, Draper, learning of this lineup, went to his coach, Dean Cromwell of Southern California, and those two had a nice little chat with Robertson. . . . [Stoller recalled that Ralph Metcalfe and Frank Wykoff began to bicker bitterly at the pre-relay meeting over which of them should anchor the team.] Imagine those boys arguing over a trivial matter as to the *position* of running when there were two boys, Marty and myself, who wouldn't see any competition at all. Well, that room was smoldering hot with dissension and ill feeling. Finally I regained my composure enough to ask for the floor.

You could hear a pin drop, it got so quiet. I told the boys that they would never run well if they were going to have so much dissension among themselves. Then I recalled to Robertson's mind how he had told me I was assured of running and how he had told me that the time trial meant everything, and then I told him softly and slowly that he had gone back on his word. . . . He left the room without answering me. . . .

Aug. 22 [aboard the SS *Roosevelt*, homeward-bound]— A teammate told me that Cromwell said I was sore at him and he wanted badly to talk with me. Well, I did talk with him, and he said that he had warned Robertson that if I didn't run there would be hell to pay in the U.S. He also said that he wanted an *all-white* relay team. He put the blame entirely on Robertson for my not running. I still am really in doubt about his story. . . .

Aug. 28—Landing Day. Alas and alack, more news

183

reporters. I've seen quite a few of them since this damned thing happened. Coach Robertson came up to me today on board ship and very apologetically admitted that he had made a terrible mistake not letting me run—in place of Metcalfe! He said that he stayed awake nights thinking of it and that his entire trip was spoiled on that account. . . .

When Lawson Robertson debarked in New York, he told reporters: "The fact that Stoller and Glickman are Jewish had absolutely nothing to do with their removal. I hope no one misconstrued the move. . . ."

And Avery Brundage, then president of the USOC, wrote a few weeks later in the final committee report on the Berlin Olympics: "An erroneous report was circulated that two athletes had been dropped from the American relay team because of their religion. This report was absurd. The two athletes in question were taken only as substitutes. Reference to the results of the final Olympic tryouts at Randall's Island will show that Owens, Metcalfe, Wykoff and Draper won the first four places. These four men composed the 400-meter relay team, won the event and broke the world's record. Their performance proved the wisdom of adhering to the rules. . . ."

And of course, that settled the controversy from that day onward and for all time.

Eleanor Holm, Interior Decorator

Another *cause célèbre* in Berlin centered on the peccadillos of Eleanor Holm, the swimmer. Although straitlaced Americans were smugly pleased with her punishment, many other people were baffled by the wrathful judgment the United States Olympic Committee dealt Miss Holm. A little glass of wine or two? Perhaps more? Did this deserve instant excommunication? Exile and humiliation? "Why, hell, the Europeans couldn't understand why it happened: I was drinking *champagne*," said Eleanor Holm not long ago. "If it had been whiskey or *gin*, well, all right. But they drank wine at their training tables, so they couldn't figure out *what* was the matter. Hitler asked to see me, and through his interpreter he said if I'd been on the German team, they'd have kept me on the team and then punished me after the Olympics—if I had *lost!* Hitler asked me himself if I got drunk—he seemed very interested—and I said no. God, look what Dawn Fraser did; she made me look like a piker. She climbed a flagpole and stole a flag and swam a *moat* in Tokyo, for God's sake, and the Australians didn't suspend her until after the Games—and after she *won!*"

Eleanor Holm is fifty-seven now, saucy as ever, still blessed with that stunning fresh *huge* glamor-girl smile radiating all the great voltage of vitality and abandon and dazzle that fascinated the world long after she was fired from the 1936 U.S. Olympic team. She is a tiny woman and looks almost too frail ever to have been the magnificent world-class swimmer she once was.

Her hair, a sort of chestnut brown color, is long and she uses bright red lipstick and applies the same color polish to her fingernails and toenails. She wears very expensive and bright Florida sport clothes and lives in a penthouse apartment in a Miami Beach condominium. It is an airy, clean, sunshiny place with a spectacular view of the causeway. The decor is artfully flamboyant—white walls, pink French Provincial furniture, magnificent carved wooden chests and bureaus and tables, some beautiful Oriental lamps. There is a Renoir on one wall and two intimate pen-sketch caricatures of her by Salvador Dali. Many of these opulent furnishings came from her second

185

husband, the tiny show business dynamo, Billy Rose, after their sensational divorce in 1954.

Eleanor Holm speaks in sunbursts and exclamation marks. Always there are gay and exuberant gestures, always a cigarette in one hand. Always that dazzling smile. Frequently she rises excitedly to her feet to do a classy little pantomime to illustrate some point. During a recent interview, she mentioned Avery Brundage's name, and said, "He's one of those heel-toe jerks." She rose immediately from her sofa and did a pompous little heel-toe strut all around the room; it was an act that had hints of Charlie Chaplin's heroic talent.

Eleanor Holm went to the Olympic Games in 1928, a girl of fourteen who had grown up in Brooklyn. Her father was chief of a New York borough Fire Department, and when Eleanor was on that first Olympic team, she recalled, "I was still at the age where it was a big kick to go out with my father and ring the bell on his shiny red car. Hell, no one will believe this anymore, but in those days I used to snitch on my roommates if they kept me up or if they stayed out too late. . . ."

Eleanor won nothing in 1928, but in 1932 she captured the gold medal for the backstroke. She also won twenty-nine national championships and held six world records for the backstroke. Surely she would have won another gold medal in Berlin.

The charge against her when she was fired from the team was that she had been drinking champagne aboard the ship bound for Europe. She also had been spending nearly all her time with sportswriters in the first-class cabin area instead of in the hold with the rest of the athletes. And yes, she also had enjoyed playing craps with her pals from the papers.

"The afternoon before I was kicked off, I won a couple of hundred dollars playing dice with the reporters," she said. "I didn't give it back either, and I'm sure this didn't sit too well with the officials. Of course, *they* were all in first-class cabins, and they didn't like my being there. I *tried* to buy my own ticket to go first class, but they wouldn't let me. I was an *athlete!* To them athletes were cattle, and they had to be fenced off. So they put us down in *steerage*, four to a room way down in the *bottom* of the boat! Everything smelled like liniment. *Yukkk!*

"It was all such a mess. I had been around; I was no baby. Hell, I married Art Jarrett after the '32 Games. He was the star at the Coconut Grove, and I went to work singing for his band. I used to take a mike and get up in front of the band in a white bathing suit and a white cowboy hat and high heels. I'd sing *'I'm an Old Cowhand.'* They loved it. I wasn't much of a singer, but I was okay with a mike.

"After 1932, Warner Brothers had signed me then as an *actress*—not a swimmer but an actress. They paid me four hundred and fifty dollars a week, and they sent me to school to lose my Brooklyn accent. Oh, I had a hell of an accent, and they had me reading the Bible to get rid of it. I was a *lousy* actress! I only made one movie—it was a Tarzan movie. *Time* said that in the love scenes I looked as if I was going to spit in Tarzan's eye. That was in '37 or '38, I guess. Tarzan was Glenn Morris, who won the decathlon in Berlin, you know.

"Anyway, here I'd been working in *nightclubs* when I made the team in '36—I wasn't a *child*. Actually I quit the band a month before the trials to go into training for the Olympics.

"On the ship, I was in first class one night, I guess it was the second night out from New York. I was sitting around with my friends, the newspaper boys, when this chaperone came up to me and told me it was time to go to *bed*. God, it was about nine o'clock, and who wanted to go down in that damn *basement* to sleep anyway? So I said to her, 'Oh, is it really bedtime? Did *you* make the Olympic team or did I?" I had had a few glasses of champagne. So she went to Brundage and complained that I was setting a bad example for the team, and they got together and told me the next morning that I was fired. The committee might have changed its mind about me, but the papers blew it up so much I never had a chance. I was dead. I was heartbroken."

Well, not *permanently* heartbroken. In Berlin, Eleanor was the belle of the Olympics. "I was listed as a correspondent for INS or someone, but, hell, I never wrote a word. Paul Gallico wrote everything under my name. . . . I was asked to all the Nazis' big receptions and cocktail parties, and of course, Brundage and all the big shots would be there, too, trying to *ignore* me! It was a *fantastic* Olympics, spectacular! I had such *fun*. You know, athletes don't think much about the politics of it all. I *enjoyed* the parties, the stadium, the uniforms, the flags, the *thousands* of cleaning ladies in their gray dresses and brooms.

"Göring was fun. He had a good personality, lots of chuckling. And so did the little one with the club foot [Josef Goebbels]. Göring gave me a sterling silver swastika. I had a mold made of it, and I put a diamond Star of David in the middle of it. . . ."

When she returned to the United States, Eleanor Holm was a celebrity. "Jarrett, my husband, was going to sue Brundage for kicking me off," she said, "but then we started getting all these fabulous offers, and, well, he dropped it. I did all right after I won in 1932, but 1936 made me a *star*—it made me a glamor girl! Just another gold medal would never have done *that!*"

And so she remained, a glamor girl, through the tempestuous years with Billy Rose and the Aquacades, when Rose made millions on his swimming show, and through a series of bizarre bulletins that kept the tabloids delighted for years: ELEANOR HOLM KO'D BY SLEEPING PILLS . . . SAVE ELEANOR'S LIFE WITH CHEST TUBE . . . OVERDOSE OF SLEEPING PILLS HOSPITALIZES ELEANOR HOLM. At the time of the sleeping pill stories, she was living at the apartment of playboy Tommy Whalen, a former nightclub owner and murder suspect. She tossed off the suicide attempt stories as being "a combination of three Navy grogs and a lobster Cantonese dinner."

She has lived in her Miami Beach penthouse for about ten years, and her life is not particularly complicated, she said. "I play golf some now—*awful* golf, 118 is my consistent score. My *best* is 106. It's very frustrating, but I keep going back. That's the way the days go now, a little golf, then a few pops at the club and it's done. Hell, I haven't been swimming in years, decades! I did some interior decorating here, and I was pretty good. I made fifteen thousand dollars a year, but my God, going up against these rich showy Jewish broads. They'd have all this jewelry dripping all over them. To impress 'em when I was trying to get their jobs, I'd run down to my bank and get out this one big *rock* that Rose gave me. I'd put it on and then go talk with them, and I'd sit flashing that big *rock* back and forth in front of my face. Oh, they'd *notice* it all right. Then when I was done, I'd hurry back to the bank and put the rock back in the vault. I couldn't afford to insure it."

She burst out laughing, and she said with that incandescent smile alight, "Life owes me nothing—I've had a *ball!*"

Gisela Mauermayer, Librarian

A homemade knit pullover sweater covers her big frame, and there is in her face a hint of the haggardness of age and loneliness, of the dry fatigue of a life filled with too much work and too little play. Gisela Mauermayer lives in the same row house in Munich where she was born; she is a spinster, and her married sister shares the house. Gisela Mauermayer, now fifty-eight, works as a librarian at the Munich Zoological Society.

Anyone who has seen any photos of the Berlin contestants will never forget Gisela Mauermayer—a six-foot blond virginal beauty who won the discus throw. The flower of fair Aryan maidenhood, she gave a stiff Nazi salute on the victory stand as the swastika rose on its staff, and the stadium roared. "The Olympics was the greatest event of my life and most probably in the lives of many other people, too," said Gisela Mauermayer. A timid, oddly nunnish smile lighted her face. "I confess that I was a Nazi, and that my main impetus came from the ardent desire to do good for Germany. This still didn't soothe my nerves. Often I felt that I was the only one in Germany who did not think I would win."

Gisela Mauermayer reached her peak as an athlete at a time when Adolf Hitler had made it a state policy to produce gold medal winners for the Berlin Games. Thus, the public pressures on her to succeed were immense. And so were the personal pressures, for she was the obedient daughter of an intensely nationalistic schoolteacher-father who was devoted to the theory that the glory of the ancient Teutons was synonymous with excellent physical performances. When Gisela was discovered by Hitler's Olympic recruiters, her father was ecstatic. She spent the year before the Games in intensive training under government coaches. Still, she recalled, "Matters were different from what they are today. I continued my studies as a gymnastics teacher. And sports, even with all the emphasis placed on them by the government, still were a pay-your-own-way affair."

Despite her resolute dedication to the Führer and his preachings, Gisela Mauermayer's gold medal brought her no material reward. After the Olympics she was given the same teaching job for which she had applied before. She taught in Munich during the war. When American forces took over the city, they robbed her home of all her medals, her cups, her trophies. She was summarily removed from her teaching job because of her Nazi Party membership. "I had to start all over again. But now I went into the natural sciences, as I had wanted long before. I started from scratch at the Zoological Institute of Munich University, and I earned my second doctor's degree by studying the social behavior of ants."

Her librarian's salary is $500 a month, but it does not afford her many luxuries. She skis. In her home a Bechstein grand piano dominates the living room, and next to it is a cello. Gisela Mauermayer plays chamber music twice a week with friends. She has traveled quite a lot and had planned a trip to Peru, Mexico and the southwestern United States, but an oil heater in the cellar broke down after forty years of service, and her trip was postponed.

For years, she was a member of the Female Executive Committee of the German Olympic Committee, but she resigned. "I sorely miss the idealism which ought to be an integral part of sports," she said. "In my time, even when I was a prominent personality, we considered ourselves lucky if we were reimbursed a small part of our expenses. Nowadays, competition sports have become too commercialized, too specialized—and, last but not least, a *hazard* rather than a boon to health.

"As a zoologist, I can attest from my scientific experience that no animal exists which could sustain the kind of protracted effort nowadays demanded by a high-performance athlete."

Gotthard Handrick, Auto Salesman

Photographs show him with eyes glinting like ball bearings, a magnificently handsome man gazing icily down a pistol barrel, his Nazi officer's cap set at an angle that can only be called arrogant, his uniform as perfectly turned out as sheet steel. In retrospect, of course, the look of Obertleutnant Gotthard Handrick was the epitome of all that was secret and sinister and chilling about the XI Olympiad. He was the symbol of all the unknowable destruction and horror that lay beyond the panoramic dazzle that overwhelmed the Berlin Games.

Gotthard Handrick won the gold medal in the modern pentathlon, a rigorous event which demands excellence in pistol shooting, swimming, cross-country running, fencing and riding. But even as he won the medal and was given a spot promotion to captain, Gotthard Handrick was secretly ordered by top Nazi functionaries to stay away from all public celebrations and Olympic parties. He was not even allowed to attend the closing ceremonies, despite the fact that his victory was even then proclaimed to be one of Germany's most impressive. "As a fighter pilot," Handrick says now with a thin smile, "I was someone whom the German government did not care to expose too much to an inquisitive outside world."

He had entered the Rewehr in 1928. Even then he was taking flying lessons from the German ace Ernst Udet, for he was determined to join the German Air Force just as soon as the Versailles Treaty was declared void and German military aviation was again legal. When the Luftwaffe was born, Gotthard Handrick was one of the first officers selected for the crack Richthofen Squadron, a band of hot pilots formed to test fly the new Messerschmitts which were then just off the designer's board. That was 1934, but Handrick's talents in the pentathlon events soon impressed the Führer's Olympic scouts as being even more spectacular than his flying skills, and in 1935 he was given a full year to train for the Games. Looking back now, Handrick says: "Admittedly, there were no commercial inducements. But the bounty of the opportunities placed at my disposal were simply inconceivable. For the fifty men picked, mostly from the armed forces, there were a hundred horses available. They were of such fantastic quality that many of them later on were sold to other countries to be used by their teams. As for my motives, I mostly was eager to beat the Swedes, who were said to be invincible. It is hard to say whether I was motivated to do this for any other reasons—for myself, for my country or for the sake of the sport.

"The most feasible answer may be that I was a born fighter."

After the Olympics, Captain Handrick went back to the Richthofen Squadron and was promoted at a dizzying rate until, at thirty-three, he was made a full colonel. He flew on Franco's side during the Spanish Civil War, participated in the invasion of Poland, flew in the Battle of Britain, then was transferred to Petsamo and Sevastopol and at the end of the war was in Vienna, commandant of the Eighth Luftwaffe Division with 3,000 men and 600 female assistants in his command. He was awaiting imminent promotion to general. He fled to the Austrian Alps and there surrendered his forces to Americans in Bad Gastein. For all his combat, Gotthard Handrick never received a wound.

He and his wife began a new life in Hamburg; he became a truck driver, hauling sacks of flour. Then he became a harbor guard, a textile buyer, an insurance man, a bank teller, until in 1951 he took a job as a car salesman for a local Mercedes agency. He prospered, indeed, succeeded splendidly; for the past seven years, he has been sales manager of Germany's largest Daimler-Benz agency, a hard-selling organization that moves 4,000 new cars a year.

Gotthard Handrick, now sixty-four, is as striking-looking as ever, a cross perhaps between John Wayne and Willy Brandt. He drives a $10,000 350 SL Mercedes, and he lives in a fine house surrounded with gardens. His three children long ago grew up and left home, and Gotthard Handrick is now the grandfather of nine.

And when he speaks of the Olympics as they have come to be, he is sanguine: "People speak much about the possible physical or moral damage caused to men who must train and compete under the stress of such intensified competition. But ultimately, there will be remedies developed against this kind of mental and physical atrophy. As far as the individual position of the competitor is concerned, one has to accept the philosophical view that the mental, intellectual or moral damage he may be exposed to is more than outbalanced by the fact that he provides a sorely needed hero image for the masses.

"Those Greeks knew quite well why, for twelve hundred years, they channeled off their aggressions in the Games. The Olympic idea still remains one of the most valid undertakings mankind has devised for his own good."

Nevertheless, Gotthard Handrick himself knows that his success since the Olympics and since the war is not typical of the fates which befell many of his colleagues on the German Olympic team of 1936. Of those who survived the war, most are living in anonymity, holding menial jobs as railroad men and postal clerks and bartenders. Many are alcoholics. Gotthard Handrick shakes his handsome head and says: "By and large, I'm afraid for most German participants the Olympics were an experience which, if they didn't possess an excellent bundle of nerves, later on gave them a lot of difficulty to adjust to."

Glenn Cunningham, Rancher

The most popular American miler of his day, Glenn Cunningham is now sixty-one, a gaunt and sharp-faced man with faded blue eyes that gaze intently out of horn-rimmed glasses. He is almost totally bald, a pinched and weather-beaten rancher from the plains of Kansas, a temperance evangelist and hard-line moralist who has come to be known by some people as "the Elmer Gantry of the track world." These days, however, Glenn Cunningham has no interest at all in the track world, none. "I seldom read the sports pages, and I never watch track on television." He was not even aware in the summer of 1971 of the celebrated troubles his fellow Kansas miler Jim Ryun had been having in winning races.

"I love hard work. I am a mule. I never get tired," said Glenn Cunningham. He now runs the Glenn Cunningham Youth Ranch twenty-six miles out of Wichita, near the village of Augusta, Kansas. He said he works sixteen hours a day there with his own twelve children (aged eight to thirty-three) and with others who are considered wayward and troubled.

In the thirties, Glenn Cunningham was perhaps the biggest name in U.S. track, a runner whose presence at a meet could draw thousands of spectators. One of the legends about him concerned the condition of his legs, which had been badly scarred from massive burns he suffered in a schoolhouse fire when he was seven years old. It was said that the stiffness of his fire-mottled skin and the pain in his scorched muscles forced him to run many, many more warm-up laps before a race than

195

ALL THAT GLITTERS IS NOT GOLD

other milers. This tale of Cunningham's endurance and rise to stardom in the face of pain from those childhood burns has long been a standard conquest-of-insurmountable-odds anecdote in the inspirational speeches of sports evangelists over the years; this includes Jesse Owens, who still tells of Cunningham's feats with such dramatic fervor one might think Glenn had been doing his running on water. Actually, it was not the burn scars at all that caused Cunningham the leg pains he suffered then. "I had been examined by doctors all over the world," he recalled. "Then I went to this dentist in the little Kansas village of Peabody, and he discovered that I had eight abscessed teeth. Apparently they resulted from my getting hit in the mouth with a baseball when I was a high school kid. I had those teeth pulled, and I've never had any trouble with my legs since."

Cunningham had competed in Los Angeles in 1932, finishing fourth in the 1,500-meter race. He lost to Jack Lovelock of Great Britain in Berlin in 1936, and his defeat was considered a stunning upset. In retrospect, Cunningham is casual, even ostentatiously detached, about what happened. "I just hoped to do my best. To me, the Olympics was nothing special. It was just the biggest track meet around that week." His silver medal, he said, is "strictly a souvenir."

"Of course," he said, "I was always conscious of being a representative of my country. After I qualified for the 1932 Olympics, doctors told me I couldn't compete because of bad tonsils, but I said, 'Oh, no, nothing is going to stop me from representing my country.'"

His patriotism was apparently no less fierce in 1936, nor was his self-righteousness. "I was always lecturing my Olympic teammates who were breaking training, and there were quite a few. I told them they were more important ambassadors of their country than were the ambassadors appointed by the President. I even lectured Eleanor Holm on her responsibility to the younger girls on the team. She was nice about it, but she said she wanted to live her life her way and let the younger girls live theirs their way.

"I think my teammates respected me for my attitude. They voted me the most popular member of the team [ahead of Jesse Owens]. My attitude toward my Olympic teammates was like my attitude toward members of the track team at the University of Kansas. I found out that the night before the Bix Six [now Big Eight Conference] track meet of my senior year, six of the track guys were out carousing around. Not one of them scored a point the next day, and that kept us from winning the meet. I went to Coach Bill Hargiss and told him to withhold their letters for the season. He said he couldn't because they had earned them. So I went to Phog Allen, the athletic director, and I convinced *him* the letters should be withheld."

His recollection of Berlin is fairly rosy. "The facilities were great, and the crowds tremendous, and I was not aware of any racial antagonism on the part of the Germans toward the American Negro athletes. The reported hostility of Hitler to Jesse Owens is in my mind mostly a fabrication. There were a lot of Jewish sportswriters there, and I think they played up the Hitler thing. I think Hitler was a rat, but as Woodrow Wilson once said, 'If you impose an unjust peace on a nation, a generation will arise to avenge it.'

"It was at the 1936 Olympics that I got my first inkling that some athletes were using drugs to improve their performances. This has grown steadily worse, and anyone found using them should be dropped from competition. I am also disturbed about the use of the Games for propaganda purposes. I resent what went on in Mexico City—what John Carlos and the others did. They showed no respect for their country and used the

Olympics for propaganda. If any individual does not want to represent his country properly, he should stay off the team. Sure, we need better racial understanding, but those who used the Games to help attain it should have been booted—fast."

Glenn Cunningham declared with vehemence that he has never, never capitalized on his reputation as a track star. With barely pent-up fury in his voice, he tells a story of being visited a few years ago at his youth ranch by a man who said he was authorized to help underwrite the expenses of the ranch (which has always been financially pressed) if Glenn Cunningham would only permit his name and his picture to be used in an advertisement for liquor. "I told him," said Cunningham, apparently still furious, "that his company didn't have enough money to get my name in their lousy whiskey ads!"

It would seem to be a case of either enormously bad judgment or incredibly careless advance research on the part of anyone who would attempt to lure Glenn Cunningham into a four-square declaration in favor of booze. His reputation and his past performances do not in any way encourage such a project. In 1948, when Kansas had an election to vote on repeal of the state's prohibition amendment, Cunningham joined other militant and well-organized water drinkers in a statewide campaign that came to be known as "The Temperance Tornado." The forces of dryness crisscrossed Kansas for three weeks, dwelling for hours on end on the consummate evils of alcohol. Among other things, Cunningham brought down the wrath of editors throughout the state when he charged that many newspapers habitually penciled out all reference to the role liquor played in auto accidents because publishers were beholden to liquor advertisers. The Temperance Tornado did not succeed in that election. Cunningham is still willing to preach a little about it now, twenty-five years later: "*We* weren't the ones who lost. It was the people of the state and their children who lost. I never saw anyone whose life was enriched by drinking or smoking. I'm interested and gratified that medical people are now substantiating what I have been insisting for forty years about alcohol and tobacco."

Cunningham was graduated from the University of Kansas in 1934, won a PhD in health and physical education from NYU in 1938, then returned to the University in Lawrence, Kansas, where he took a job as a lecturer and public relations man at the then stunning salary of $300 a week plus expenses (top professors at Kansas were then getting $4,000 a year). He became athletic director at Cornell College in Mount Vernon, Iowa, entered the Navy as a physical education officer in 1944, divorced his first wife. He acquired some 2,000 acres of Kansas prairie and 700 head of cattle during the war. Then he plunged into youth work, and for the last quarter century he has had his ranch for youngsters who needed help. The youth work has not been financially rewarding. At one point, he purchased a menagerie of strange animals—bison, wild sheep, water buffalo, yaks, llamas, a couple of bears—with the hope of building a roadside zoo that would attract people traveling along busy Route 54 past his place. The Glenn Cunningham zoo did very poorly. However, there are still some of the animals around the ranch, and the aroma of a zoo is still in the air.

Cunningham charges fees for helping youngsters according to their parents' ability to pay, but he has still had to sell off much of his land and cattle to make ends meet. Awhile ago, he incorporated his ranch in hopes that he could raise funds as an officially recognized charity. He hired a professional fund-raising group, but it was a failure, too. "In thirty weeks they didn't raise enough money to pay for the postage they used," he said. Then, late in 1969, the state of Kansas moved against the Glenn

Cunningham Youth Ranch, Inc. It denied him a permit to solicit funds, ruling that the ranch did not meet standards for caring for minor children and that its housing facilities did not seem sanitary or safe. In supporting the legal moves against Cunningham, the secretary of state pointed out that in February, 1969, Glenn Cunningham had been convicted of boarding children under sixteen without a license and that he had been fined $50.

Cunningham admitted that his facilities may have been inadequate but said that was precisely why he wanted a permit to raise more funds. He still did not have the permit at the end of 1971, nor did he have a license to board children under sixteen. However, he does have some youngsters over sixteen, sent to him by their parents, and he has attained the legal guardianship of some under that age. His ranch covers sixty-eight acres, and the main house is a frame building with a dozen rooms. There are also two house trailers. Cunningham said that besides his own twelve children, he has had as many as eighty-eight staying in that house and in the two trailers at the same time. He was asked if the crowded conditions were not beyond the limits of human comfort. He said, "I stack them up in bunk beds in the bedrooms, and they love the place so much they're indifferent to where they sleep."

Cunningham has horses, sheep, hogs and cattle around his ranch, and part of his income comes from selling them. The kids in his care help keep the animals fed and healthy. "My theory is that what kids need most is hard work," he said, "and I see that they get it." He is a hard disciplinarian also. "I use a leather belt on the kids as I do on my own kids. Certainly, I'm in favor of corporal punishment." He said that he does not force the children to go to church, but added, "If they don't go to church, they can't go anywhere else either."

So it goes with Glenn Cunningham. He is scarcely discouraged by his troubles, although he said he is heavily mortgaged now. "When I started my youth work, everything was paid for, not a mortgage on the place," he said. "But it is worth it because I'm convinced you can cure most children of their problems by hard work, discipline, no liquor, no tobacco, no boy-girl relationships, being honest with them and setting a good example. One example is worth volumes of words. The principal problem with youth today is that the kids say to their parents, 'Your actions speak so loud to me that I can't hear a word you are saying.' "

Yasar Erkan, Restaurateur

Yasar Erkan of Turkey, sixty-one years old now, is a prosperous restaurateur in Istanbul. In 1936, when he weighed 132 pounds, Yasar Erkan won a gold medal in Berlin in Greco-Roman featherweight wrestling. Since then he has become rich. Never tall, he now weighs 200 pounds and seems squat. He is bald, and his head shines. His face is usually wreathed in smiles. His restaurant, specializing in fish, is called Olympic Restaurant, and he has bought a farm to breed cattle; it is called the Olympic Farm. Recently Yasar Erkan spoke of his prosperity: "I am, of course, the first wrestler in Turkey who has ever been an Olympic champion. Of course, my title has been of great use to me. I was loved by all.

"I owe everything I possess to the Olympic Games and my gold medal. When news of my triumph in Berlin reached Turkey, Ataturk, the first President of Turkey, then retired, was dining with President Bayan. They drank toasts to my health for three minutes. Then Ataturk sent me a cable which said, 'You have entered history. Long live Yasar.'

"Being an Olympic champion has been for me a magic key, opening all doors—opening my life to good fortune and prosperity."

Ilmari Salminen, Retired Soldier

Ilmari Salminen was born on a tiny farm near the small railroad junction town of Kouvola in Finland on September 1, 1902. He grew to be a calm, rawboned young farmboy. At twenty-one he entered the Finnish Army for his compulsory service, and he began to run long distances as a part of military conditioning. When his service time ended, Ilmari Salminen returned happily to his family's farm and tried competitive running in small events around the village. He did well. In 1926 a friend told him that if he rejoined the Army, he would have more time for running than he did working on the farm. Ilmari Salminen reenlisted, became a champion runner and continued to run competitively for more than a quarter of a century, including his gold medal race in the 10,000 meters in Berlin in 1936.

Ilmari Salminen said, "I won always without doing real training. I ate anything I wanted, but only good solid food. The only thing I ever tried to avoid was too much fat. I never smoked, and I drink very little. I have never had a serious illness. When I started training for Berlin, there was deep snow and we had no indoor halls, so I could only take a long walk twice a week. In spring, I had to be on parade at seven thirty in the morning, so I got up at five thirty and went for short walks and runs along the forest tracks and across the rough forest floor. In the evenings before dusk, I went into the forest again for one and one half hours.

"Today some men take no time for work; they only train.

They have to train very hard today, much harder than I did, and perhaps they are much better. But it means you must make yourself a slave to training. In my time we did it for fun. We were not out to make martyrs of ourselves."

In Berlin, Ilmari Salminen ran the 10,000 meters in a trio with two other Finns, Arvo Askola and Volmari Iso-Hollo. All three had identical blond haircuts, sheared to the skin around the ears and blooming into cockscomblike disarray on top. They ran so close to each other and with such similar fluid strides that they seemed connected to a common motor. As they circled the track again and again, they came to resemble three grim over-sized roadrunner cuckoos attached to a shooting gallery track. They finished first, second and third in the race, and one of the unforgettable, dramatic scenes in Berlin occurred when those three farmerish Finns stood together on the podium. One after another, three Finnish flags slowly ascended the victory staffs above Berlin Stadium, and the Finnish anthem was played three times in succession. "Well, I had got what I had come for," said Ilmari Salminen. "Yes, I wanted our country's flag raised, but I had come to run for myself."

When he returned to Finland, he was promoted to senior sergeant, then to sergeant major. Friends took up a collection to build Ilmari Salminen a sturdy two-storied wooden house in Kouvola. At sixty-nine he is living there still. He retired from the Army in 1953 and has a small, not very tidy garden behind the house with apple trees and a flower bed and a vegetable plot. Salminen putters there while his grandchildren play near him. Inside, there is a television and a tableful of scrapbooks and a glass cupboard filled with trophies that are badly tarnished. His only physical ailment is that he must wear glasses to watch TV.

The only cloud shadowing his old age, he said, is that his

beloved Olympics house and his garden were to be demolished soon to make way for an apartment building. Ilmari Salminen has been promised an apartment in a nearby building, but he is not enthusiastic about making a change now.

Fritz Pollard, Civil Servant

Fritz Pollard, fifty-five, works in the State Department in Washington, a civil servant in a civil servant's office with the mandatory photograph of a shiny-eyed Richard Nixon on one wall and a warm-looking Secretary of State William Rogers on the other. In 1936, Fritz Pollard was nineteen, son and namesake of the first black man to make the college football All-American team, and he won the bronze medal in the 110-meter hurdles in Berlin. Pollard is a very pleasant man, with a bright smile which makes him almost as handsome as Harry Belafonte.

To recall Berlin was mostly a pleasure: "They were the greatest Games I could imagine. Of course there was the trouble at home, and a lot of Jewish people were trying to organize a boycott, just like the blacks tried to do in '68. But in those days all we were concerned about was getting proper treatment and in competing. I was a hurdler—politics be damned. I just wanted to run against the top guys, whether they were from Alaska or South Africa or wherever. Because of Hitler, I wanted more than ever to go to Germany. I wanted to go and run in his backyard and show him what black men could do.

"In Germany I kept hearing all those stories about what Germans did to blacks—the 'black auxiliaries' they called us. Well, I had to have a tooth pulled while I was there. My God, people said, a *black* going to a German *dentist!* You're crazy! I got to wondering about it myself, but the tooth hurt like heck, so I went. I never felt a thing. He was the gentlest dentist I ever had.

"We were given the keys to the city. You realized that the people were different from their government. And, you know, the farther we got from the metropolitan areas, the less propaganda there was around. At the Games I felt fine! It was one of the greatest of times in my life."

Rie Mastenbroek, Housewife

Rie Mastenbroek is an invalid, nearly crippled from an auto accident and unable to work, although her family could use more money. She is fifty-three, heavy and seemingly very tired as she tries—unsuccessfully—to dig out souvenirs of her Olympic celebrity. She shrugs. "I do not even have pictures here anymore, I guess, though I would have had thousands of them once. For the signatures, you know. It has not been such fun since the war."

Rie Mastenbroek was the most famous woman swimmer in Europe in 1936. She won three golds and a silver medal in the Berlin Games, and everyone in the world knew her name, and everyone could pick her face out of any crowd. "I am forgotten now," she said. "No one remembers who I was. Though at the Swimming Hall of Fame in Fort Lauderdale, Florida, they have my picture hanging behind glass, and they even have prints of my feet, I have been told, like the stars of Hollywood." She lives with her second husband and a fifteen-year-old son from her first marriage. They have a bland, very neat Dutch apartment in Rozenburg, a suburb of Rotterdam where the sky has turned tan from pollution that blooms from nearby refineries and chemical plants.

Bitterness hangs like the smoke of the factories over Rie's life. Her first marriage was a "disaster," and she was forced to work fourteen-hour days for a cleaning company after the war in order to feed her two eldest children. The only time she has actually been in the water of a swimming pool in decades occurred recently when she waded in a therapy pool at the hospital in an attempt to ease a headache that constantly pounds at the base of her skull.

There are no medals, no mementos of triumphs past, on the walls of her apartment. Rie Mastenbroek said wearily, "I do not stick much to those things; they have brought nothing to me. But now sometimes I think, 'Oh, dear, oh, dear, how good I must have been, how really *good*.' Especially when I know how much guidance and coaching the girls receive today. I had to do everything on my own as a small fourteen-year-old kid. But after me not one lady swimmer, nobody—not one—ever did it again: three times gold and once silver. Oh, how good I must have been.

"Now I have lost all contact with swimming. I am not interested. Ah, and Ada Kok [who won a gold medal in swimming for The Netherlands in 1968] is as disappointed as I am. She thought that any Olympic champion will be put into a castle of gold—just like that. No, it is only as long as you do exactly as the swimming associations and coaches say. Everything goes right until you go against them."

Rie Mastenbroek's swimming feats are even more impressive in retrospect, for it was not until 1955 that Dutch doctors discovered she had a chronic blood disease that meant her system had always suffered from a critical shortage of oxygen. "Now I don't know how I survived those years," she sighed. "I nearly drowned once during a meet in 1935, but they laughed it off. I never told anybody, but I was always troubled. Always. I sometimes fainted suddenly. Or my legs became very thick. Perhaps I should have been dead long, long ago."

None of Rie Mastenbroek's three children was encouraged to be swimmers by their Olympic mother. On the contrary. "We lived nineteen years near a canal in the city of Amsterdam," she said. "The water attracted little boys tremendously, and everybody was always in fear for them, but they always went to that damned canal. I warned them and warned them; then once after all those warnings when I saw my son near the canal side again, I dragged him home. I held his head in the bath water. I held it there for such a long time that he got all blue. He never went to the canal again. . . ."

1948

Held in London from July 29 to August 14. 4,468 athletes from 59 countries competed. A rather melancholy festival. Drizzle. Bomb rubble. Japan, Germany, Italy banned. King George VI reigns over British Empire. Harry Truman and Alben Barkley upset Thomas E. Dewey and Earl Warren in U.S. election. Mohandas Gandhi was assassinated.

When Americans first arrived in London, they were astonished that news of the Olympics barely made the London sports pages. There was no sign that the British were even aware of the Games. There was no new stadium—old Wembley would do—and no money for a posh Olympic Village—a sprawling former RAF barracks was thrown open. People were worried that the whole thing might simply be ignored by the British. But, no, on opening day, with the temperature a melting 93 degrees, Englishmen filled the stadium with 83,000 people—and it went on like that day after day, with 70,000 sitting sodden in a drenching rain one afternoon.

The star of '48 was the doughty Fanny Blankers-Koen, Dutch mother of four children, who was referred to *ad nauseam* as the Flying Housewife. She won four gold medals—in the 100-meter dash, the 200-meter dash, the 80-meter hurdles and the 400-meter relay. When Fanny returned to Amsterdam with her medals, she was cheered in the streets as she rode through town in an open coach drawn by four white horses. They named a rose after Fanny Blankers-Koen and a gladiolus and a candy bar.

Another track star who might have got similar honors in his country—had he not stumbled over the rules of amateurism of the day—was the magnificent Swedish miler Gundar Hagg, a gaunt and determined runner who flirted with the mystic four-minute mile for much of his career (his best time was 4:00.2 in 1946). Almost certainly, Gundar Hagg would have won the gold medal in the 1,500-meter race in London and gone home a hero.

He and Arne Anderssen, another Swede, had fought many a memorable duel in the mid-forties. But by the time the 1948 Olympics arrived both had been summarily disqualified for taking money, and the Olympic medal went to yet another Swede, whom both had beaten.

Gundar Hagg, now in his fifties, and a traveling salesman for a manufacturer of fur hats, is no longer gaunt; he has ballooned to a monumental 223 pounds and is obviously a man untroubled by his inability to win an Olympic medal. "The decision to disqualify was correct enough, if you followed the regulations," said Gundar Hagg. "In a good running season as an amateur, I could make thirty thousand crowns [$6,000] which was paid under the table by promoters who knew Arne Anderssen and I would draw thousands of people whenever we ran.

"However, the penalty was arbitrary, and many lesser known breakers of the same law went without punishment. In a certain way I'm thankful because the decision forced me to quit while I was on top."

Delfo Cabrera, Physical Education Instructor

There was a time when he was known as the Exotic Gaucho, but he is fifty-three now and white-haired, and he likes nothing quite so much as puttering in a tiny garden behind his rather shabby home in heavily industrialized Avellanada, a suburb of Buenos Aires. Delfo Cabrera won the gold medal in the marathon in the 1948 Olympics in London, and life has never been the same since.

He was born to a family of rural laborers in Santa Fe Province, a family so poor that it did not even own a horse. Thus, Delfo Cabrera began running because he had to. He eventually moved to Buenos Aires and competed for a sports club which gave him a shirt and running shoes to use—but demanded that he return them to club officials after each race. By 1944 Cabrera was the champion of Argentina, and he was given a nice job with the Buenos Aires Fire Department. In 1948, when he went to London for the Games, the Fire Department granted Delfo Cabrera a three-month leave of absence with pay and $3 a day living expenses in London. He immediately gave the salary advance to his wife, who was pregnant. The

Cabreras then lived in two shabby rooms in a Buenos Aires tenement, a rickety building that was scheduled to be torn down. On the day Delfo Cabrera won the marathon in London, the Eva Perón Foundation immediately called Cabrera's wife and summoned her into the presence of Evita herself, the wife of dictator Juan Perón. Evita told the dazzled Señora Cabrera that the foundation was making a gift of a brand-new house to her husband.

Evita demanded that the house be finished by October 17, which was Peronist Loyalty Day. It was done, a full construction job of a two-bedroom home completed in just seventeen days. Cabrera was, of course, a national hero. When Señora Cabrera's baby was born, Eva Perón was present at the christening, as was Hector Campora, president of the Argentine Chamber of Deputies, official representative of Juan Perón himself. The child, a girl, was named María Eva after Evita, her godmother.

Ah, but bad times awaited the Exotic Gaucho. When Perón was deposed in 1955, Cabrera immediately lost his job with the Fire Department. He was let go without either severance pay or pension. The Cabreras did not lose their house because it was decided, after a vindictive anti-Peronist lawsuit, that it had come from Eva's foundation rather than directly from Perón's government treasury, but Cabrera was flat broke and hungry for a long time.

Though he has taken much abuse from the bitter legions of anti-Peronists in Argentina, his life has finally become brighter. He now works fairly steadily as a physical education instructor at a number of schools and with the National Highway Department. Besides his tiny garden, Delfo Cabrera's pride and joy is a huge glass showcase, which overwhelms his tiny living room. It is filled with about 500 trophies he has won, including 150 great silver cups and, of course, his Olympic gold medal. Gazing at the medal, Delfo Cabrera said, "I would compete a thousand times if I could. Still, nowadays the Games have come to signify 'social movements,' and the spirit is different. They tend to be a fight between Russia and the United States. They are too political and too commercial. "I would not like it as much now as I did then."

Micheline Ostermeyer, Pianist

Micheline Ostermeyer is forty-nine years old, an ample, athletic woman with gray hair and horn-rimmed glasses, a graceful lady with a hint of that certain hauteur which connotes an artist's sublime and polished ego.

At the Olympics in London, Micheline Ostermeyer competed for France and won gold medals in the shot put and the discus, plus a bronze in the high jump. She was twenty-five when she won the medals, but two years before, she had had a solo piano recital in Paris, and there was no real doubt where the realities of her life lay. One day, after the Olympic competitions, she went to a concert for the athletes and thought, "Why, I have three medals. I should be up there." She smiled at the memory, then said seriously, "You know, at that concert in London for Olympians, the pianist chose an all-Mozart program. I would not have done that. Not that I don't love Mozart, but I think the Romantics would have been better for such an occasion.

"The Olympics were the biggest moment of my life," she said, "but you must not forget, life is not a moment. I look at it perhaps as the most important moment of my childhood. Yes, in a way, the Olympics was a prolongation of my childhood. I have nostalgia for it now because I am older, but it was the single most thrilling moment of my life. Still the whole thrill of that kind of moment was prolonged in my career in music. . . ."

Mme. Ostermeyer was born in Berck, in the north of France. Her mother was a piano teacher. Her grandfather was a composer and virtuoso, Lucien Laroche. Victor Hugo was her great-uncle. She attended the Paris Conservatory of Music, where she practiced the piano five or six hours each day. She practiced track five or six hours a week, usually at night. Yet she won the French championships in 1946 and 1947 in the high jump and the shot put. She said: "I think the training now is too much for women. Look at the weight throwers—they are fat, too gross, too big, too much like great whales. If that's the result of all that training, I don't think it is a good thing. It must be horrible for a woman to look as fat as that."

Mme. Ostermeyer was married for many years to an American-born kinesitherapist, Ghazar Ghazarian. He died six years ago, and she now lives quietly with two children in a pleasant apartment in Versailles. She teaches piano at the Conservatoire Claude Debussy at St.-Germaine-en-Laye and rarely gives concerts, although she admitted that she had written a note to Count Jean de Beaumont, a French member of the IOC executive council, asking that she be allowed to play for Olympic competitors at Munich. "I've had no reply, alas. It could be something unique—and very significant for me—to give a concert in honor of the Olympic Games."

Her own career as a concert pianist was not particularly enhanced, she felt, by her Olympic medals. "Some people were a little apprehensive about my playing recitals. They thought that I was an athlete who happened to play the piano. In reality, I was a pianist who competed in athletics. It was the opposite with musicians—if I had played tennis or something mundane like that, it might have been all right, but other musicians thought, what was this track and field? An athlete playing the piano? There was prejudice. I had to show them my diplomas. "When I became an Olympic champion, the musicians had respect, but it was not healthy. They were jealous of all the articles about me. I didn't have a friend in the conservatory." The Olympics even influenced her selection of musical programs. "Well, I couldn't play Liszt, for example. He was too *sportif*. I knew that other musicians would say, 'Well, of *course*, what else *would* she play?' So I had to play Debussy, Ravel, Chopin. I never did dare play Liszt, although the fact was that he suits me. In 1954 or 1955, I finally played Liszt at a recital, and I had such a success with it that I thought, 'Oh, *why* didn't I play it before?' "

Gaston Reiff, Minister of Physical Education, Sport and Recreation

Gaston Reiff, fifty-one, the fine Belgian long-distance runner, won his gold medal in the 5,000-meter race in London, barely defeating the brilliant Czech Emil Zatopek, and he said, "A world record is made to be broken, but an Olympic title is forever. Only experts know record holders, but Olympic champions strike even people who are not at all interested in sports and have confused memories. They often greet me, saying, 'How are you, Mr. Zatopek?' or 'Hello, you were that splendid Olympic skater, I will never forget you.' Yes, they get mixed up, but the title is remembered, and public esteem is attached to you forever."

M. Reiff believes that times have changed greatly for the athletes of the world, that an Olympic runner must now make his training a career in order to excel. "When I was in training,

213

I worked in a government office with another Olympic runner. One day we left half an hour before the usual time the office shut, which was five o'clock, in order to begin training. We had hardly arrived at the track when our boss telephoned us. He called us back urgently to work. We quickly changed out of running clothes into office clothes and arrived at full speed in the boss's office. It was four fifty-eight P.M. With quite a theatrical gesture, he produced his watch and sat looking at it in utter silence for two full minutes. Then, when it had ticked precisely to five P.M., he said, 'Now you may go.' That would not happen today when athletes are getting a minimum of hindrances— and a good thing, too!"

Gazanfer Bilge, Bus Czar

> From Olympic champion to a kingdom of buses. . . . On the verge of death, then to prison. . . . In spite of tuberculosis, jaundice, infarctus and bullets perforating liver and lungs, the man is alive and standing on his feet. . . . But this man, a businessman and a millionaire, is guarded day and night by an army of volunteers. . . .

Thus does the Ankara journalist Mehmet Ali Kislali put into elegiac thumbnail summary the life and recent times of the celebrated Turkish wrestler and bus mogul Gazanfer Bilge. These have been bitter and bloody years for Gazanfer Bilge, now forty-eight, a far cry from the shining hour in London when he was awarded the Olympic gold medal for winning the featherweight division in free-style wrestling. "When our flag went up and the Turkish national hymn was played, I trembled very much," he recalled. "My knees were like cotton. I was nearly falling down—a thing that the greatest wrestlers had not been able to do to me during the Olympic Games matches. . . ."

Gazanfer Bilge is a man of immense self-confidence and diamond-hard egotism. When he was asked who had helped him the most in his quest of the Olympic gold medal, he replied, "Nobody did. I have learned every game by myself. The secret of my success is my strength and my intelligence."

All the more reason to wonder over the state of affairs which have brought Ganzafer Bilge to the point where the journalist Kislali can report that "clouds of anxiety have come to fill his eyes."

All Turkey has been shocked over the gunslingers' violence which has rocked the bus business of the nation, as well as the serenity of Gazanfer Bilge's rich life. It is all the more bizarre because the chief parties in the violence are all Olympic wrestling medal winners. One could say that Gazanfer Bilge should blame only himself for what has happened. It was his generosity which helped the other Turkish wrestlers get started in the bus business.

Before Bilge won his gold medal in 1948, he worked as a mechanic and, later, as an Istanbul policeman whose salary was .145 Turkish liras a month. After the triumph in London, the Turkish government rewarded him with a gift of 20,000 Turkish liras ($1,333), and gave the same generous prize to all Turkish Olympic champions. (Ironically this largess resulted in the 1948 Turkish medal winners being declared ineligible for the 1952 Olympics in Helsinki.) Gazanfer Bilge used his Olympic money to buy a sheep and cattle farm near Istanbul. He sold it for a profit in 1950, returned to his hometown of Karamürsel, where his father had once been mayor, and there he purchased two minibuses.

His entrance into the bus business was a kind of larky, quasi-spiteful act. "I am a stubborn person and know what I want," he said. "One day I was to travel with the minibus belonging to a friend of mine. When I came to take my seat, I saw that he had given it to a pretty young girl. Upon that—just to make him mad—I bought two minibuses and started operating them in competition with him. Later on we became friends again, and I helped him a lot. That was the turning point in my business life."

He began running his buses on the line between Karamürsel and Yalova, a distance of thirty kilometers, and he prospered. Within a year he sold the minibuses and bought a full-sized bus. Today there is scarcely an important route in all Turkey that does not have the buses of Gazanfer Bilge. On the busy Ankara-Istanbul line, one of his buses starts every fifteen minutes, day and night, twenty-four hours a day nonstop.

They are easy to tell from his competitors, for they are brightly painted with the famed five-circle Olympic symbol, along with his name in large letters.

Because Gazanfer Bilge is very wealthy, he regularly is able to indulge his taste for Japanese fish, for nightclubs, for luxurious hotels and for American cowboy movies. He has a chauffeur-bodyguard to drive his chocolate-colored 1970 Oldsmobile. During Ramadan, a month so sacred to the Mohammedans that each day they fast from sunrise to sunset, he gives food and clothing to 100 people daily, and he donates hundreds of thousands of Turkish liras to hospitals and charities. He owns two splendid gardened villas in Istanbul and a good deal of other valuable real estate, including a piece of land he recently purchased in Ankara that is worth 20,000,000 Turkish liras ($1,300,000). Still, there are those "clouds of anxiety."

The main reason for them is Adil Atan, forty-two, who won two bronze medals and a silver for wrestling in the Helsinki and Melbourne Olympics. (His brother Irfan also won a bronze at Helsinki.) Adil Atan started in the bus business in 1958 and owns fifty buses, most of which run on the same routes as Gazanfer Bilge's. Adil Atan is a fierce-looking fellow who has become very bald and has put on a massive amount of weight since his Olympic days. He is reputed to be afraid of nothing and to be as strong as a bull. Nonetheless, his hobby is keeping canaries. There are many of them in his home, and he is said to be as gentle as another canary when he is around his feathered pets.

There is understandable confusion over precisely what triggered the feud between Adil Atan and Gazanfer Bilge. Adil Atan will not discuss it at all, saying, "There is no need talking about these sad events." Some say that the war started in Helsinki in 1952, when Gazanfer Bilge met and fell in love with a Finnish girl of Turkish origin, Yildiz Bey, whose father was chairman of the Turkish-Moslem Society in Finland. Adil Atan also met and fell in love with the fair Yildiz then. In 1954, Yildiz married Gazanfer Bilge, who took her to Istanbul to live. As the journalist Kislali records it, "It was upon the recommendation of Yasar Dogu, the greatest Turkish wrestler of all times, that Tahir Bey gave his daughter to Gazanfer, and that is when the cold war began between him and Adil Atan."

But let us hear the entire chronicle of blood and intrigue as narrated by Gazanfer Bilge himself to the journalist Kislali. Certainly, this is a prejudiced version of events, but it is nevertheless the truth as Gazanfer Bilge understands it:

"I had opened for Fethi Atan, the youngest of the Atan brothers, a bus office in Adapazari in the name of my company. The Atan brothers are Abazas, a branch of the Circassians. My mother is Circassian, too. We knew each other since we were very young. After that I started operating the Istanbul-Ankara line. One day, the Atan brothers came to see me. They started swearing and asked for half the share of my company. Of course,

I gave them no share whatsoever. I am not a man to surrender to threats.

"Upon this they left my company. They started beating and threatening my drivers. I complained to the prosecutor, to the mayor, to the police, even to the governor. It was useless. Nothing was done to protect me. In the meantime, I'm telling the Atans, 'Do not be stupid, cease bothering me. . . .'

"It was in 1963. It was election day. The law stipulates that on election day, nobody is to carry a gun or any other kind of weapon. That very day, presuming I carried no gun, they made me fall into an ambush. That morning at eleven o'clock I was waiting for a friend of mine in front of my office at Kadiköy [in Istanbul]. Fethi Atan came up and started attacking my nephew, who was standing nearby. I immediately told my nephew not to attack back. Thereupon, Fethi assaulted me. Suddenly I saw *all* of the Atans.

"Adil and Irfan were starting to attack me. One of them was holding my arms from the back and the others were striking. A policeman tried to interfere, but he only succeeded in getting a blow too.

"I was falling to the ground. In the meantime I pulled out my gun. I started to fire. The bullets entered in the arm and the hip of Fethi Atan and in the belly of Adil Atan. Whilst I was trying to charge again, they got scared and disappeared. Thereupon I went to the police station and gave myself up.

"In the meantime, I was informed that I had slightly wounded a young girl I did not know, and I was informed that Adil's condition was serious.

"I learned also that they had hired as an assassin a man who was not normal. Thus, he could not be sentenced even if he had succeeded in killing me.

"Then I was arrested. I stayed in prison forty-eight days. I lost twelve kilos [twenty-six pounds]. I had tuberculosis of the lungs, and that is why I got so thin. Finally, I was released after paying a bail of ten thousand Turkish liras.

"Two years elapsed from that day. One night I was passing by the Kadiköy post office. All of a sudden I had the impression that a bus was running on me. The bullet fired from the back had put my liver into pieces, had gone through my lung and come out my chest. When I turned to face the assassin, a second bullet wounded my arm.

"I immediately ran behind a minibus that was stationed there, and I started firing too. But the assassin ran away. Later he was captured and sentenced to twelve years. He was the son of the eldest of the Atan brothers. His name was Bahtiyar Atan.

"I was put into the hospital. Siyami Ersek, the world-famous doctor who has undertaken a heart transplant for the first time in Turkish history, operated on me. I was hospitalized for months. My life was in real danger. In the meantime, I had jaundice. I was under treatment for three, four years. The hearing of the lawsuit for the events of 1963 was also going on. The decision was rendered in 1968. I was sentenced to two years.

"In spite of the certificates issued by the hospitals stating that I could not be imprisoned, that my life would be in serious danger, I was thrown into prison. I suffered very much at the Karamürsel prison. The prosecutor was horrible, he treated me like a beast. When I became seriously ill, I was sent to the hospital. Finally, after one and a half years I was released because of my 'good conduct.'

"A short time ago I had an infarctus crisis. Again I suffered from jaundice. In the meantime, Hamit Kaplan [who won an Olympic gold medal in 1956 and was also a medalist in 1960 and 1964] and the Atan brothers started quarreling about the cafeteria to be opened at the new bus terminal at Harem. The bid had been given to Hamit Kaplan, but the Atans occupied the adjudication room, and all formalities had to stop. They did not allow Hamit to participate in the second adjudication, and the cafeteria became their property for a ridiculous price.

"Thus the Atans are also fighting the Gulhans who are owners of a bus company. This proves the Atans are dangerous people. I have always been good to them, of course.

"Irfan and Adil are my friends from the time we were all on the national team."

In April, 1971, gunfire and zipping bullets were exchanged between the forces of Hamit Kaplan and the Atans around the cafeteria at Harem.

Gazanfer Bilge, scarred and weakened from his encounters with the Atan brothers and from his months in prison, is taking as few chances as possible. The journalist Kislali reported after a visit to his office at Harem:

"There are iron bars at the windows. Volunteers are guarding the doors. To be able to see Gazanfer one has to overcome four or five obstacles. One has to make an appointment months in advance. The only thing they do not ask is a password. As for the rest, you have only the impression of entering a top secret military zone."

1952

Held in Helsinki from July 18 to August 3. 4,925 athletes from 69 countries participated. Modest, but charming Games. Among best. Juho K. Paasikivi President of Finland.

U.S. exploded world's first hydrogen bomb. Cold war at iciest. Senator Joseph McCarthy had begun Red witch-hunt. Fearful times.

Bob Mathias, Congressman

In 1948, he won the gold medal in the decathlon as a seventeen-year-old schoolboy, and he repeated the victory in Helsinki. Perhaps even more than his stunning triumph in London, Mathias' performance in 1952 launched him as an authentic American hero. For despite the relative coziness and the air of sincerity and warmth that pervaded the Helsinki Games, there was also a confrontation between differing national ideologies, and there were many people who saw this Olympics as a rather decisive battle in the cold war between the Communist East and the relatively free West.

As Mathias himself recalled, "There were many more pressures on American athletes because of the Russians than in 1948. They were in a sense the real enemy. You just loved to beat 'em. You just had to beat 'em. It wasn't like beating some guys from a friendly country like Australia. This feeling was strong down through the whole team, even members in sports where the Russians didn't excel."

Whether it was because of the intensity of the cold war or simply because of his sensational performances, Bob Mathias is one of America's best-known Olympians. And he has, quite without shame, cashed in on that reputation handsomely. He is now the Republican Congressman from California's Eighteenth District, which is located near Los Angeles. He is a staunch supporter of the Nixon administration; nevertheless, he does favor extremely zingy clothing, such as flowered bell-bottoms, sashes and boots. Congressman Mathias said:

"Winning an Olympic gold medal helps in business or politics or anything. If people know your name, it's a big help—like an astronaut or a fellow who climbs Mount Everest is well known. Business is just that—getting the name known sells the product. Oh, the individual still has to produce, but people without a name have to spend a lot of money and energy to get themselves known.

"Some people will vote for any name on the ballot that is familiar."

This was the Soviet Union's first Olympics since 1908, when Czar Nicholas sent a man to London. The Russians were straightforward about planning to use the Olympics as a propaganda tool. Pjotr Sobolev, secretary-general of the Russian Olympic Committee, said, "Sports will be a weapon in the fight for peace and the promotion of friendship among all peoples."

When a Russian pinned a hammer and sickle emblem on rower Dick Murphy of the U.S. Naval Academy, the Soviet joked, "If you should wear this in the United States, they would put you in the electric chair." When a Soviet put an emblem of a dove of peace on the chest of diver Sammy Lee, then a major in the U.S. Army, Sammy snapped, "I can't wear that Red propaganda!"

Horace Ashenfelter was a skinny, intense twenty-nine-year-old FBI agent, and he was entered in the 3,000-meter steeplechase, an event he had run only eight times before the Olympics. The favorite was Vladimir Kazantsev, who held the world record. Astonishingly, Ashenfelter won. Almost immediately an exuberant cable arrived from the world's No. 1 anti-Communist

and American patriot, J. Edgar Hoover, saying, ALL YOUR
ASSOCIATES IN THE FBI ARE PROUD. . . .

Feelings were high back in the States even before the team
left for Finland. There was a definite sense that the American
team had to do well or the entire nation would lose face. Nevertheless, there had been problems over raising enough money to
finance the team. In large part because of fears over the "Red
Menace," Avery Brundage, then president of the U.S. Olympic
Committee, managed to arrange for an Olympic Fund Telethon
on June 21 starring Bing Crosby and Bob Hope.

It was to be Crosby's debut on television (he had only
recently turned down $50,000 for a one-shot appearance), and
he said, "This is one time I can't refuse. I think every American
should get behind our Olympic team and send our athletes across
at full strength and in the finest style possible." Hope, ever the
cold war chauvinist, cracked, "I guess Old Joe Stalin thinks he is
going to show up our soft capitalistic Americans. We've got to
cut him down to size. This is the most exciting thing I have
ever undertaken and, brother, Bing and I are going to throw our
best punches."

The goal was to raise $500,000 toward the $850,000 needed.
The telethon lasted fourteen and a half hours and was seen by
50,000,000 people. Crosby and Hope exchanged insults. Cameo
appearances were made by a galaxy of stars—Frank Sinatra,
George Burns, Gracie Allen, Abbott and Costello, Eddie Cantor, Martin and Lewis, Edward G. Robinson, Dinah Shore,
Ginger Rogers, etc. When it was over, there were pledges for
$1,000,000 in the bag. Only $353,000 was actually collected, and
the Olympic fund wound up with $310,000. Far from fully
financing the trip, the telethon actually slowed down the cam-

223

paign because many potential contributors thought the TV show put the USOC over the top and would not open their wallets to give more.

The Russians, who had no trouble financing their team since it was an arm of Soviet foreign policy and thus subsidized by government funds, refused to live with athletes from other nations in the Olympic Village. At first, the Russians planned a daily airlift of competitors from Leningrad. Finally, they gave up that idea and erected their own Olympic Village in Otaniemi, near a Russian-owned naval base. They hung eight-foot portraits of Joseph Stalin and other Soviet leaders and surrounded their premises with barbed wire.

At first, they were a glowering, isolated group, and the West wondered if Russia had raised some kind of superrace of athletes in the decades since the nation last appeared in international competition. Parry O'Brien, then a twenty-year-old who would win his first gold medal in the shot put, recalled, "We had no idea what to expect. They might have been like a population from another planet. For all we knew, the Russians had a guy who could throw the shot eighty feet and another who could high jump nine feet and another who could run the mile in three and a half minutes. They didn't, of course, but we didn't know that at first. They were a total mystery to the world."

As it turned out, the Russians were remarkably human. Eventually their icy demeanors thawed, and they allowed Western athletes behind their barbed wire. In actual competition, there was nothing remarkable about them either. The Russian men did not win a single gold medal in track and field competition. In contrast, the United States picked up fourteen gold medals—the most Americans had won since World War I.

Nevertheless, despite the much ballyhooed confrontation between the United States and the USSR, the real hero of Helsinki was neither a Russian nor an American.

Emil Zatopek, Insulation Installer

Emil Zatopek ran each step of every long, long race he entered as if there were a scorpion in each shoe and a python wrapped around his chest. The antics of his pain were grotesque beyond belief, and Red Smith wrote after Zatopek's gold medal in the 10,000 meters in London, "Witnesses who have long since forgotten the other events still wake up screaming in the dark when Emil the Terrible goes writhing through their dreams, gasping, groaning, clawing at his abdomen in horrible extremities of pain."

In Helsinki, Emil the Terrible simply let his grand agonies, which were almost entirely a matter of theatrics, transport him to victories in the 5,000 meters, the 10,000 meters and the marathon. No man had ever done such a thing, and it was the more astonishing because Zatopek had never before run a marathon in competition. When it was over and he had won by more than two and a half minutes, he said, "The marathon is a very boring race."

He often wore a bedraggled white painter's cap when he raced, and he frequently joked and toyed with other contestants by running far ahead, then dropping back to chat with those struggling in the rear. But he was a man of sensitivity and expressiveness. In 1967, which was the last year he was seen outside Czechoslovakia, he spoke of his interpretation of the Olympic Games: "For me the 1948 Olympics was a liberation of the spirit—after all those dark days of the war, the bombing, the

225

killing and the starvation. The revival of the Olympics was as if the sun had come out. I went into the Olympic Village in 1948, and suddenly there were no more frontiers, no more barriers. Just the peoples meeting together. It was wonderfully warm. Men and women who had lost five years of the full life were back again. . . ."

Emil Zatopek's wife, Dana, won the women's gold medal for the javelin in 1952, but when they returned to Prague from Tokyo in 1964, she said, "Oh, Emil, it is very tough now. We were lucky to be champions when we were. Today I would have been afraid, for the whole world seems to run and throw. . . ." But Emil the Terrible would not admit to being afraid. "I would still try to be a champion if I were young again," he said. "You have something inside you which makes you always try, however hard it may seem. The Olympics are the one true time. At the Olympics you can say, 'These men are the best.' It is a big truth. I have many memories, but we must keep busy. We can never stop running. And when the sun comes out at Olympics time, all will be well."

All is not well for him now. In his days of fame he had been promoted to a colonel's rank and was the toast of the Communist Party; he attracted crowds in the streets, an intense and high-spirited man, the kind of hero the Czechs adored. Then in 1969 his colonel's commission was taken away from him because he had signed the famed rebels' 2,000-Word Manifesto during the fleeting, hopeful days in the spring and summer of 1968 when the Czechoslovakian leaders tried to grant their people new freedoms. Zatopek spoke too soon and too openly, for after the Russian tanks snuffed out the fires of rebellion, he was a marked man. He was given a job as a trainer in an Army sports club, fired from that. He was expelled from the Communist Party, dropped from the Army, and given a pittance for a pension. He worked for a time as a well tester, then lost that job too. He found employment as a garbage collector in the streets of Prague.

This, too, turned bad. The people recognized him at his work; they helped him to carry the garbage cans; they slapped his back; they greeted him as a lost friend. The authorities regarded these responses as symbols of solidarity against the regime. So Emil Zatopek was fired from his job as a garbage collector. Now he has been ordered to work in a place where the public will not see him, installing insulation in half-finished buildings in Prague. He is almost never seen in such a job.

1956

Held in Melbourne from November 22 to December 8. 3,539 athletes from 67 nations appeared. A troubled, yet successful Olympics. Prime Minister Robert Menzies headed Australian government. Nikita Khrushchev denounced Stalin at Communist Party Congress. Egypt seized Suez Canal, triggering world crisis. Brave Hungarian freedom fighters snuffed out by Soviet force.

There was great alarm in the IOC over whether or not the Australians would ever be ready for the '56 Olympics. When Avery Brundage said he'd like to visit Melbourne to see how they were doing, Arthur Coles, the chairman of the host committee, said, "Don't waste your time." Coles then told reporters "If Brundage came now, there would be nothing to show him.

227

All we could do would be to put him in a plane and fly him over the Melbourne Cricket Ground. Then we'd say, 'There is the finest cricket ground in the world.' " That was late in 1953. In the spring of 1955, Brundage did travel to Melbourne, and he was shocked at the complacency—and the nearly total lack of Olympic construction under way. He said flatly, "Melbourne has a deplorable record of promises upon promises. For years we have had nothing but squabbling, changes of management, bickering. Today more than ever the world thinks we made a mistake in giving the Games to Melbourne. I hope that the Games don't have to be taken away, but I would like to leave with the assurance that the job will be done. . . . Too much is still in the planning stage." While Avery was in Melbourne, building workers struck at the Olympic Village, and no sooner had he left than the carpenters went on strike at the stadium.

Yet his barbed words did some good, apparently, and the facilities were completed soon after his departure.

Perhaps the most emotional scene in Melbourne occurred when the Hungarian team arrived at the airport and was met by thousands of weeping countrymen who had emigrated to Australia. The crowd wore black armbands of mourning and shouted, "Long live free Hungary!" The Hungarian Olympians replied with revolutionary slogans.

And the U.S.-Russian cold war was still a powerful force on the Olympic scene. A few months after the Games, the Soviet newspaper *Literary Gazette* charged that Russian athletes had been under constant pressures of corruption by members of the U.S. Central Intelligence Agency, then headed by Allen W. Dulles. The paper said Dulles' "team of professional American spies and provocateurs also tried to subvert the Russian sportsmen by attempting kidnappings, sneak-thievery and frameups on espionage charges. . . . American agents tried to palm off 'secret documents' on our girls and boys. They tried to give them photographs of military objectives in order to convict them later of espionage. . . . The American intelligence service did its utmost to force upon Soviet athletes an acquaintance with young women. Its agents more than insistently importuned them 'to have a good time.' "

The *Literary Gazette* did not say whether such temptations were strewn in the paths of Russian champions to encourage potential defections or simply to divert them from serious training, the better for Americans to win gold medals.

Shirley Strickland De la Hunty, Housewife

Shirley Strickland (now Mrs. De la Hunty of Perth) won her first gold medal in the 80-meter hurdlers in Helsinki, set a world record for 100 meters in Warsaw in 1955, and won two more gold medals in Melbourne at the age of thirty-one. She probably would have run in Rome in 1960 if she had not been pregnant. Some Olympians find their motives for victory in patriotism or personal profit or ego or simple devotion to sport, but Mrs. De la Hunty said of her accomplishments: "I could not have done it without the help of my family, but I did not do it *for* my family. I did it because it was self-testing. I did it because I regarded my body merely as a piece of machinery. I wanted to see if I could make my machinery work better than others."

Betty Cuthbert, Shoe Representative

She was Australia's Golden Girl, the world's outstanding female sprinter, the recipient of three gold medals at eighteen in Melbourne, a fourth in Tokyo at twenty-six. "I've been invited to visit the queen, and I've met people who have achieved so much in other fields. I feel the respect of people, you see, and it makes me feel good inside," said Betty Cuthbert. "I sometimes can't help but wonder what I would be like if I hadn't worked so hard to succeed at running. I suppose I'd be married to someone and have babies and a house to care for."

The blond curls that once turned frizzy when she ran are now shaped in a long gamin cut, and she has learned to apply makeup to emphasize her enormous blue eyes. She still lives at home with her parents in the outer Sydney suburb of Ermington, in the same house where she has lived since she was five. Her father has a nursery there, and Betty has worked at his side for years. Once there was nothing but rural paddocks all around, but now there are houses as far as the eye can see, and two doors down from the nursery there is a Colonel Sanders franchise selling finger-lickin' chicken.

Betty Cuthbert recalls her years as the Golden Girl as little less than agony, particularly right after she became a national heroine with her brilliant sweep in Melbourne. "I detested being a public figure. I suppose it was because I was only eighteen. I think I get more of a thrill out of those three gold medals now when I read the old clippings than I did at the time. But I hated the attention. I wanted to quit. By the time I got to Rome, running was only a chore. I was living for that Olympics so I could get it over with, so I could quit and do things other girls did, go to dances and shows and parties whenever I felt like it. And stay out late at night.

"But I felt that I had been blessed with a gift as an athlete. I felt I had a responsibility, an obligation, a duty to keep running because of that gift."

In Rome, the Golden Girl tore a muscle in her leg, and she won nothing at all. Finally she could quit, a blessed event. "For almost ten years my life had revolved around athletics," she recalled. "It was a case of just eating, working, training, sleeping, eating, working, training, sleeping. I worked in the nursery from eight A.M. to four-thirty P.M. and trained five nights a week from six to eight P.M., had tea, took a bath, and went to bed. For the first twelve months after I retired, I did everything I'd always wanted to do. I loved it. It was terrific.

"Then I began to feel uneasy, as if something was missing in my life. It wasn't that I missed athletics, the competition or the winning. It was that I needed a feeling of accomplishment, a direction. I needed the feeling you get when you work very hard for something, and then you achieve it."

She began running again, and in Tokyo she astonished everyone by winning the 400-meter race. "In Melbourne it had happened so quickly I hadn't time to think of it. But in Tokyo the fact I had won came over me right away; I felt it inside. It was splendid—it was like losing something you love very much and then finding it again. I felt tremendous gratitude.

"I guess I believe in destiny or fate. I believed I was going to win that race. I don't know why, but I thought it was God's plan for me, and when I crossed the line and saw it actually happening, I was so thankful. I still wonder why I was meant to do it, but I think I will figure it out in time. Sometimes it takes a long, long while for these things to come clear."

Alain Mimoun, Civil Servant

When the mother of Alain Mimoun was carrying him in her womb, she lived in a village in the mountains of Algeria. One night, far into her pregnancy, she dreamed that she was walking across a mean and stony landscape lighted only by the moon. The moon was a comfort, and soon she stopped walking

231

and gazed up at it. The moon seemed to drop a little closer to her. It became brighter, more silvery, and it began to descend, lower and lower, glowing gently, until at last it loomed so near and so large that she reached up and embraced the moon with her arms and held it to her bosom. She awoke, then fell asleep and dreamed no more. In the morning she found she was troubled by the dream. She could not forget it because she could not understand it. She walked down the village street to a shabby little hut to consult an old crone who interpreted dreams.

The old woman considered the import of the vision for a time and found it full of happy tidings. She said to the mother of Alain Mimoun: "The child you carry will someday do a magnificent thing."

Alain Mimoun has often told this story, slowly and respectfully, because it carries echoes of the stark, baked mountain ranges and the occult peasant beliefs that encompassed his life before he became an Olympic champion. Now Alain Mimoun lives in a fine two-story home in the well-to-do Paris suburb of Champigny-sur-Marne. His home has a wine cave stocked with remarkably good Beaujolais and a fine champagne which he purchases from his private supplier. A prosperous civil servant, an adviser on French national sports programs, Mimoun is fifty years old and perhaps the most popular sports personality in the history of France—overshadowing Carpentier, Cerdan, Killy in the minds of many.

He is cheerful; there is something childlike in the light of his smile and the buoyancy of his laughter. His brown eyes blaze or twinkle or well up with tears when he talks, and his face is always filled with shadows or sunshine, depending on what subject he is discussing. Few men are more devout in their belief in the Olympics, for all his fame and his livelihood and his way of life have come to him because of his Olympic achievements. "The Games are sacred, a religion," said Alain Mimoun. He named his daughter Olympe and calls his home Olympia. He has a room filled with his medals and he calls it the "museum," although he soberly admitted, "If the Olympics is a religion, then this should be a chapel."

Alain Mimoun entered four Olympic Games from 1948 through 1960. He won one silver medal in London, two more in Helsinki; he finished behind the magnificent Czech Emil Zatopek in the 10,000-meter run in 1948 and in both the 5,000 and 10,000 in 1952. In Melbourne he was thirty-six years old, yet he won the gold medal in the marathon. In Rome he was forty, and he was injured and did not win anything.

Alain Mimoun left his native village when he was eighteen and joined the French Army. He was named a chevalier in the Legion of Honor for courageous service against the Nazis. But his mother did not mention her dream when that happened. He became a fine runner—"I wanted nothing but to run; it was my only profession"—and after World War II he began winning one national long-distance championship after another even though he nearly starved and was working sixteen-hour days as a busboy while he trained. In all, he won thirty-two championships, and he was named captain of the French team for eight consecutive years. Still, he was told nothing of his mother's dream after those honors were his. Nor was he told after he won his medals at London and Helsinki. Nor was he told after he became a physical education instructor in a government school in France (a teacher's position would be one of almost kingly importance to the peasants of his mother's village).

In 1954 Alain Mimoun was stricken with sciatica, and he could no longer run. Newspapers ran morose columns mourning the finish of his career. He visited countless physicians, innumerable chiropractors, and at last a friend cautiously sug-

233

gested that perhaps Alain Mimoun might try to cure his illness by making a pilgrimage to the Basilica of St. Theresa of Lisieux. He did. That was in October, 1955, and within two months after his visit to the Basilica Alain Mimoun ran a race which broke another French record. When he speaks now of his cure, Alain Mimoun can barely finish the tale. His voice becomes strangled, and his lips tremble. At last, overcome, he simply walks to the mantle of his fireplace, tenderly picks up a miniature of St. Theresa and whispers, "A miracle."

Then came 1956, and though he was thirty-six years old, he was still running fifty kilometers a day, and he entered the marathon. "I knew I was older, and I was losing speed. I am a realist. But I also knew my resistance was good, as good as ever."

So he ran in Melbourne, and only one journalist and his old competitive friend Emil Zatopek predicted that Mimoun had a chance to win. Zatopek was running, too. Alain Mimoun ran almost the entire race without once looking back, and when at last he pumped into the stadium and was going into his last lap, he turned to see if Zatopek was gaining. "I was sure Emil was there at my heels," said Mimoun. But there was no one, no one at all when he crossed the finish line. Mimoun shook off the astonished officials who tried to congratulate him and stood gazing at the stadium entrance. "I was hoping Emil would be second; I was waiting for him. Then I thought, well, he will be third—it would be nice to stand on the podium with him again. But Emil came in sixth, oh, very tired. He seemed in a trance, just staring straight ahead. He said nothing. Nothing. I said, 'Emil, why don't you congratulate me? I am an Olympic champion; it was I who won.'

"Emil turned quickly and looked at me, as if waking from a dream. Then he snapped to attention. Emil took off his cap—

234

that white painting cap he wore so much—and he saluted me. Then he embraced me." Alain Mimoun weeps again as he relives the scene. "Oh, for me that was better than the medal."

Then came the ceremonies, the podium and the applause. Alain Mimoun is nothing if not a patriot, and he said, "I carry France on my back in all my races." In Melbourne, with his gold medal in hand, the French anthem was being played. "The 'Marseillaise'—ah, for a Frenchman, monsieur, it was a marvel. And the flag rising. Three times before, I stood on the Olympic podium and the flag of France was on the right. This time it was in the center. And it stayed there for *three days* because, you see, the marathon was the closing event of the Olympic Games."

The gold medal he won in the marathon was precisely what the mother of Alain Mimoun had been waiting for. "She said to me, 'That's it! That's what my dream meant!!' And then she told me about embracing the moon and of the magnificent thing that she had been waiting for me to do. I suffered much, but I know the real Olympics to be religious games as the Greeks had planned them. You can't fabricate an Olympic champion. You are an Olympic champion in your mother's womb."

1960

Held in Rome from August 25 to September 11. 5,902 athletes from 84 nations competed. Splendid Olympic setting. Lots of East-West goodwill. Games construction gave *much-needed urban renewal to Rome. Giovanni Gronchi President of Italy. U-2 plane, downed in Russia, sabotaged Eisenhower-Khrushchev summit conference. Bomb shelters; civil defense; fear of nuclear attack grips United States. CBS paid $660,000 for first Olympic TV rights.*

The Roman Olympic Organizing Committee made a deal with the Association of Roman Thieves to refrain from street thefts during the Olympic Games. As a result, the Olympic weeks produced the fewest complaints over pickpockets, purse snatchers, car thieves, muggers and holdup men in a long, long time.

In addition to that bit of charity, the Roman Games were fraught with reasonableness, good cheer and friendship. Despite the tension between the United States and Russia over the U-2, there was no major conflict in the world (the Korean War had fizzled out, the Hungarian Revolution was nearly forgotten, the angers of Vietnam had not yet been loosed). There was a great deal of fraternizing between athletes of the East and West. The chairman of the Russian Olympic Committee, the pudgy Constantin Andrianov, was even moved to say, "Politics is one thing, sport another. We are sportsmen."

Roger Moens, Police Inspector

Chief Police Inspector Roger Moens of the Brussels criminal investigation branch won a silver medal in the 800-meter run in Rome. He was the favorite in the race, but Peter Snell of New Zealand raced past him in the last meter to win. Roger Moens might have had a gold medal in Melbourne in 1956 except that one dank rainy day, his spectacles suddenly steamed up and he sprinted full tilt into a post, which left him too lame to run that year's competitions. When people ask Inspector Moens if he wishes he had a gold medal, he tells them, "Not really. Some athletes who don't deserve one have one. I prefer people to say of me that I don't have one, but that I deserve one."

Roger Moens says that he specializes in "violent deaths, the bloody cases." His photograph is often carried in Belgian newspapers, almost always with a thin smile on his sharp face and a thug handcuffed to his wrist. People constantly ask Roger Moens, if he has ever had to pursue a suspect on foot. "I have had to chase after guys who were getting away only three times in my twenty years of police work. I caught them each time. But once the young villain—who might well have had a good career in athletics—nearly got away from me. I told myself that my honor as a runner was at stake, and I caught him up with an enormous effort."

Inspector Moens said that his career as an Olympian has definitely been of help to him in police work. "My job is thrilling and absorbing," he said, "but mostly it is a question of methodically working through investigative research or intensive questioning. My past helps me. In sport, I have a starting point for conversation, and after that, it is easier. People confide in me more readily, perhaps. They like to talk about the 800 meters in Rome. Some criminals have told me that they were glad to meet me. They make it clear, of course, that they would have preferred different circumstances. . . ."

Herb Elliott, Sales Manager

When he was twenty-two, Herb Elliott was on the threshold of one of the most promising long-distance careers since Paavo Nurmi. He won an Olympic gold medal in the 1,500 meters in Rome, and he held the world record in the mile and the 1,500 meters. He had never lost a race. Then he quit.

Now Herb Elliott is thirty-four, and it is as if he had never been famous, never anything but what he is now—an ascending and very ambitious sales manager for Australian Portland Cement Ltd., living with his wife and six children in the middle-class Melbourne suburb of Moorabbin. Herb Elliott is a tightly disciplined fellow who speaks grimly of his view of life: "I believe life falls into categories. When you are a youngish sort of bloke, as I still class myself, your career has to be developed to a level which makes you happy. I am not happy by any means. There is a family to educate and a home to build and be paid off. The first fifteen to twenty years of married life must be a selfish sort of existence where job and family come first."

Herb Elliott was asked what interest he has in track now. He said rather sharply, "Nil."

He was asked if his reputation as a medal winner and champion had helped his career, and he said, "No."

He was asked if he ever appeared before athletic associations, and he said: "I accept those invitations only if they are for a very close friend or if they will help me in my job or if they will pay me."

Herb Elliott was remarkably dispassionate when he discussed his brilliant running career. He spoke with reluctance and with such detachment that it was almost as if he were discussing a stranger. "When I first started running, my only ambition was to be better than I was. This gradually leads you on until such a time when you are satisfied with what you have done. I didn't realize what my goal was until I felt satisfied. I felt satisfied when I won an Olympic gold medal and broke a world record. Once that hunger had been satiated, I lost interest altogether. Once the sense of achievement in winning races and breaking records had been tasted, it was just a drag. A real drag."

Even when he was competing regularly however, track was not an ecstatic experience. "Every time I ran it was an enormous strain on me, even if it was at a little country meeting. I hated the four or five hours before a race. People thought I was a bad sport because I didn't shake hands and all that sort of thing. But it was that I was just so twisted up and knotted up inside. It was a ghastly feeling. The nervousness and the pressure increased as my unbeaten record got longer. The pundits, the damned journalists, would say, 'Today's the day Elliott's going to be knocked off,' and in England and all over the world tens of thousands of people would turn up just to see if I would be beaten."

Herb Elliott said, "If I were training athletes, my message would be to emphasize intensive training sessions. The race itself is very intense. You have only a very short time—thirteen minutes in 5,000 meters or three and a half minutes in 1,500 meters. You must pull every ounce of energy you have in your body out of yourself without dying. That's the essence of it."

Don Bragg, Boys' Camp Owner

Kamp Olympik is in the pine barrens of New Jersey, nine miles west of the town of Gretna and far off the nether end of the Garden State Parkway. In cold early spring, before the ground cover fills out, you can see a man watching you from perhaps a quarter of a mile or more back among the trees in those sparse thickets. In the summer, Kamp Olympik overflows with 200 boys, but in the cold early spring it is a waiting wilderness.

The owner of the camp and of several hundred acres of

surrounding desolation is Don Bragg, thirty-five, the hulking, handsome ex-Army private who won a gold medal in the pole vault in Rome. The medal is now displayed on a large velvet-bedded, glass-covered tray along with many, many other ribbons and badges and precious-metal bric-a-brac won by Don Bragg for his pole vaulting. The tray is on exhibit in a barnlike wooden building which is the dining hall at Kamp Olympik.

In the early spring, the dining hall was empty, and Don Bragg's bellowing, exuberant voice made hollow thunder up among the log rafters of the building. Outside, it was growing dusky over the empty miles of pines, and inside the echoing dining hall, it was even darker. Don Bragg peered at his Olympic gold medal and shouted, "Of course, all I ever really wanted to be was Tarzan. It was my dream and my obsession. Listen, I broke the world's record because I *was* Tarzan. I won the gold medal in Rome because I wanted to be Tarzan. I knew Hollywood would believe I was Tarzan if I had that medal.

"All my life, I was emulating Johnny Weissmuller—he's the guy. I was constantly swinging on trees; I built up my forearms that way by swinging through the woods behind my house. My house was in Penns Grove, New Jersey."

Don Bragg became excited as he talked about being Tarzan. He is an enormous man, easily big enough to be a linebacker for Green Bay, easily big enough to be Johnny Weissmuller. Bragg has thick curly black hair and thick sideburns which have already turned snow white. In a business suit he could easily pass for an insurance executive or a very classy *maître d'hôtel*. His hair seemed almost to stand on end when he spoke of being Tarzan, and he lumbered agitatedly around the gloomy dining room.

"People started calling me Tarzan, which I loved. In the

240

Garden, I'd compete, and they'd be yelling all the way up in the peanut galleries, 'Go, Tarzan! Win one for Cheetah!' Once one of those pale little stuffed shirts from the AAU came up to me and said I was gonna jeopardize my amateur standing because I had *Don 'Tarzan' Bragg* printed on my traveling bag. Ridiculous. I laughed at him and said I'd do what I wanted.

"So in Rome I won the gold medal after eight hours of vaulting. Eight hours! Jesus, I'd gone from a hundred and ninety-eight to a hundred and eighty-seven pounds, but I won and I let go with this fantastic Tarzan yell. It echoed all over the stadium, and the crowd went wild. The Italians loved it!

"The gold medal did it for me; Hollywood called. I moved out there to be Tarzan. At this point I *know* I am Tarzan; it is in my bones. They wanted to straighten my nose and cut my vocal cords. My wife was about to have our first baby, and she went home to New Jersey. I was living with Horace Heidt, the bandleader, and one night I took this girl home from some party and some guy took a shot at me. God, the headlines! And then I got to thinking about what the hell am I doing in *Hollywood*—Don Bragg from Penns Grove, New Jersey? What the hell am I doing with nose jobs and voice-box fixes? I figured it's all too rich for my blood, so I came home."

Bragg paused for a moment, then spoke in hushed tones: "I am home for a week, and I went down to the local swimming hole, and some little kids asked me if I'd make like Tarzan. Could I resist? No, I could not. So I swung out on a rope and dropped a hundred feet, and I landed on a huge jagged piece of glass and cut my foot so badly I needed eighteen stitches and was supposed to stay off the foot for six weeks. Six weeks! Naturally, at this point I got a phone call from my old friend

241

Sy Weintraub, the producer, and he said, 'Don, Don, we want you to play Tarzan in *Tarzan Goes to India*.' I was lying in bed with my foot wrapped up and I just gulped. 'Don, Don,' said Sy, 'we'll pass on fixing your nose and your vocal cords because we don't have time and we're leaving for India right now. You ready to go, Don? Don?' I said, 'Well, ah, er, Sy, I can't walk because ah, er, I got this foot problem. . . .' So he hired Jock Mahoney to play Tarzan.

"Then in 1964 I was talking to some television types about playing Tarzan in a series. They'd tested Weissmuller's son for the part, but he was too tall, so I got it. Yeah, I was going to *be* Tarzan. We went to Jamaica to film it, and one day there I was, standing on a cliff in my little Tarzan briefs, and the cameras were all below me, and the director was sitting there in his chair, and I look out at the horizon and I puff out my chest and I think, 'This is my dream—I'm a *star!* I'm Tarzan in the *movies*.'

"Not two days after we started shooting, they slapped a subpoena or an injunction or something on the whole thing—a huge legal screw-up over whether we had the *rights* to do Tarzan. The company shut down on the spot. I was crushed. I came home to New Jersey, and I took a job selling drug supplies for sixty-two hundred dollars per annum. What humiliation—people'd say to me, 'Say, aren't you Don Tarzan Bragg? What are you doing selling drug supplies?' Oh, it was one hell of an ego adjustment. But it still wasn't the worst.

"I was having bad back problems then. My leg had been going numb, and the doctor said I had no choice but to go into the hospital for spinal surgery. So I was packing my stuff to check into the hospital when I got this phone call from South America. It was Sy Weintraub. He was calling from Rio, and he wanted to know if I could fly down there and be on location in forty-eight hours. They were shooting *Tarzan the Impostor*. Sy said he wanted me for the impostor, which could lead to the real thing pretty soon. I gulped again and told him I couldn't make it just then because I, ah, er, had this *back* problem. Weintraub couldn't believe it. He hired Ron Ely to be the impostor, and damn, if Ron Ely didn't end up playing the *real* Tarzan on the TV series."

Don Bragg shook his head and gazed at the lavender murk that had fallen over Kamp Olympik. "I'm no fatalist, but I just was not meant to be Tarzan. Hell, I could have been a Tarzan equal to Johnny's. . . ."

Later, in the small warm living room of his house, which Don Bragg said he had built himself ("My father was a carpenter") and which he filled as a bear in a doll's house, his wife Terry brought out a small snack of cookies and Coca-Cola. She is from Penns Grove, New Jersey, too. There are four Bragg children. "They love it here a hundred percent," said Don. "The woods and the trapezes in the trees, it's perfect. Terry loves it, maybe sixty percent. She likes conveniences around." Until the family moved to the barrens in 1969, they had lived in Trenton, and since he had not become Tarzan, Don had worked in the administration of Democratic Governor Richard Hughes. It was not a job he cherished much of the time.

"I was an athlete, and this was politics," he said. "In sports things are black and white, there's no bull shit. You do fifty push-ups, you get a certain result in return. Sports are true, truer than anything in the world. I hated all that on-again-off-again political crap around the governor's office. You may think a guy as outgoing and enthusiastic as I am would love politics. Listen, when I was a child, I was an introvert. I could hardly bring myself to go out in front of people at little high school track meets and vault. Even at my first track meet in college when I went to the Boston Garden, I remember they called my name to vault. I pulled down my sweat suit, and my pants came down with them. My God, I was demolished! I wanted to die; I wanted to quit college and track and never see anyone again. I passed on that jump and ran and hid in the men's room for a long time before I could get up my nerve to go back out in front of that crowd. I finally learned to psych myself by believing—actually believing—that I was in my own backyard. That worked. It even worked in the Olympics in Rome."

When Bragg spoke of the Olympics and of his own path to the gold medal, his voice was much softer, gentler, perhaps even reverent. "I was so big that I could never eat more than one meal a day or I'd weigh so much I'd break the poles. I lived on skim milk and honey. I did that for ten years because if I went over two hundred pounds—*crackkk!*—the poles would go. Well, I hardly went out with girls until I was twenty; pole vaulting was my life. The Olympics were my whole life. In fact, ever since the Olympics everything in life has been anticlimactic.

"To get to the Olympics, I lived like a monk when I was in college. Vaulting was my life. The Olympics were like a religious pilgrimage. Well, I missed the team in 1956 with a pulled muscle and don't think I didn't contemplate suicide. I locked myself in my room and cried four hours every afternoon for four or five months. I just *bawled!* Then I got it so I locked myself up to cry only a couple of days a week, then once a week, then once a month. Finally I pulled out of it—after a *hell* of a long time, and I decided there was nothing to do but start all over again."

The nearest good restaurant to Kamp Olympik is about a forty-five-minute drive. It is called Zaber's, and it is a sprawling, many-tiered, dimly lighted establishment which caters to the Atlantic City trade in the summer and has souvenir-trinket shops tucked away in any corner of the restaurant which does not have tables. It serves a memorable cocktail—"The Zaberized Martini"—which comes in a sixteen-ounce pitcher. Don Bragg had a Zaberized Martini, and his spirits rose suitably, enabling him to cover a wide variety of subjects in a short time:

"If I lived in Europe, I would be a millionaire. So could Parry O'Brien or Rafer Johnson or Bill Toomey. They know all of us over there—we're celebrities. We're like Mays or Mantle or Namath there. Here it's always, 'Hey, Don, drop by and see us when you're through competing; we might have something real good for ya.' But when you do that, it's always, 'Hey, jeez, Don, I'm sorry but we're all filled up, man.'

"I thought about going into teaching here, but I didn't because I didn't want people pointing at me and saying, 'Hey, he's an Olympic champion, and he's only making eight grand a year.'

"There's a change in sports today. You have lots of second-rate athletes going into track. You have the individualists, the kooks who can't adapt their personalities to team sports. Hell, if a kid can sign for millions going into pro sports—which are all team sports, incidentally—why should he knock himself out being in track, the poor man's sport?

"You want to hear what athletes are really like? Let me tell you, we're like little boys who won't pass up a dare. We are *so* competitive it is insane. I remember once I stopped my car in the middle of a bridge somewhere, got up on the railing in the middle of traffic, took off my shirt, and dived in. I didn't know how deep it was, I didn't know if there were sharks or a thousand-pound jewfish down there to eat me up. But the guy I

245

was riding with dared me to jump, so I had to. Of course, I had dared him, too, and he jumped, too.

"I remember another time at a meet in Greece I was with Parry O'Brien [the shot putter] and Al Cantello [a javelin thrower], and we bet each other we couldn't swim out to a yacht that was about four thousand miles offshore. Well, we swam out there, all right, all three of us. Then, once we're there, Cantello says, 'Hey, I bet I can swim under this boat.' Well, God, it was a boat like the *Queen Mary* or something—it must've gone forty feet below the surface. But Cantello goes. O'Brien says, 'Well, I can't let that bastard beat me,' and he goes. Naturally I couldn't just stay there treading water, so I went under, too. It got darker and darker, and I couldn't get under that thing. I kept cutting my head on the barnacles on the bottom, and I was terrified that the blood would attract sharks. Finally, I got under the hull, and it started getting light again, and I finally hit the top with the last ounce of air in my lungs. We all started laughing. We were all bleeding from the barnacles, and the blood was streaming down our faces." He laughed again at the memory.

"But if you *really* want to know what athletes are like, let me tell you about this time in Texas when Parry O'Brien and I are staying together in this motel room the night before a meet. I'm doing some exercises on this night, and one of them is to do handstand push-ups—push-ups while I'm on my hands with my feet propped on the wall. I'm doing these things, and Parry says, 'Hey, man, let me see you do some more.' So I do about thirty of them. I then bet Parry he can't do any. So he gets himself propped against the wall, and he grunts and groans, and he gets himself down and up once. Then he says, 'Okay, lemme see you do some more.' I do about forty more; then Parry strains and grunts and does one; then I do about thirty and Parry does two, and I do twenty-five and Parry does two. By now I can hardly move; I've done about a hundred and fifty to Parry's six or seven. I get up on my hands, and, damn, I can't do any more, not one. So Parry kind of painfully gets up on his hands, and he's sweating and bright red in the face, and his veins are popping out, and by God, if he doesn't manage to do one more push-up. Then real quick, he stands up, brushes his hands together and says, 'I won.'

"That's what athletes are about."

On the return drive from Zaber's to Kamp Olympik, with owls hooting in the black distance and the sudden gleam of small animals' eyes in the headlights appearing in the dark along the road shoulder, Don Bragg was asked if he still had any desire to leave the pine barrens and be Tarzan. "Nah," said Don. "Listen, I'm so happy here I wake up in the morning and think I must be somebody else." Then he paused. "Well, maybe I have a thirty per cent desire." After perhaps two minutes of further silence, he said, "Make that forty-five percent."

1964

Held in Tokyo from October 10 to October 24. 6,600 athletes from sixty-four nations participated. Considered one of best Olympics ever. Charming. Lovely. Efficient. Hayato Ikeda Premier of Japan. Khrushchev deposed by Brezhnev and Kosygin in Moscow. Warren Commission released report pinning assassination of President Kennedy on Lee Harvey Oswald. Red China exploded first atomic device. Avery Brundage celebrated seventy-seventh birthday at Games, was described as "giant of ethics misplaced in an age of nationalism, selfishness and mercenary greed."

Not since Berlin, 1936, was an Olympics so blatantly used as a vehicle of a nation's advancement and recognition as a worldwide power. Rather than the uncomplicated festival of sports-*cum*-brotherhood that Olympic mythology insists it should be, this Olympics was the springboard for Japan to become one of the most powerful economic forces on earth.

"It was a national crusade for Japan to host the Olympic Games. We were still struggling under a defeated enemy nation syndrome in the eyes of most of the world. Without the magic of the Olympic name we might not have gotten the investment we needed to rise as a world trade power. Our national prestige was tied to it and, yes, it was a governmental policy to make the Olympics our announcement to the world that Japan was no longer a beaten nation, that Japan had regained confidence in herself."

So spoke Dr. Ryotaro Azuma, sixty-one, now president of the Japanese Red Cross but during the sixties the chairman of the committee which sparked and ultimately masterminded the Olympic Games of 1964. Dr. Azuma was also the mayor of Tokyo during this period—and the Olympics and politics were never far separated in *his* particular approach to life. "A very significant part of my first election campaign in 1959 was to remind people that I would try to bring them an unforgettable Olympic Games—and, in doing that, to remake our city. In my reelection campaign of 1963, I said, 'Now of course you must vote for me again since I am the perfect man to carry out my own promises about the Olympic Games.'"

The motive for bringing the Olympics to Japan was double-edged: (1) to offer a spectacular launching of its arrival as a power in international trade and (2) to be the catalyst for a badly needed major urban renewal overhaul of the ticky-tacky tumbled labyrinth that Tokyo had come to be after it was nearly destroyed in the catastrophic earthquake and fire of 1923. Dr. Azuma is brisk and articulate in his use of English, and he sounded quite proud of all that had come after the XVIII Olympiad—and of his part in all that had come before.

"The Japanese had, of course, been given the Olympics of 1940 by the International Olympic Committee," said Dr. Azuma. "But the militaristic policies of the government then caused the Games to be canceled eventually. To many Japanese, this was a supreme disappointment. So right after the surrender in 1945, there was much agitation to try again to have an Olympics in Tokyo. Frankly, I was rather conservative on the matter. I wrote an article in a paper saying that we should reach a point where Japan could *compete* again in the Games before we sought to act as host.

"At that time, of course, all of the international sports federations had expelled Japan from their membership. Because of the war, you know. However, as has always been the policy of the IOC, we retained our seats on the IOC. They did not expel countries for political purposes. Nevertheless, we were not allowed to participate in the London Games of 1948 because we had no membership in the world federations of sport."

In 1950, Dr. Azuma was appointed one of Japan's delegates to the IOC. This was just before the committee's annual meeting, which took place in Copenhagen that year. "I wanted badly to go to Denmark," he said, "because I wanted to contact members of the various world federations and plead the case for Japan's being reinstated. The war had been over five years, and I thought perhaps they would feel we had been punished enough.

"However, this was 1950 and the U.S. Supreme Command still frowned on the idea of a Japanese leaving the country. Then Avery Brundage intervened with General MacArthur—who was the supreme commander of the U.S. occupational government, as you know. And so did Sigfrid Edström of Sweden, who was then president of the IOC. As if a magician had waved his wand, I was suddenly granted a passport, which was personally approved by General MacArthur.

"So I was free to travel. But I had no foreign currency, and I could get none easily. I arranged for a plane ticket to Hawaii, and there a dentist of Japanese ancestry met me at the airport. I had never seen him before. But he gave me money he had collected from other Japanese in Hawaii. He took me to a department store and bought me a new suit. Oh, I was a charity case, all right. And as it turned out this dentist from Hawaii was the real hero of the Tokyo Olympics because my trip to Copenhagen was a success and Japan was allowed back into most of the federations. Our first international competition took place during the Asian Games of 1951. Indeed, that meet was Japan's first official institutional contact with the outside world since the occupation.

"The country began to regain its confidence almost immediately. And from that day on, now that we were accepted back in the world, the people began to talk constantly of having an Olympics in Tokyo as early as possible."

The Japanese began applying to the IOC for their own Games right after Helsinki in 1952, then again after Melbourne in 1956. They were turned down, but they arranged for the IOC's annual meeting in 1958 to be held in Tokyo—in conjunction with the Asian Games. The IOC was impressed with the way the Japanese ran the meet. In 1959 Dr. Azuma, now the mayor of Tokyo, confronted the IOC once more with his "Olympic platform." As he recalled it, "Through certain politicking and various manipulations very subtly done, Tokyo was duly selected for the 1964 Games."

The city then launched one of the most monumental urban construction projects of the twentieth century. "We planned to rebuild Tokyo for the Olympics," said Dr. Azuma. "It really had to be done, and there was no other way but the Olympics to get the people behind it. Of course, no one really believed we could do it."

Construction work went on on a twenty-four-hour schedule from the beginning. There was a constant air of feverish efficiency about the projects and the entire operation soon earned the name the Banzai Charge Construction Company.

Japan spent nearly $3 billion on the Games—six times more than had been spent on any Olympics before. The Olympic Village alone cost $1.9 billion, which is more money than was spent on the first nine Olympics all together. Miles of new superhighways were installed, and the driving time from the Ginza in downtown Tokyo to the airport was slashed from ninety to twenty minutes. An eight-mile monorail was built, and hotel space in town was tripled. A new 72,000-seat stadium, a new natatorium, a new rowing course and a new equestrian park ninety miles out of the city (with a new expressway covering the entire distance) were completed.

The whole project took three years. But it was of such stupendous size that most people despaired of its ever being finished. Only eighteen months before the Games were to begin, a poll was taken throughout Japan and it showed that 73 percent of the people believed that it was impossible for all the Olympic projects to be completed in time. But they were.

"I became a great expert on deadlines," said Dr. Azuma.

251

"But it was worth all of it. If it were not for the Olympic Games, I'd hate to think of the situation Tokyo would be in today. We would perhaps be dying under our own inefficiencies. Oh, certainly, I feel it would be better for the Olympics itself if the Games were simpler and less expensive. I think it would be excellent if the Olympics were small enough so that a nation's full prestige is not necessarily at stake each time it produces the Games.

"Yet of course, for Japan I think it is possible that we would not be so prosperous today if we had not been so ambitious in presenting the Olympics of 1964. We were greatly challenged by it—and we were greatly advanced by it. Otherwise, I imagine that we would not have volunteered to do it."

The Japanese people threw themselves into the Games—in every way. One problem which nearly panicked the authorities was Tokyo's appalling shortage of public toilets. The city had but 1 for every 12,000 people (compared to London's 1-to-800 ratio, for example). To help clear up the crisis, several companies donated mobile "toilet cars" at a cost of $10,000 each, and civic groups arranged to post signs around many subway stations saying: LET'S STOP URINATING IN PUBLIC—THE OLYMPICS ARE NIGH. A major loss of face occurred at the Olympic Village when two Japanese firms sent 650 bicycles free of charge for use of the Olympians living there. More than 100 of the bikes fell apart instantly under the weight of heavy foreign athletes. Hundreds of free bamboo umbrellas also collapsed in the heavy rains which plagued Tokyo during much of the Olympics.

Twenty percent of all seats were saved for schoolchildren by the Olympic Committee. The children adored it all. Their particular favorite was the only Olympian from Niger, the boxer Issaka Dabore. He received thousands of letters with good-luck paper storks folded inside. Alas, Issaka Dabore did not win a gold medal.

Dawn Fraser, Swimming Coach

"The newspapers were full of all sorts of things then. They said I swam the emperor's moat—in the nude. Have you ever seen the moat? Ugh. It's full of green slime. None of the things they said were true. I finally sued on the grounds of defamation, and they had to apologize to me, and they lifted my suspension from amateur competition."

The apologies came in 1965, a year or more after that infamous escapade at the Tokyo Olympics, but by then Dawn Fraser was past her peak, married and able to swim competitively no more. She has always been a relatively old lady by modern swimming standards which cause most champions to be burned out and finished before they are twenty years old. Dawn Fraser was seventeen when she won her first Australian national championship in 1955; then she went on to win a gold medal in the 100-meter free style in Melbourne '56, another in the same event in Rome '60 and yet another in Tokyo '64, when she was twenty-seven. She also collected one gold and two silvers in relays.

She is now thirty-four, divorced several years ago and living with her six-year-old daughter in Balmain, a Sydney suburb, in the same terrace house in which she was born and reared. Dawn Fraser is a coach for about fifty students at a Sydney pool, about half of whom are children just learning to swim. Dawn herself learned to swim when she was five at the Balmain Baths, a neighborhood hangout near her home. When

253

she was fifteen, she began serious training—leaving school and taking a job in a dress factory so she could afford it. World records began to fall around her, but it was the Olympic Games that fired her spirit. "Every four years a swimmer gets the chance to prove she's the best in the world. That's what the Olympics stand for," she said. "You've trained all those years, done all that hard work, and it all has to prove itself there or it's not worth it. You want to represent your country in the Olympics, but you really do it for yourself. If you win, all the sacrifices are worthwhile. Nobody can ever take it away from you. They can break your records, but they can't take your Olympic medals. You are *always* the Olympic champion."

Dawn Fraser is proud of her independence. "I supported myself all during my career," she said. "I didn't get any help. If I wanted to buy a new frock, I couldn't afford to. My parents had too many responsibilities to help." But it was this same streak of independence that ultimately got her into trouble with the Australian swimming hierarchy. After the Rome Olympics, she was named to the national team, even though she had refused to wear the official green Australian Olympic track suit during the Rome Games. Instead, she favored an old baggy outfit because it was more comfortable. She was also accused of being involved in a fierce dispute with a teammate, Jan Andrews. "I never slapped her as the papers said," recalled Dawn. "I threw a pillow at her because she used some bad language in front of a chaperone."

She was not picked for the team in 1961, although no formal charges were ever made. "It's probably why I stayed in swimming so long," she said wryly. "I wouldn't let them push me out. I've always had these problems. I say things. I'm outspoken. I can't be told what to do—but I can be *asked*. Nobody has to *tell* me to go to bed the night before an Olympic race.

I'm not going to waste twelve months of my life working to win a race and then throw it away for one evening in the rec hall. I know when to go to bed. I know how important it is. I resent an official telling me to go to bed at seven thirty.

"I also like parties. A few beers. Especially after a big race. Especially an Olympic race. I always like to have a bottle of beer. If I had to swim the next day, I would just have a glass. You're keyed up for months before an Olympics. You've trained four years for it. You're jumpy. When I'm like that, the greatest relaxation for me is a glass of beer and a cigarette, but I always drink it in front of the officials. I wouldn't sneak away and drink."

During the Tokyo Olympics, when she was accused of the wildest sort of celebrations and ultimately banned for ten years from amateur swimming, Dawn Fraser was under more pressure than the mere tension of Olympic competition.

"Times were most difficult for me there," she said. "Mentally I had a lot to get over. In March, 1964, I was in a bad car accident and my mother was killed. I had a broken neck, and I had to wear a collar for the next three months, twenty-four hours a day. Physically I was hampered by the collar, but the worst thing was my mental condition. I was very shaken up. *I* had been driving the car, and now my mother was dead.

"Fortunately, I was living with some people in Melbourne, and he was a psychiatrist. I was nearing a mental breakdown, but he helped me so much by letting me talk to him. It saved me. By the time I got to Tokyo I wanted to win very much.

"I wanted to win the gold medal for my mother."

Dawn Fraser is a tall, striking-looking woman now, stylishly dressed and sure of herself. She is hoping to launch an ambitious project in Adelaide—a Dawn Fraser Sports Center with pool, squash courts, saunas. Eventually, she would like to open

255

a series of such businesses throughout Australia. She could well succeed, for she is known as a quick-witted, sharp businesswoman. She credits her swimming for this side of her character: "You learn to use gamesmanship; you have to outguess your opponents in a pool; you have to anticipate their reactions. It changes your whole way of thinking. Swimming makes you a lot shrewder."

Anton Geesink, Judo Studio Owner

Perhaps the most stunning event of the Tokyo Games occurred when a Dutchman named Anton Geesink won the gold medal in judo from the Japanese champion. Judo was an event widely understood by students of the Olympic Games to be the traditional "house sport" for the XVIII Olympiad, meaning a sport the host country introduces into the program which should guarantee it at least one gold medal. But Anton Geesink defeated Ako Kaminaga, the Japanese heavyweight champion, in the final—a result that was tantamount to a national disaster for Japan. "The moment I had beaten him, the poor Japanese felt it was the most humiliating event to happen to Japan since losing the Second World War," said Anton Geesink. "I feel sorry for them."

Anton Geesink was born in the slums of Utrecht and began working in his early teens as an unskilled construction laborer; he was a crude kind of urban yokel whose tongue was so heavy with the local Utrecht accent that he even spoke his native Dutch badly. Today, at thirty-eight, his old mates are amazed at Anton Geesink. He has taken speech lessons from a retired Dutch actor and has been tutored in the proper way to move at social gatherings. Anton Geesink now speaks elegant Dutch, excellent English and enough good Japanese to make speeches in Tokyo ("I am probably more famous and more popular there than back home; they still know Anton Geesink all over Japan, even today"). He has a prosperous judo studio in his hometown of Utrecht and a fine farmhouse outside town, and he is known as a warm, gentle fellow despite the ferocity of his sport. "I do not like trouble," he said. "I remember once that I caught two pigeons, and I ate them because I was hungry. Later I felt so guilty that I began keeping pigeons as a hobby, and I am still keeping pigeons today."

Abebe Bikila, Emperor's Guard

He will have a seat of honor at the Munich Olympics, but it will be a sad and futile tribute of the type that healthy men habitually pay to the cripples whose still, gleaming wheels line the field sides at professional football games. They seem so dead and the football players so quick that the tableau comes to represent some kind of crude testimonial to the waywardness and whimsy of fate.

It will be this way with Abebe Bikila in his chromiumplated wheelchair . . . more so because he was so graceful and so strong before he was paralyzed.

Now thirty-nine, Abebe Bikila is an Ethiopian national hero who ranks not far below the Emperor Haile Selassie in the hearts of his countrymen. He became a historic figure in Rome when he won the gold medal in the marathon: it was the first such prize ever captured by a man from black Africa. Bikila was unforgettable when he ran through the ancient streets of Rome. He was barefoot, and his stride was loping and easy, though his legs seemed far too thin to carry him over so many

257

miles. His face was set in a gaunt brown mask that somehow also seemed beatific at the same time it was so grim. When he won, the mask cracked and burst into a radiant smile.

He made Olympic history again in Tokyo, when he won his second consecutive gold in the marathon; there he did an exuberant handstand just after he broke the tape. He might have done the impossible in Mexico City, except that he ran with an injured ankle; he dropped out and did not finish.

Now Bikila is a paraplegic and he cannot move from his waist down. In the winter of 1969 a Volkswagen he was driving near Addis Ababa overturned after Bikila was blinded by the headlights of an oncoming car. He was crushed behind the dashboard and steering wheel of his car. He was immediately flown to England for special treatments at the famed Stoke Mandeville Hospital near London, and Emperor Haile Selassie even made a trip to visit him there. But the doctors could do nothing, and his chances of ever moving his legs again are a million to one.

Though he is helpless, Bikila still holds the rank of captain in the proud imperial guard of Emperor Haile Selassie. He was a private in the Army when he went to Rome, was instantly promoted to corporal in the emperor's guard after that gold medal, won promotion to sergeant before Tokyo, was made a lieutenant following that triumph, and became a captain after the Games in Mexico City. In the Ethiopian pattern of military careers this represented a lightninglike ascension. "My life was enriched by the Olympics in that way," said Bikila matter-of-factly.

Bikila lives with his wife and four children in a wooden cottage, high among groves of tall gum and eucalyptus trees on the outskirts of Addis Ababa. All around his sturdy house there are the mean and tumbled shanties of his peasant neighbors. A seven-foot fence of corrugated iron surrounds Bikila's property, and inside, on brilliantly green grass, half a dozen sheep graze with a few chickens pecking about their feet. The wooden floors of the house are polished to a fine sheen, and the walls are hung with Ethiopian war shields made from the hides of oxen. His trophies, stained and discolored by the damp mountain air, are displayed in a cupboard. A heavy scent of incense permeates the rooms.

At home, Bikila is wheeled about by his brother. He speaks in Amharic, through an interpreter. There is an almost incandescent intensity about the man; he frowns gravely at each question asked, and his long, tapered fingers frequently make nervous sketches in the air as he answers. He is brave and fatalistic and enormously dignified when he speaks of his fate.

"Men of success meet with tragedy," he said softly. "It was the will of God that I won the Olympics, and it was the will of God that I met with my accident. I was overjoyed when I won the marathon twice. But I accepted those victories as I accept this tragedy. I have no choice. I have to accept both circumstances as facts of life and live happily."

He said, "God gives, God takes away."

Bikila was asked if his victory in Rome was all the sweeter for its historical symbolism—that an Ethiopian had triumphed in Italy, the nation that had crushed his country so brutally in the thirties. He was stiff when he answered, "I think there must be a clear distinction between sport and politics. Sport is for international friendship. The Olympics have nothing to do with war—not with *any* war."

Bikila, the patriot and the idealist, was disturbed about the increase in commercialism around the Olympic Games. He said, "An Olympic athlete is first an amateur who is going to compete for the flag of his country. Now and again, a sportsman appears on the scene who seems unable to make the distinction between competing for his nation and gaining personal profit.

259

'Amateurs should not be paid—not to advertise products or anything else. I do not agree with any profit-making devices allied to the Olympics. In some places when an athlete who has won in the Olympics returns home, he is able to profit in different ways. So he's not interested in working hard for the next Olympics—so he's slowly destroyed as a sportsman. . . ."

Bikila is almost priestlike in his devotion to Olympic ideals and idealism. Even his most memorable scenes fit the scriptures as written by Coubertin: "The most wonderful thing at the Olympics for me is that, at the end of everything, all the competitors from all over the world who have not known each other before get together for the closing ceremony. They hug each other. Usually some of them cry. It is as if they were really brothers and sisters, a family, about to separate. . . ."

The mud and stone path leading to Bikila's door is almost trod flat by the dozens of Olympic aspirants who come to their paralyzed hero for inspiration and advice. Ragged little boys and rough rangy soldiers arrive daily to visit Bikila. They wish to run as he did; they wish to win as he did. Theirs is a pilgrimage to Ethiopia's Olympic oracle.

And of course, the honor is more profound than any he will receive in Munich.

1968

Held in Mexico City from October 12 to October 27. 6,082 athletes from 109 nations competed. A pleasant Olympics. Bright, excited though marred by deaths of hundreds of *students rioting shortly before Games started. Gustaro Díaz Ordaz President of Mexico. Student riots in Paris. Robert Kennedy assassinated. United States explodes with antiwar sentiment. ABC paid $4,500,000 for Olympic television rights.*

Like Japan, Mexico gained greatly from the Olympics of 1968. Pedro Ramírez Vázquez is one of the finest architects in Mexico—which makes him nearly a saint, for Mexico abounds in geniuses in that field. Señor Ramírez Vázquez was chairman of the '68 Games, and he is a patriot, a pragmatist and a man who speaks his mind. "I am an architect; I know nothing about sports," he said. "The only Olympics I have ever seen is our own. If you ask me why Mexico wanted the Games, I will tell you that a major purpose was the advantage of having people throughout the world see a true and honest vision of Mexico as it really is. We wanted everyone to see our true image. . . . The diffusion of television across the world resulted in fine advertising for our nation. . . . Foreigners knew only the folklore, sombreros, siestas, mañana. They knew of the violence of our revolutions. We had never taken the opportunity to explain to the world what contemporary Mexico was. The Olympics told Mexico's story to millions. . . ."

The white gloves of Albin Lemursiaux perhaps went all but unnoticed at the first Games in Athens. Not the black gloves of the American sprinters John Carlos and Tommie Smith at the Games in Mexico.

Fistfights erupted in sections of the stadium in Mexico City when Carlos and Smith stood upon the victory steps, each with his head bowed and a clenched fist in a black glove raised high, as "The Star-Spangled Banner" was played. One spectator

261

said: "My God, fifty people started fighting all around our section. It was mostly full of Americans. Some guys yelled, 'Kill the SOB's and some yelled, 'Let 'em be!' We had to pull guys apart. It was like fifty lunatics fighting for a foul ball. . . ."

Recently John Carlos, now a player for the Montreal Alouettes of the Canadian Football League, spoke of that day of protest: "Tommie and I were just telling them that black people and minority people were tired of what was taking place in the U.S. and all over the world. We were telling them about roaches and rats and diseases that plague the poor because those things can spread like a brush fire. They can burn up the world. I don't think we were very successful. The press and TV blew it all out of proportion. They made it a huge harmful thing, like some kind of fire-spitting dragon."

The third man on the stand was Peter Norman, an Australian sprinter who had finished a surprising second to Smith in that 200-meter race. He spoke of Carlos and Smith: "They believed with such fervor in what they were doing that I have to support them for having the courage of their convictions. I knew they would demonstrate before the ceremony. They were most open. They were both supposed to have a full pair of black gloves, but Carlos forgot his. Smith was loath to give one up, but John begged him and finally Tommie gave him one glove. I don't think they spoiled or soiled anything by their demonstration.

"I had earned the right to be on the platform. So had they."

American officials disagreed. Carlos and Smith were expelled from the Olympic Village. Their visas were canceled. They were ordered out of Mexico. There was a great deal of fulminating about their display, and most people felt they had desecrated something by injecting "politics" into the Olympics.

John Carlos said, "Ours was not a political act, it was a

moral act, and that is all right. When else can you do something like that? Only at the Olympics or when you land on the moon. Then everyone is looking at you."

Al Oerter, Computer Programmer

Al Oerter is thirty-five years old, a big, serious-looking fellow who works as a designer of computerized business systems for the Grumman Corporation. His office, in a long, low white cement building that is called Plant No. 40, is located in a section of suburban wasteland in Bethpage, Long Island, and it is enclosed behind a high wire-mesh fence. Everyone needs an identification badge to get in or to get out.

Al Oerter is one of the greatest Olympic competitors who ever lived. He has won four gold medals as a discus thrower in four consecutive Games—at Melbourne in 1956, at Rome in 1960, at Tokyo in 1964 and at Mexico City in 1968. No other man has ever matched this superhuman feat.

On the Ides of March in 1971 Al Oerter reluctantly decided that he would retire from the rigors of Olympic competition. "My neck was hurting, and I couldn't double my weight-lifting program to put on the weight I needed, okay? I weigh two hundred and thirty-five pounds now, and I had to get it up to two seventy-five or maybe three hundred pounds to compete properly. I don't believe in steroids, and I think I've proved you don't have to take them. It's no secret that most of the weight guys used steroids in Tokyo and in Mexico, but I don't believe in them, okay?"

For all his triumphant times in the Olympics, Al Oerter rarely competed without pain or suffering. "In Rome in 1960 the nervous tension was so bad it was like physical pain. I

263

injured my neck in 1962 and had to wear a brace. In Tokyo in '64, I ripped the cartilage in my rib cage. I had to use novocaine. I was wrapped up in bandages like a mummy, but the pain was still fierce, and I was popping ammonia capsules to clear my head. In Mexico I pulled an abductor muscle in my leg a week before the Games, but the doctors were good. . . ."

His training regimen has always required enormous discipline, plus profound expertise in physiology, particularly his own. "It is all a matter of body weight—are you as strong as you're *supposed* to be? It's the number of hours of effective throwing every day. It's applying more pressure from throw to throw. It's also heartbeat, pulse. I know how to read my pulse, I've been at this sixteen years, okay? I know when to increase the salt in my diet. . . ."

When the Ides of March arrived and Al Oerter decided that the ordeal of his fifth Olympic Games would be too much, he telephoned his wife. "Honey," he said, "I think I'll be home a little early tonight. Okay?"

1972

The Olympiads fly by. We are back to Germany. What can one say about then and about now? Today the leader of Germany, Willy Brandt, stands decorated with a Nobel Peace Prize, a paragon of good intentions in the world's eyes as the XX Olympiad arrives in Munich. In 1936 Hitler was laying plans for a holocaust, assembling in secret a machine so barbaric in its purpose and so efficient in its function that most men still cannot assimilate the magnitude of its brutality. History has clanked on. Perhaps there is really no comparison at all between these two Germanys. Perhaps everything has come to be so changed that only the name of the nation is the same.

Adam Nothelfer was a press officer during the Berlin Games, and he is once again a press officer for the Munich events. In the years between, many sad and many good things have happened to Adam Nothelfer, and he is now white-maned and frail-looking, though alert and always affable. He was critically burned during the Battle of Britain when his Heinkel bomber was shot down over England. He was captured and hospitalized, and once recovered, he entered a POW camp. In 1944, in the only British-German prisoner exchange of the war, he was returned to Germany and was immediately drafted and shipped to fight in the chill and bloody futility of the Russian front. When the war ended, Adam Nothelfer and his wife plodded through Germany in the great river of refugees flooding the country. They ended up in Dortmund with a peddler's pushcart, which they ultimately built into a prosperous department store.

Adam Nothelfer recalls that there was an oddly sinister feeling in Berlin during the Olympics: "Though I truly believed that in 1936 the butterflies were indeed more speckled and less rare than they are today, and I didn't know then as yet what life had in store for me, I still am convinced that Berlin marked the dividing line between the good and the bad. Its drive for perfection, beauty, virtue and idealism was a pretense for a propaganda line which Hitler successfully seeded—and which has persisted ever since. If the Olympics want to continue in the right spirit, something will have to be done about it. This was the reason that I, at my age and a recent widower, let myself be persuaded to return to the Olympic harness.

"From the outset the Munich Games were planned as a

265

gay, joyous, relaxed event, with none of the hecticness, super-nationalism and occasionally fierce antagonisms which so frequently have evolved since Berlin. What we all ought to strive for is something reminiscent to the mood of the 1952 Helsinki Games. They were, spiritually at least, the best ones ever.

"Right now, however, the indicators show a steady influx of hysteria. I hope this is due only to the anticipation and not yet a harbinger for a deep-seated further deterioration of the Olympic spirit. . . ."

The site of the Munich Games—700 acres, manicured and lovely with the newest architectural miracles and hundreds of evenly planted trees—is in an area that was a refuse dump after 1945, a place where they swept wreckage and rubble, the tons of smithereens that remained after 50,000 homes were demolished by Allied bombing raids over Munich during World War II. Atop this desperate trash pile, the Olympic Grounds for 1972 have been spread like the layer of a prehistoric cave floor—new life atop homes and artifacts of a civilization that did not survive.

If there is to be something predictably memorable emanating from the XX Olympiad, it would seem—beforehand certainly—that it will be the plethora of technological marvels, miracles and tricks that Munich has produced. Such a legacy seems to be comfortably far from the cynical and calculating motives that powered the political Olympics of Adolf Hitler. Yet the Munich Games may hold rather ominous intimations of their own. For never has there been an Olympics so totally born, bred and built in synthetic environment, never one so dedicated to the proposition of an artificial life. In a sense the XX Olympiad is a true harbinger of that world which Richard Brautigan calls "the cybernetic ecology," a place set in a time when mankind is "all watched over by machines of loving grace."

From the beginning, the Munich Games have been shaped to fit the electronic retina of television's Cyclops eye. Setting, lighting, seating—all are geared to the presence and the influence of cameras and microphones. Rather than have TV as an eager junior partner which fits its needs to the human exigencies of the Games, Munich put TV in as chairman of the board. The central landmark at Munich is the television tower, a great steel needle with a rotating restaurant halfway up. Perhaps it is practical and perhaps it is economical and perhaps it is even necessary, but there is always a plastic quality to any production which is totally oriented to the simplicities of TV. For the camera cannot encompass reality, only a facsimile of reality. Thus, in a sense the entire XX Olympiad becomes little more than a television studio, complete with colored billboards to make the commercial messages snap to life, as well as rigged perhaps with prerecorded sounds of wild cheering, enthusiastic handclapping, even booing to hype up a dramatic moment when the "real" spectators do not respond with enough verve. Still, there are advantages. Because Munich has cut back so greatly on "real" spectator space, its facilities are 20 percent smaller than either Mexico City or Tokyo, and officials do not anticipate the horrendous traffic snarls that have cursed other Games.

Perhaps most memorable of all the sights at Munich will be the massive translucent tent roof, a plastic mini-Alpine landscape whose grand peaks and drooping valleys form a big top over almost the entire Olympic Grounds—an area which includes the 80,000-capacity main stadium, the entire swimming hall and the hall where fencing events will occur. The tent is made of heat-insulated material and is illuminated by spotlights which are said to "approximate daylight." The tent is guaranteed to be strong enough to withstand all sorts of storms. Indeed, rains will be welcomed, for they clean the crystalline luster of the tent. Afterward rain is led off the roof through a network of troughs which directs it into a gigantic lagoon. There rain is ushered through another labyrinth of pipes and squirted back—*splat!*—high into the sky whence it came. Once aloft, the former raindrops are lighted in a series of electric colors for the entertainment of the television audience. You see, even rain gets a synthetic treatment at Munich.

This huge tent, designed by Frei Otto, is the largest in the world,—although the confident Herr Otto foresees much larger ones to come. He envisions the day when such roofs can be stretched over entire harbors to keep the waters unroiled in bad weather and over vast Disneyland-like tracts to keep them snug year round for the tourist hordes. He also envisions the possibility of his great insulated tents being stretched over entire cities which will be built in formerly unsuitable climes such as the Sahara or Antarctica. Soon all the world will be an incubator.

Of course the lighting under the Olympic big top is artificial—halogen spotlights because they are best for TV. The track will be artificial, *Rekortan*, which is a German-made substitute for Tartan. The infield grass will be real, surprisingly enough, but its roots will be artificially warmed by a well-organized maze of pipes, so the grass will grow green even when it is cold on the surface. All measurements at all events will be made by electronic devices—timers that bite off time in atoms of one/one-thousandth of a second and optical scanners that see distances in one/one-hundredth of a centimeter. Television monitors hover with omniscient Big Brother scrutiny over every finish line; their viewings are developed in seconds, then fed to a computer for instant evaluation.

There will even be a computer-encyclopedia crammed with 2,000,000 individual sports facts which can be spewed out at the request of noncomputerized sportswriters in need of data. In the Olympic Village cafeteria, where some 12,000 athletes, coaches and trainers will dine, there will be a computer which will automatically flash directional lights showing stray and hungry tray carriers where to go to find an empty seat at a table. Perhaps the ultimate in automation: The food will be prepared mechanically without human contact of any kind. A press release from the Munich committee said, "Large automatic cookers will enable delicious meals to be prepared untouched by any cook's hand. The ingredients enter the automatic cookers at one end and come out ready to eat at the other. . . ." There will be a "spice dispensing machine" which is plugged into a computer which is programmed to release just the proper pinch of oregano or red pepper or thyme into the soup as it gurgles through the spicy section of the cooking machine.

And so on and so forth.

All this is going to cost $612,000,000, to be shared by the Federal Republic of Germany (50 percent), the state of Bavaria (25 percent) and the city of Munich (25 percent). One might wonder if governments embark on such ambitious and expensive projects merely for the joy of having a quadrennial sports festival around the country for a couple of weeks. Of course, the answer is no; there are rewards far richer than medals to be found in the Olympic Games.

Hitler's Germany was able to present an impressive, yet innocent image to the world through its Olympics and that served his sinister purpose perfectly. There are people in Australia who say that the Melbourne Games brought that rough-diamond nation to the world's attention and spurred the development of natural resources and more trade. Japan, of course, sprang into world affluence from its Olympics, and the Mexicans are certain that they have been welcomed into the adult world of the twentieth century largely because of their Olympics.

And Munich? Germany's defeated nation syndrome vanished long ago, and its reputation for economic efficiency and fine products needs little improvement. Politics would appear to be beside the point (although there are always Byzantine patterns being drawn in the sandboxes of world power which do not become apparent for years). But already people are beginning to refer to this as "the businessmen's Games," for the profit motive seems to be the major drive. The Olympic Village, for example, is a product of private enterprise. It will probably bring a pretty penny; already penthouse apartments with swimming pools have been sold for 2,000,000 marks ($60,600).

The baroque city of Munich is very much a tourist town, and it was badly in need of new transportation systems. The Olympics has resulted in a new subway, plus many miles of wide new freeways and boulevards. New hotels and nightclubs and restaurants and specialty shops have all sprung to life in a hectic building boom that burst over the last three years. Walter Noel, personal secretary to Munich's Lord Mayor Hans Jochem Vogel, said, "Obtaining the Olympics has brought advantages of immediate benefit for the future. It has accelerated achievements which otherwise would have taken at least twice the time to be gained."

The commercial rewards for Munich can scarcely be guessed at yet. But the annual *Oktoberfest* arrives soon enough—within a week after the 1972 Olympics leaves town. And then the merchants of Munich will be rubbing their hands, for the renovation of the town will make it all the more pleasing for all the more tourists who will bring all the more money when they come.

270

Ah, but if Munich's profit-oriented motives seem to miss the Olympic spirit, we must not be too critical. For it is true that the major factor in holding an Olympic Games these days is money. A profit-and-loss mentality must now dictate the sense and the direction of the Games. We are talking about vast sums and grand debts when it comes to producing an Olympics—or merely producing an Olympic *team*, for that matter.

The U.S. Olympic Committee has steadfastly refused to ask the U.S. government for money to send its teams to the Games on the assumption that soon the entire Olympic program would fall into the hands of bureaucrats. The astronomical expenses incurred by Olympic Americans are supposed to be covered by voluntary contributions. In 1964 it cost $2,000,000 to finance the American Olympic and Pan-American teams; in 1968, $2,500,000; and now the price has skyrocketed to $10,000,000.

A few years ago, with the pinch for money desperate as usual, the USOC concocted a scheme whereby a few extra hundred thousand dollars could be gained by dealing American big business a piece of the U.S. Olympic effort. Thus, instead of falling into the hands of government bureaucrats, it would fall into corporate hands. The program works like this: If a company donates $30,000 to the Olympic team, it is allowed to print the U.S. Olympic seal in its advertisements, the assumption being that the seal might lend credence to the implication that any product good enough for American Olympians is good enough for American consumers. For a $100,000 gift to the team, a firm can print the Olympic seal *and* instigate an advertising campaign using the Olympic team itself as a hard-sell promotional gimmick. It could, for example, announce that part of the cash a customer pays to buy a product will be siphoned off to the Olympic team. Gillette does this with its Olympic Razor, and so does Bank of America with its traveler's checks ("Fred

271

Hansen Would Be Grounded Without You"). It is a pretty ingenious sales promotional idea, for it allows a company to put itself plainly on the side of the Olympic angels at the same time it is pursuing profit for its products. It has, however, not been free of controversy.

Recently the people who make Coppertone Sun-Tan lotion had paid their $30,000 to include the Olympic seal in their ads. Their campaign on billboards and in magazines featured a cherubic little girl with golden ringlets and a healthy tan on her back. The child was pictured with a tiny, cute puppy pulling playfully at the trunks of her bathing suit, thus exposing a lot of her white bare bottom as a striking contrast to her tan back. The U.S. Olympic seal appeared not far away in the ad. This caused dissent, for several members of the USOC complained loudly when the revered Olympic seal appeared in such proximity to the child's bare derriere. They felt this desecrated the Olympic ideal.

Other than that, there have been no significant protests about the scheme. It is running smoothly, organized so that bids to be the official brand are now submitted in rotation by specific industries. For example, one day in May, 1971, there was an air of tension around "Olympic House" as administrators of the USOC awaited the bids of the ice cream industry. ("Olympic House," incidentally, is an opulent Park Avenue mansion that was once owned by J. P. Morgan and occupied by his mistress, Maxine Elliott, the actress. It was not called "Olympic House" in those days. It is now because it is used as an office building by the USOC staff of twenty-seven.)

As he awaited the ice cream offers, Arthur Lentz, the executive director of the USOC, spoke rather gravely about the critical state of United States Olympic finances: "We are running a ten-million-dollar business here," he said. "We feel big business should be involved since it helps them to benefit the kids. Our procedure is to send out letters soliciting offers to contribute, and we mail the letters on a staggered basis—to the toothpaste people one week, the shaving people the next, the ice cream people the next. Ice cream is officially open right now. Eskimo Pie has called," he said. "Eskimo Pie is the first to call. I'm positive we'll also hear from Howard Johnson soon."

Olympic House coolly handled a set of eager bids from a series of other industries, too. When they had been duly sifted, it turned out that Gillette is the official razor of the XX Olympiad. Eastman Kodak is the official camera supplies company, Coca-Cola the soft drink, Bank of America the traveler's check, Sears, Roebuck the mail-order house and, of course, Coppertone the official sun-tan lotion.

1976, ET AL.

One of the tense and more exciting decisions that the grandfathers of The International Olympic Committee periodically face is the selection of a city for future Olympiads. This has come to be a complex, even a dirty business at times. It used to be very competitive with a dozen or more cities vying to be picked. Lately because of the enormous costs involved, as well as the municipal disruptions and possible corruptions that accompany the Games, the number of cities seeking the nomination has steadily declined. In fact, even a decision to volunteer to be a host city has come to be a matter of extreme controversy. Take the case of Zurich.

273

In the winter of 1969, the mayor and the city council of that fair Swiss city were considering issuing an invitation to the IOC for the Winter Games of 1976. Though perhaps such an idea may seem bland enough, acceptable and uncontroversial on the surface, it did, in fact, generate an unholy tempest among the citizenry of Zurich. No sooner was the mayor's plan made public than Zurich broke into hot debate, and soon there was no choice but to put the issue to a referendum.

In the days preceding the vote, the campaign became increasingly intense. People argued the pros and cons of global prestige and tourist profits which might be expected to follow from the Games. The high cost of it all was fought about, and critics constantly pointed out that the Winter Games in Grenoble, France, had cost $202,400,000, far above the estimates and that citizens of that city would be paying taxes for ten years to make up the deficits. The ugly commercialization of the Grenoble Olympics by ski manufacturers was also brought up.

When the vote was taken, it was not at all close. Only 40,912 voted in favor of having an Olympics at Zurich; 145,437 voted no, a ratio of 3½ to 1. Of course, the monumental cost of it all was the most popular reason for saying no in Zurich. But newspapers ran editorials which encompassed a few other factors that have come to plague the Winter Olympic Games in recent years. They said:

> Behind the financial considerations, the Swiss hide their judgment of the moral values. They see, in the Olympic Games, a symbol of corruption of today's sport, and they sneer at financing them. . . .
> Sport has become a commercial enterprise and the Olympic Games are masters of sport. . . .
> It is possible that the Swiss repugnance is a foretaste of an attitude which will increase and the IOC will have, with-

out doubt, difficulties organizing competitions in the future. . . .

Whatever the reasons, the fact was that the first time the Olympic Games was put to a ballot, it lost by a fat, fat margin.

The historical antithesis to Zurich would have to be Detroit. No city has been so tenacious in trying to catch the Olympic Games. Seven times Detroit has been to the well; seven times it has gone home with an empty bucket. Perhaps the man closest to this long losing record is Douglas Roby, formerly of the American Metal Products Company and now a U.S. representative on the IOC.

"I got into this Olympic thing trying to get the Games for Detroit. Our first bid was in 1939. Since then we've spent, my God, I guess around two million dollars! And no Olympics." Mr. Roby spoke with profound sadness. "The first time was in 1939, and I remember I stayed at the Dorchester Hotel across from Hyde Park. It was June. Everything was so green, but they were putting in air-raid shelters everywhere. We asked for the 1944 Olympics, and I had with me one scrapbook about Detroit. It was a nice scrapbook. That was big stuff in those days.

"London bid against us and won. Of course, there weren't any '44 Games, so London got them for 1948. We tried in 1947 for the 1952 Olympics, and lost to Helsinki. In Rome we made a really strong pitch for 1956, but the IOC was determined then to give them to a country in the Southern Hemisphere. Juan Perón from Argentina had put in a strong bid for Buenos Aires, but on the fourth ballot it went to Melbourne, Australia. The British Commonwealth—they had a lot of countries then—did it for them. We were never in the running, I guess. It was lucky, though, that Argentina didn't get it because Perón was out of

275

a job in 1956. No South American country has even bid for the Games since.

"Detroit kept bidding for almost thirty years. But it's funny, you'd take it over as a Detroit bid, and at the IOC, it'd become the U.S. bidding. The IOC has always had a tendency not to give a country that has everything anything more. In 1963 in Baden-Baden we lost to Mexico—the Russians delivered some votes there that made the big difference. We had a great video tape that time, and President Kennedy gave a beautiful pitch. We also had Henry Ford and other international names rather than just the mayor and City Council of Detroit. We still lost.

"We didn't try for 1972. We had the riots in 1967, the climate had changed. Detroit had problems, and no one really thought an Olympic Games would help.

"You know, campaigning for the Games is really not like anything else I can think of. Well, maybe it's like courting a beautiful girl. People make all those subtle little approaches, offer little gifts. The Japanese were past masters at this subtle approach, with really good-looking trinkets. It is now a rule that IOC members can't take anything worth more than a hundred dollars. Members are still wined and dined and given round-trip tickets to come and visit potential sites. For some guys these trips are the chance of a lifetime."

This is not a simple story; it is fraught with intrigue, strange twists of fate, threats, flattery, humbug and perhaps some distortions of the truth. It is about the manner in which the 1976 Olympic Games were lost by Los Angeles and Moscow and won by Montreal. Many elements and many men were swept together in the tangled mesh. All seventy of the princes and rajahs and blue-suit fellows of the IOC were involved, for it was their difficult duty to vote for the city which would host the 1976 Games. Also swept in were many high-echelon American businessmen, lots of top Russian Communists, President Richard M. Nixon and the Canadian Parliament, the U.S. State Department and Mayor Sam Yorty of Los Angeles and Mayor Jean Drapeau of Montreal and Mayor Vladimir Promyslov of Moscow and a fellow from Henry Kissinger's office in the White House and quite a few American ambassadors around the world, to say nothing of people worried about international conditions involving Iran, North and South Vietnam and Russia, as well as those professional merrymakers who are waiting in the wings to cater a really unforgettable two hundredth birthday blowout for the United States of America in 1976. (The United States did land the Winter Games in Denver, but they are not considered quite the bicentennial frosting that the Summer Games would have been.)

In affairs of this nature, reputations are stained and lifelong feuds are triggered. For example, in the course of the battle for the 1976 Olympics, Avery Brundage may have ruined his last chance to gain a significant award from his native land in recognition of his work as the world's leading Olympian.

Over the years Avery Brundage has received enough national decorations to cover the chest of a much bigger man. Such medals as Japan's Order of the Sacred Treasure (1st Class) and Norway's Commanders Cross with Star of the Royal Order of Saint Olav and Germany's Great Cross of Merit with Star and Portugal's *Grandeoficial da Ordem de Instrucao Publica.* The Congo and Korea and Finland have honored him, and the Republic of San Marino pinned him with its *Caveliere Grand Ufficiale dell' Ordine Equestre di Sant 'Agata* and even issued a stamp bearing his portrait.

Yet in all his years in the public notice Avery Brundage has never, never received any medal or honors at all from the government of the United States. Indeed, the only decoration from America included in his official IOC biography is the Order of Lincoln, which is given by the state of Illinois to all sorts of people.

The truth is, Mr. Brundage was more or less in line to receive from President Nixon the most coveted civilian medal the White House gives—the Presidential Medal of Freedom. In the past it has gone to Ralph Bunche, Felix Frankfurter, Marian Anderson and Robert McNamara to name a few. However, Avery Brundage's opportunity to gain honor in his own land was perhaps snuffed out in the spring of 1970, when the IOC meeting in Amsterdam failed to select Los Angeles as the site for the 1976 Games. Some Americans felt this defeat was Avery Brundage's doing, that he had purposely undermined the Los Angeles cause. Some *important* Americans apparently felt that way. "It'll be a goddamn cold day when Nixon pins a medal on *that* SOB after what he did to America," said one fellow in Washington who was close to all that happened. "What kind of man is it who'll shoot down his own country?"

If that is true, it is a sorry fact. But this is a story full of sorry facts, so let us proceed.

The techniques for campaigning used by Moscow, Montreal and Los Angeles were diverse and cunning—some involving overt muscle, others fragile diplomatic cajolery, others titanic public relations pressures, others the sheerest sentimentality. In Moscow, for example, the Russians came on strong with an old and proved gimmick of the free world—a press conference and cocktail party. They brought out the chief architect of Moscow, several government ministers, quite a few Soviet athletes and Mayor Promyslov, who said the city was prepared to spend $45,000,000 on the Olympics, including building some desperately needed new hotels. Each correspondent was given a good-looking photograph album titled *Moscow '76* along with color slides. The Minister of Communication said the Iron Curtain would turn to rose-colored glass for the Olympics, with full and free transmission of journalists' copy, as well as uncensored live television. And the Minister of Culture, Mme. Yekaterina Furtseva, rose before the reporters, flirtatiously bobbed her long blond curls, promised that no nation on earth could equal the festive cultural delights of Russia and then cooed, "Have sympathy for me, give me your assistance and your propaganda to have the Olympics in Moscow." The Russians mailed brochures to all members of the IOC and used other techniques of persuasion, including pointedly reminding Iran that it shares a long mutual boundary with Russia and that there were some trade agreements in the works.

Montreal was almost entirely dependent on its mayor, the Chaplinesque little Jean Drapeau who had produced the unforgettable Expo 67 despite a general belief it could not be done. Esthetic success that it was, Expo 67 operated at an abysmal financial loss. Not only that, the Canadian Parliament had refused to pass a resolution promising that it would underwrite the Games if they were held in Montreal. Nevertheless, Drapeau kept up a steady barrage of brochures in the mail to IOC members, and he had some of them visit Montreal for Olympic briefings and other forms of entertainment. When he had to appear for his final sales talk before the IOC in Amsterdam in May, 1970, he was faced with the embarrassing prospect of putting up a financial guarantee. In a moving and dramatic speech, he told the committee: "The history of Montreal is our guarantee. It is a history of meeting and beating challenges. That is our guarantee. If there is any doubt you have about Montreal, then do . . . not . . . choose . . . us." And so forth and so on. That speech—plus the reluctance of the IOC to get into a blatant cold war confrontation by choosing between Russia and the United States—won the day for Canada.

However, the American campaign had been in high gear for about three years by the time those final days of conflict occurred in Amsterdam. The Los Angeles group was chaired by Sam Yorty, the mayor, plus a number of politicians, plus some influential Southern California businessmen. The operative leader of this determined band was John B. "Jim" Kilroy, who is not accustomed to failure and has made several million dollars with his own real estate development firm, Kilroy Enterprises.

One radiant afternoon in the summer of 1971, Mr. Kilroy arrived for a luncheon interview at the California Yacht Club at the Marina Del Ray in Ventura. The club was a cool and swanky place, almost fully walled with windows which looked out on sparkling water, sun-washed docks and several luxurious acres of varnished decks and neat masts bobbing, bobbing in unison. Mr. Kilroy fit the setting. He was tall and lean and athletic, his dark tan contrasting nicely with his white hair and —particularly—with his white teeth when he smiled. He seemed confident and relaxed, walking lightly on his blue sneakers, flashing the smile at a few people. He wore a blue shirt with the words KIALOA II stitched in white above the pocket. The *Kialoa II* is Jim Kilroy's deepwater yawl, computer designed with an all-aluminum hull and a reputation as one of the finest seagoing yachts in California. Kilroy's reputation as a skipper is equally sterling. He had just flown in from Honolulu after a 2,225-mile race from Los Angeles in which *Kialoa II* finished sixth. The bartender at the California Yacht Club said as he passed, "We heard it on the radio, Mr. Kilroy. Nice race." But Mr. Kilroy shook his head and said, "There's only one place to finish in a race—first," and the white smile again appeared briefly—and tightly.

Mr. Kilroy seated himself at a round, shiny, varnished wooden table and ordered a draft beer and shrimp salad. The Del Ray marina shimmered in clean sun at his back, and speaking in a pleasant, deep voice, Mr. Kilroy began to relate the saga of his involvement with the Olympic Games of 1976:

"We decided to take a hardheaded businessman's approach. We all happened to feel that business can do it better, can do almost *anything* better, than government. So we laid out our concept on the basis that it would never put a burden on the taxpayers. I understand how taxpayers feel—you might say I'm a *professional* taxpayer with all I've contributed over the years." He smiled fleetingly.

"We wanted the project to sustain itself and not burden the community, because we saw it as a way of keeping Los Angeles together, of unifying this big sprawling place. Then too, we figured we'd put in an urban renewal feature by forming a nonprofit corporation that would operate the Olympic Village and then take the proceeds from the Games and turn it into equity. We had a potential profit on the drawing boards of thirty million dollars from the Village; it would be used as a catalyst for urban renewal. It would cover a hundred and twenty acres at a place that now very much needs to be redeveloped."

Mr. Kilroy ran through some more complex figures which he seemed to have memorized. Projections indicated the Olympics would cost L.A. barely $40,000,000—about one-fifteenth of the Munich Games in 1972—since most of the facilities were already there. All things considered, the '76 Olympics in L.A. could have generated a profit of $1,291,000 he said. In all, the Los Angeles committee spent $314,000 to get the bid, but Mr. Kilroy emphasized that this did not include the donations of many loyal and wealthy businessmen who contributed their

281

corporate planes and pilots, plus personal travel funds and personal time, as well as the time of certain junior executives and secretaries.

"I understand Denver spent a million dollars to get the Winter Games," said Mr. Kilroy, not without pleasure.

"I got into this thing in 1967 when Sam Yorty asked me to look into having the Games in L.A. It was all Sam's idea, you know, not Washington and not the two hundredth anniversary people. It was Sam's doing.

"We had some static here and there about things. One nut wrote letters saying everybody in real estate in Southern California has to be a crook. One group said that the Games should be held in Vermont because of the smog in L.A.

"We had the L.A. '76 campaign under way during the Games in Mexico City. We'd have eight A.M. breakfast and plan the day's schedule—who was going to work on which delegation, who'd have lunch with the Japanese or who'd have a drink with the Nigerian. We had round-trip air ferries to Acapulco for IOC members—we'd been given the use of some Hughes Aircraft planes and pilots. We had one large reception in Mexico, and I guess three, four hundred people came. Then afterward we had some IOC people up to see Disneyland and some movie sets and things like that. A Japanese and a Czech and a Rumanian flew back with us from Mexico, I remember. We had no federal government help at all in any of this—not in transportation or in printing. We had a great brochure finally, and a movie that cost us thirty-seven thousand dollars. We had about five thousand brochures printed and we sent one to every state and federal elected government official in the U.S.—assemblymen, state senators, the Congress. Then, for the IOC, we mailed each member one copy, and we sent one of our own envoys from the committee to hand deliver another copy to each member.

"In the beginning Montreal was against us and a couple of other so-called competitors—Florence, Italy, was one. The Russians weren't in then. We were really sailing along. All systems were *go!*

"President Nixon sent a personal letter to every member of the IOC, guaranteeing that L.A. had the backing of the U.S. government in trying to get the Olympics. Oh, the White House was very involved in our campaign. We never brought up Nixon's name because we thought everyone would accuse him of doing it just for publicity purposes. But he was with us, believe me. We went to the President at one point and told him our problems, and he very generously gave us—full time—a man from the State Department and one of Henry Kissinger's men to help in our checking around the world.

"We had access to intelligence on how the votes were going from our embassies all over the world. If we needed any input from them, all we had to do was ask, and they'd give us a head count on how we were doing. The fellow from the White House traveled with our own Los Angeles emissaries when they went out to hit all the IOC countries during the winter of 1970—just before the vote. We had Americans down helping organize an international meet in Panama. At our suggestion, the State Department sent American coaches to Africa to hold symposiums and clinics there. We had people all over the world those last months to help sell the idea of an L.A. Olympics."

A number of American athletes have suggested they were the wrong people, that the Los Angeles campaign might have done better if there had been some U.S. Olympians, such as Jesse Owens or Al Oerter or the Connollys, involved. Mr. Kilroy

283

scoffed at this. He said, "Now what would an athlete have done with those IOC members? What the hell could Jesse Owens have to say to King Constantine or the Duke of Luxembourg? Athletes can't sit down and talk with the kind of men who sit on the IOC—no, we had the right people."

Mr. Kilroy then recounted how Moscow had entered the competition late in 1969 and how Montreal stayed in regardless of the troubles in getting money. "There was a kind of dress-rehearsal presentation before a number of sports federations in Munich early in the winter of 1970. We were told that Montreal fell on its rear end and that Moscow had no feel for making that kind of presentation. So these federations were going to make a strong recommendation to the IOC that L.A. be selected since we had good facilities already. But the Russians then moved in with the idea that there shouldn't be any recommendation because in six years, all three cities could easily have the proper facilities for the Olympics. The Commonwealth countries went along with that because of Canada, and that was a very great tactical loss for us."

The meeting in Amsterdam began May 12, 1970, and the American delegation was confident. "Our input indicated that we had thirty-six votes on the first ballot for sure," said Mr. Kilroy. "We counted the Soviet bloc with twenty-seven votes and the Commonwealth bloc with England, Ireland, South Africa, Kenya, Canada, New Zealand, and Australia, plus a couple more. So we figured the other thirty-six in our pocket for sure, and so did the White House. Needless to say, the White House was very involved toward the end. The timing was not the best for our bid, and the White House was concerned. We had just invaded Cambodia, and the kids had just been shot at Kent State a week before the IOC vote. It was very touchy, but we were prepared to face it and to talk about it. Vietnam, too.

"Now in Amsterdam we were housed in a downtown hotel, quite a way from the IOC hotel, so there wouldn't be any late pressure on the members. But when we arrived, I wanted to see Avery and tell him our plans, show him our guidelines. I told him that we were prepared to talk about Cambodia and Kent State and Vietnam—that we *welcomed* any questions. By God, that SOB slammed his fist on the table, and he said—oh, he was livid, in a rage—he said, 'There will be *no* politics in this. I will not *permit* a word to be said about Vietnam or Kent State or any other discussion along those lines!'

"Well, I was surprised," said Mr. Kilroy, "but I said fine, okay, Avery, if that's the way you want it, that's fine. Now look what the bastard did when he got home. . . ."

Mr. Kilroy held up a clipping from the Cleveland *Plain Dealer* sports page dated June 2, 1970. The headline, eight columns, was WHY LOS ANGELES LOST OLYMPICS and the subhead was "War, Kent State Killings," and in the body of the story there was a quote from Avery Brundage, who had just been in Cleveland, saying, "The Kent State situation made headlines all over the world, and it came just about the time of our meeting. It didn't help. Neither did the Vietnam War. We spend so much money all over the world, and yet when it comes down to counting our friends, we have very few of them."

Mr. Kilroy said, "Brundage is an unbelievable hypocrite. He will retain his office as long as he sells off a little bit of the U.S. each time. One reason he hates this country is that he's received like a head of state, a goddamn *king* everywhere he goes except here. That infuriates him."

Mr. Kilroy was flushed red beneath his tan, for Mr. Brundage had plainly infuriated him, too.

"We were prepared to talk about *all* the conditions in the U.S. We were ready to talk about the black situation. We had

285

blacks on our committee, and we were going to let them speak. We had an administration man, from Kissinger's office, for God's sake, and he was going to talk about Kent State. We said we were *delighted* to talk about our problems. Sure, and we would also be delighted to have the Russians talk about what they had done in Prague. The Russians tried to attack us about our smog. And we said, sure, we have smog, but so do you —what about that Fiat plant in Moscow and all the smog it blows around town?"

Mr. Kilroy stopped talking for a moment and turned to gaze at the peaceful marina, the clean sunshine on the masts outside. He seemed refreshed when he turned back to the conversation.

"Well, there was plenty of infighting going on. You think you've seen politics? Try an IOC meeting. The Russians were threatening to boycott Munich if the Germans didn't vote for Moscow. General Clark [the late Joseph del Flores Clark, then the IOC vice-president from Mexico] told us that he had to vote for Russia on the first ballot because they had promised to vote for him to replace Avery as IOC president next year. Then there was the tragedy with black Africa; they asked us to promise that we'd repudiate South Africa and Rhodesia if they voted for L.A. We had to tell them that we were *nobody* until we were actually selected by the committee, and we couldn't promise that because we were just there to sell Los Angeles— and I guess we lost 'em.

"The Russian tactics were incredible. At one party given by Queen Juliana in Amsterdam, there were these two burly Communist bastards, and they had a member of the IOC in a corner, and every time the poor fellow tried to get away, they'd slam him back in the corner. Another IOC member from a Russian bloc country, said he'd really like to talk to the L.A. delegation, but he was terrified to do it at the party. So we all kind of sneaked out to a little restaurant and met him there. He sat way in the back of the room, with his back to the door, kind of slouched over the table, and he raised his glass and toasted L.A.

"We knew we had some problems after we'd been in Amsterdam for two days. Drapeau was hanging around the elevators at the IOC hotel all the time, and he'd buttonhole every delegate who came out—which was against the rules. The Russians had a few of those big burly guys who never smiled standing at all four corners of the balcony over the lobby. They were making notes on who was talking to whom. I thought I was in some kind of a weird foreign spy movie.

"Once a couple of Russians even started pushing me around —physically. Well, I'm a pretty big guy, and I can take care of myself, and I told one, 'Get the hell away from me or I'll knock you on your ass.' I said the same thing to the other one. They left me alone after that.

"For our actual presentation, we had a booth, and we were told ours was best. We also had a half hour to make the pitch to the committee assembled. Our film ran twenty-one minutes, Yorty spoke for three minutes, Preston Hotchkis [vice-president of Los Angeles Committee] for three, and I spoke for three minutes and answered a few questions. We weren't allowed to watch the other countries' presentations, but I understand Russia's was about forty years behind the times.

"We were criticized for our cash-flow analysis. Brundage said it was 'high-dollar pressure.' But we really used a very low profile. Russia was not a low profile. I think we comported ourselves with dignity. Sure, it's hard to come on like a small, meek nation when you're the United States of America, but we geared our presentation to the fact that the Games would not be too big. We did not make any negative cracks. It was purely

287

positive selling of L.A. We pointed out that TV would be live worldwide—prime time in Europe—and that this would be worth forty million dollars in revenue. We pointed out that when it comes to TV, L.A. is the hub of the business."

Jim Kilroy sipped glumly at another draft beer, then shrugged and spoke as if the memory were too bitter to discuss much longer. "Well, it comes to be the day of the vote. The Social and Cultural Minister of Holland—Madame Klompe—opens the Sixty-ninth Congress of the IOC, and she makes this speech welcoming everyone to Amsterdam, and she says she knows all the IOC guys know that the true spirit of the Olympics was shown forty-two years ago when the Netherlands—a *small country*—hosted the Games, and she says it is her fond and fervent dream that the Olympics can be returned to the *small countries!*

"God, then they show a movie about Amsterdam, and there, big as life, is this shot of a plane from *Air Canada.*

"Then Avery gets up and he said, 'Why, to my great *surprise*, Madame Klompe, you have given my speech.' This is a goddamn lie because I was in his office two days before, and I *saw* Madame Klompe's speech on his desk, but anyway, Brundage launches into this talk about returning the Olympics to the *small* countries. Then Avery did a little more bad-mouthing about the U.S.—anarchy in the streets and the horrible things happening in Cambodia. . . . I wasn't there, but this is what I was told by a number of people who attended.

"And of course, after that it was just a matter of counting the votes." Kilroy simply shook his head at the memory. His tight white smile had not broken through his tan in a long while.

Jim Kilroy shrugged. "We had a power play going, and it didn't work for us. Our input was not great; our intelligence

288

broke down. It didn't work for Russia either. But a lot of those IOC guys took the chicken way out. We take the position that you stand up and be counted. They didn't dare come out straight for America or for the Commies. They finked out when it came to the showdown. They went for Montreal—a negative, no, a neutral vote. They ignored the fact that Canada doesn't have the dough. They ignored *all* the facts."

For the record, the final facts were that on the first ballot, the vote was Moscow twenty-eight, Montreal twenty-five and Los Angeles seventeen. A majority of thirty-six was required. On the second ballot, only Moscow and Montreal were included, and the Canadians won with forty-one votes. Jean Drapeau wept long and without shame. The Russians sulked, and Sam Yorty delivered a characteristically weightless remark. "Well, if we couldn't get the Games, I'm glad at least they stayed in the free world," he said.

Since the Los Angeles '76 effort fell so short, the consensus among men who chart the Olympic winds around the world is that there is no point in the United States even trying to land another Summer Games until—well, until 1988. Most everyone assumes that Moscow has the 1980 Olympics sewed up and that an African nation will play host in 1984.

Epilogue

WELL, what have we wrought?

The Olympic Games are a mighty institution, influential and far-reaching, no doubt. But the world is too much with them for mythology to prevail. The opportunistic and transparent politicking of the Sam Yortys and the Nixon administrations and the Kremlin bureaucrats have tracked indelible footprints upon the "sacred Olympic territory." The routinely avaricious forces of commerce have put this "twentieth-century religion" to working for their own purposes in too many ways—peddling beer or publicizing ski brands or cashing in on the Olympics as merely a branch of the world tourist industry. The powerful exigencies of television have come to affect the drift and the tides of the "world's greatest social force" too much.

Most athletes of Olympic caliber have been forced to invest their young lives with very *un*young attributes to reach an Olympic peak, for their training demands personalities which combine the relentless persistence of a machine, the grim devotion of a monk, the single-mindedness of a miser. That is the heartbreaking part—the sacrifice of youth and freedom to an Olympic medal. Then comes the demeaning part. Usually, an Olympic athlete must lie about himself and swear to an oath in which he hears no truth in order to meet the specious standards of amateurism set down by the IOC.

Still, the Olympic Games are not an intrinsically bad institution. It is their mythology which makes them seem such a force for cynicism and hypocrisy. It is the attempt to clothe the Games in grand ideals they could never realize which makes them seem so fallible, so undermined and so corrupted by man's meanest motives.

Instead of pretending—or propagating the myth—that the Olympics is "sacred" or a "religion" or even a "force for good," it would be wise to call it what it is: a mere quadrennial carnival of sports where the world's best athletes compete for their championships.

To invest the Olympics with intimations of absolute peace on earth is to make them seem the sheerest folly in reality; the best that happens (and it does happen) is that Olympic athletes of myriad faiths, ideologies and nationalities simply make friends with each other. They do not do much to influence the course of the world.

To insist on "pure amateurs" in the competitions is to insist on corruption. Either let the Games be an open competition in which the world's best are included—be they professional or not. Or reduce the entire scale of Olympic excellence to the caliber of *real* amateurs; this means that this multimillion-dollar spectacle would be staged for fresh and callow schoolboys competing at the intense but scarcely expert level of an Andover-Exeter track meet. (And perhaps that wouldn't be so bad.)

To deny that politics is an integral force in the staging of the Games and the creation of the teams entered is foolish and dishonest. So is the denial of commercialism and materialism. Without television's money and the glinty-eyed profit hunger of the tourist industry, no Olympics would take place, for there is no institution, nation or municipality in the world so desperately motivated toward the "religion" of the Olympic Games that it would spend several hundred million dollars for the sheer propagation of the Olympic "ideal."

The Games fill many needs in the twentieth century, and their appeal in the world is still strong—and universal—for several reasons beyond the synthetic mythology that has grown up around them.

The Olympics help satisfy man's need for ritual, for pomp, for thrilling carnival times. Flags. Bands and parades and marching throngs. There is medieval pageantry in the Olympics to rival a Pope's inauguration or a king's coronation, and perhaps there are even intimations of immortality to be found in the constancy of ceremonies handed down over 2,500 years from the halcyon days of Greece.

The Olympic Games seem to return to good, old-fashioned establishmentarian simplicities, and the fact they *seem* so is refreshing to many people. For there is no mistaking an Olympic winner. He stands on a real pedestal. He hears a thunder of applause for himself. He is serenaded by his own national anthem. He is saluted by his own flag being raised in his honor. He is given a piece of gold.

In a day of sliding ethics and adjustable verities, such a clear and unmistakable example of cause and effect is a soothing event, for it revives that wishful belief that life can proceed without a plethora of metaphysical and moralistic uncertainties. The Olympic Games give the spectator the illusion of seeing men succeed or fail without a complexity of doubts and questions and rationalized explanations. There is a beginning of the conflict, an end to it; there is a winner and a loser; and if only life could really *be* that way. Of course, all sports offer this simplistic illusion, but the Olympic Games have practically deified it.

What we have wrought here in the Olympic Games of the twentieth century is no myth, no religion, not even an easily definable ideal. No, the Olympics is simply a large and colorful sports festival which amuses several million spectators at their TV sets, inspires several thousand athletes on the Olympic playing field, and perhaps enriches several dozen other people here and there who have used the Olympics for quite another kind of profit. The Olympics is as imperfect, as poignant, as foolish, as funny, as admirable, as fallible as any—as *all*—of the thousands and thousands of mere humans who have at one time or another engaged in the Olympic game. It is no more and no less, but, of course, that is quite a lot.

Index

Index

297